The Journey of a Tzotzil-Maya Woman of Chiapas, Mexico

Book Twenty-Six
Louann Atkins Temple Women & Culture Series

The Journey of a Tzotzil-Maya Woman of Chiapas, Mexico

PASS WELL OVER THE EARTH

Christine Eber and "Antonia"

University of Texas Press   Austin

The Louann Atkins Temple Women & Culture Series is supported by Allison, Doug, Taylor, and Andy Bacon; Margaret, Lawrence, Will, John, and Annie Temple; Larry Temple; the Temple-Inland Foundation; and the National Endowment for the Humanities.

Requests for permission to reproduce material from this work should be sent to:
    Permissions
    University of Texas Press
    P.O. Box 7819
    Austin, TX 78713-7819
    www.utexas.edu/utpress/about/bpermission.html

∞ The paper used in this book meets the minimum requirements of ANSI/NISO Z39.48-1992 (R1997) (Permanence of Paper).

Library of Congress Cataloging-in-Publication Data

Eber, Christine Engla.
The journey of a Tzotzil-Maya woman of Chiapas, Mexico : pass well over the earth / Christine Eber.
        p.   cm. — (Louann Atkins Temple women & culture series v. 26)
    Includes bibliographical references and index.
    ISBN 978-0-292-72665-9 (cloth : alk. paper) — ISBN 978-0-292-73539-2 (e-book)
    1. Tzotzil women—Mexico—Chenalhó—Social conditions.   2. Tzotzil women—Mexico—Chenalhó—Political activity.   3. Feminist anthropology—Mexico—Chenalhó. 4. Chiapas (Mexico)—History—Peasant Uprising, 1994–   5. Chenalhó (Mexico)—History.   6. Chenalhó (Mexico)—Social conditions.   I. Title.
    F1221.T9E23   2011
    972'.75—dc23   2011018270

I dedicate this book to my children.

Antonia

Contents

Acknowledgments

The process of writing this book has involved many people. Foremost among them is Heather Sinclair, Antonia's and my friend, who joined us in conversations in 2005 and 2006, and enters the narrative at several points. Heather gave intensive feedback on early drafts, and I am indebted to her for her insightful comments and support.

Antonia and I are also indebted to her husband, Domingo, and her children for bearing up with Antonia's absences when she was working on the book in the United States. I am also grateful to my husband, Mike O'Malley, for taking care of our home and animals during my trips to Chiapas and helping me keep a balance in my life.

In addition, I am deeply grateful to Bill Jungels, who gave generous and insightful feedback and much encouragement on early manuscript drafts. Several of his photos of life in highland Chiapas grace this book.

Furthermore, my heartfelt thanks goes to Carter Wilson for his encouragement and careful critiques and for inspiring me through his pathbreaking writing about life in indigenous communities of Chiapas in the past and present.

I also thank Susan Bagby, Christine Kovic, Marilyn Moors, and James Taggart for providing invaluable help with restructuring and clarifying the book's main contributions, and Joanne Hand, LeeAnn Meadows, and Heidi Moksnes for being so encouraging and helpful to me during the revision stage, especially in their suggestions for clarifying chapter introductions.

I was blessed with support throughout this project from many other individuals and groups, including Gerrie Casey, Carol Charnley, Louanna Furbee, Jeanne Laberge, Linda Laughlin, Crystal Massey, June Nash, Rosaceli Ortega, Evelyn Phillips, Mayra Valtiérrez, Rebecca Wiggins, Mary Wolf, students at New Mexico State University, the Desert Writers of Las Cruces, participants in the 2009 Sociocultural Workshop sponsored by Washington University's Anthropology Department, participants on a panel and roundtable on writing at the 2009 Society for Applied Anthropology

Annual Meeting, and the editorial team at the University of Texas Press, especially Lynne Chapman and freelance editor Alexis Mills. I am also grateful to New Mexico State University for providing financial assistance for travel to Chiapas through several research awards.

Finally, I thank Theresa May for believing in this book.

Prologue

My backpack and duffel bags sit by the door, bulging with what remains after paring down to essentials. I couldn't bring myself to eliminate any gifts. They are my most important cargo, a way for me to reconnect with friends and share something with them from El Norte. This time I'm carrying photos of my godson for his parents. He has been in the United States for almost a year working on farms and in Chinese restaurants in five different states. A few months ago I sent him a disposable camera to take photos of his life. When the photos arrived, there he was, shoveling snow outside his apartment in West Virginia and posing inside in his new sneakers and cutoff pants, arms folded, feet astride. I wonder what Antonia and Domingo will think of their son. When he left Chiapas, he was much thinner. He says he's gained weight because he doesn't get much exercise. He no longer plays basketball as he did at home because he's afraid of *la migra* (immigration authorities).

I hoist the pack on my back and lift the two bags to see if I can carry them even a few steps. I can. I check to make sure a few dollar bills are handy to give the porters I may need to help me in the airport in Mexico City and El Tapo, the station where I'll catch the bus to Chiapas.

The phone rings. I really don't want to talk to anyone now. I've already said my goodbyes.

"Madrina [Godmother], it's me, Alberto."[1]

I'm surprised to hear his voice since we talked just yesterday. He's called to ask for one last favor.

"Madrina, I just want to ask you to bring me a tape of my parents talking to me. I want to hear their voices."

"Of course. I'll make sure to ask your parents to do that. I'll send the tape along with some photos when I get back."

"Thank you, Madrina. I just want to ask you for that. That's all."

I tell Alberto to take care of himself and be sure to go to the emergency

room if the illness he's been suffering from doesn't clear up. I hate leaving while he's still sick, but I must go. It's not as if I help him that much, living half a country away, but we talk a lot on the phone.

After landing in Mexico City I take a taxi from the airport to El Tapo, where I board a bus that will take me through the night to San Cristóbal de las Casas, the major city in the highlands of Chiapas. Most of the thirteen-hour ride I sleep, until dawn breaks and the falling temperature tells me that we are ascending into the cloud forest. The sun has yet to pierce the clouds. I long for it to reveal the green forests and end the chilly night ride. My seat-mate still sleeps, scrunched against the window, hooded sweatshirt pulled tight around his face. He is a young man from Yajalón, a rural township in Chiapas. He told me that he has been cleaning restaurants in Mexico City for a few months and is returning to visit his family.

How different this seatmate is from those who made this trip with me in the 1980s. Then they were young, European tourists venturing into the exotic rain forests of Chiapas, or so the guidebooks promised. Today they are mostly Mexican migrants who must find work wherever they can, no matter how far away.

Once in the city of San Cristóbal de las Casas, I settle into a room that has just become vacant in the home of Antonia's brother Francisco and his wife. Francisco and Marta know my routine, and that I'll head out to Chenalhó as soon as I'm settled in. I want to see Antonia and Domingo, not just to deliver the pictures of their son, but because being with them is like com-ing home. I lived with the couple for a year in 1987 when they had only three small boys. Now their four boys are grown. Felipe and Sebastian are married, each with two children; Mariano has a job in another Mexican state working with computers; and Alberto, the youngest, is working in the United States. In the early 1990s, two girls were born. Paulina is now married with a baby boy, and Rosalva is in high school.

I pack up just what I'll need for a few days and make my way to the mar-ket, where I'll find a taxi to Chenalhó. My ears slowly adjust to the mixture of Tzotzil and Spanish as I wend among the throngs of vendors and buyers. I haven't spoken Tzotzil in over a year and struggle to get back into the groove of this language, so different from English and Spanish.

I slip into the back seat of a VW taxi and place my backpack between my legs. After a half hour of practicing Tzotzil and watching people pass by, we have the four passengers required to make the trip to Chenalhó.

I take some hope in the ride being slower than usual because the driver is

(FACING PAGE): Photo by Christine Eber, 1987.

middle-aged, but he proves to be as much of a risk taker as his younger colleagues. I close my eyes to contain the nausea rising inside me as we careen around one more curve, just missing two little girls herding sheep along the side of the road. When the driver slows down for a speed bump, I open my eyes to take in the land and people of Chamula and Mitontik, the townships that lie between Chenalhó and San Cristóbal.

We are moving down into the valley, and the ridge of mountains where Antonia lives is nearly visible through the fog. After the Spaniards took control of these lands during the campaigns of Diego Mazariegos in 1527 and 1528, they forced the native people onto the mountainsides and built cities and farms in their fertile river valleys. Now the mountainsides of Chenalhó are dotted with about a hundred communities, each with its own primary school, a few family stores, and a chapel or two. As we speed along I am delighted to see the tops and sides of many houses decorated with paintings of animals and plants. The birds and flowers remind me of pictures I've seen of designs that my great-grandfather painted on houses and barns as he traveled throughout the countryside of central Sweden in the late 1800s.

We arrive in Chenalhó, and I get into the back of a truck that will take me to Antonia's community. Our climb along the mountainside is faster and easier each year since the road was paved in the early 1990s. Before, we'd often bog down in mud, and passengers would eventually abandon the bus and start walking, always the surest and safest way to get anywhere in highland Chiapas.

I don't know if I'll find my *compadres* at home, but I'm lucky this time. It's February, coffee harvesting season, and I find them picking the last of the beans just above their house.

I call out the traditional Tzotzil greeting. "Me li oxuke?" (Are you there?)

"Li une (I am here)," Antonia answers. A big smile fills her face as she puts her basket down and descends the trail.

She is glad for an excuse to stop working and welcomes me into her kitchen, where a pot of beans simmers on the fire. It's winter, which can be cold in the highlands. Like the scrawny cat that my *compadres* abide to keep the rats at bay, I stay as close to the fire as I can without singeing myself.

It has been a year and a half since we've seen each other. My face is more creased and my hair more like I remember my grandmother's, grayish brown with glints of gold. Antonia's face is more drawn than I remember, but her eyes and mouth are as warm and expectant as always. Her more sedentary life has put pounds on her, a common occurrence in middle age in both our cultures. But as she repositions logs to rekindle the fire, she seems as much at home in her body as when she was a young woman.

Each time I visit I bring the gifts out right away. I want to wait, but something inside me doesn't trust that I'm enough. So the gifts come out—the Obama calendar and baseball caps, gifts from Antonia's other friends in the United States, and the little photo album of Alberto.

Soon Domingo joins us and the couple flips through the album pages searching for clues about their son's life, just how bad his sickness is, how much he is really drinking.

Rosalva and Paulina join the huddle around the photos. They, too, point out how heavy their brother looks. They must envy all the food he is eating. They have learned about the abundance of things to eat in the United States from the influx of imported goods and from their mother's stories about her visits there.

I have come to Chiapas to reconnect with friends, but also to work with Antonia on her life story. We have only been able to work together during summers and now, during my sabbatical, so the book has come together slowly. It means far more to me than anything I have done in my academic career, allowing me to explore issues that I just touched on in previous writing. Most importantly, I have been able to explore the complexities of cross-cultural relationships shaped by extreme power differences, but also the fundamental similarities that connect us to other humans despite how differently we live our lives.

Books have never been very important to Antonia. When I lived with her and Domingo in 1987, they didn't own a single one. I gave them a Bible, which they appreciated, even though Domingo was just learning to read. The next book they valued was *La otra palabra* (The Other Word), about the massacre in Acteal, Chenalhó, in 1997, with photos of people who died in the massacre, some of whom the couple knew.

During our conversations in New Mexico in June 2006, Antonia explained how books relate to other aspects of her life. She was recalling a visit the day before to the Mesilla Cultural Center, which has a collection of rare books by Chicano and Mexican writers. While visiting the center we sipped tea and talked with writer Denise Chávez. All the while Antonia embroidered a piece of fabric that she hoped to sell during her visit. At one point Denise asked her if she liked to read. Antonia recalls her response:

> I told Señora Chávez, "Yes, I have books, books that my *comadre* has
> given me. The problem is that I don't have time to read because we
> have to work very hard in our homes. We can't count on a salary so
> we have to work. Just as I'm embroidering right now, I always have
> to work as that brings an income. I'd like to sit back with my arms

crossed, but I can't because I know that I won't earn any money that way. At home we have many things to do—care for children, wash clothes, cook. There's no time to read. I want to read, to take a walk. But no, walking happens when there's a meeting to attend.

Our work is going well, despite the demands of coffee harvesting and the numbness in Antonia's face, which the doctor says is neuralgia of the trigeminal nerve. He tells her that it may take a few months to cure. We fill the prescription, which costs over $300. I am shocked, and realize that if I hadn't come, Antonia's problem would have gone untreated.

We work inside Antonia's store so she won't lose any business. Like many women in her township, Antonia has a small store next to her house to bring in a little income. We are surrounded by shelves loaded with bags of salt, sugar, pasta, soap, animal crackers, neatly stacked cans of sardines, and sodas in plastic bottles. On the floor are crates of bananas, limes, apples, oranges, and flats of eggs. On one side of the store, cascading from hooks on the ceiling, are hair ribbons and weaving threads; on the other side hang clumps of candles of different lengths and thicknesses. Domingo and his sons built this store using wooden planks for the walls, metal for the roof, and cement for the floor. The structure and its contents are a source of pride for the whole family.

In between customers I read Antonia the words that I've transcribed from our conversations over many years. Sometimes she adds additional thoughts or provides an update. Occasionally she says, "We better not put that in the book." The words that prompt her to say this usually involve criticism of someone she doesn't want to offend or information about her involvement in the Zapatista movement, which we are still figuring out how to handle.

One day I broach the topic of our motivations for writing her life story. I explain that I hope that her story will do many things, including provide an opportunity to learn about the lives of women in her community and deepen awareness about the process of mutual discovery that cross-cultural relationships entail. I end by saying that I hope that her book will increase solidarity connections between her people and people in the United States and other nations.

I ask Antonia to sum up her motivations. She gathers her thoughts and says, "I want to write this book to conserve my story so that when I am gone people will know what I thought and what happened in my life. I hope that other women will be inspired to have the same rights that I have had, to leave their homes, to know another world, and to have many experiences."

Over the course of my month in Chiapas I finish reading all of Antonia's words to her. Just before I leave, I lend her my tape recorder so she and Domingo can send a message to Alberto.

After my return I send the tape to Alberto in West Virginia. He calls to tell me that he was happy to hear his parents' voices. But he adds sheepishly, "They gave me advice, you know." I wondered how Alberto would take his father's lecture. Domingo spoke first and preached about the evils of drinking.

As I expected, Antonia's words to Alberto were comforting; they embody the local belief that mothers are guardians of their sons' souls, as fathers are of their daughters'. Her words also reveal the difficulties of protecting children's souls in a globalized world when one has little knowledge of the cultural worlds where they live. Antonia has repeatedly told me that the only way she knows something is if she experiences it in her body—if she lives it on a daily basis. Her words convey wisdom about knowing which is confirmed by what anthropologists have learned by accompanying people in their daily lives.

Antonia's Words to Alberto

K'ox,[2] I want to talk to you. I'm going to tell you that I want you to be happy in your work, where you are working. May you have good spirit in your work. Save your money because you only crossed over to the faraway land once.

I only became sad about you one time. You, too, only suffered once from walking, from hunger, from thirst, from fear and all the suffering as you crossed. Thank God that you could do it.

I console you because you were suffering. You didn't have money, you didn't have clothes. You suffered a lot because I couldn't help you with everything.

But now be content. You're earning a little.

I only tell you to be content for that. I'm also content. That's how I always am.

May God accompany you in your work, on the road wherever you may find yourself. And also may God heal your sickness. That's all my talk. We'll see each other later. You stay there.

Background Notes

A ntonia's story starts with Chapter 1. The background notes below describe the main contexts of our work on this book and key challenges we faced in respect to language issues, the politics of representing another's life, and gathering and assembling the material. Readers who would rather continue reading Antonia's story without interruption are welcome to return to this section at points in the story.

CONTEXTS OF ANTONIA'S STORY

Antonia and I first talked about writing her life story in 1996 and began to work on it in 2002. We have known each other since February 1987, when I lived a year with her and her family in a rural community of San Pedro Chenalhó, a township in the highlands of Chiapas, Mexico. My goal at that time was to conduct research for my dissertation in anthropology about indigenous women's experiences with their own and others' ritual drinking as well as problem drinking. Although neither Antonia nor her husband, Domingo, were currently drinkers, Domingo was a heavy drinker as a young man and often counseled others to stop drinking.

In 1988, just before I was to return to the United States, I asked Antonia what I could do to repay her and other women in her community for all that they had given me. She told me that I could help them sell their weavings for fair prices in my country. Our collaboration began in earnest in 1989 after I returned from my Ph.D. fieldwork and began working with friends to sell weavings in the United States for Tsobol Antzetik (Women United), a weaving cooperative that Antonia and her family members had formed. This work continues today under the auspices of Las Cruces-Chiapas Connection, a volunteer organization that assists two weaving co-ops in highland Chiapas to find fair trade markets (www.lascruceschiapasconnection.com).

Another context for Antonia's life story is the solidarity movement with indigenous people of Chiapas that developed in the wake of the Zapatista uprising in 1994. Antonia and Domingo became Zapatistas soon after the uprising. Their passion for the movement inspired me and many others throughout the world to assist Zapatista supporters to create a more just relationship between indigenous people and the Mexican state. This book is very much a part of global efforts to foster social justice and create understanding and solidarity between indigenous people and people of other ethnicities and nationalities.

Yet another context for Antonia's story is the movement of researchers and activists across the globe exploring the significance of women's diverse experiences. Many scholars have written about the Zapatista movement's focus on women's rights, unique among Latin American social movements.[1] Antonia has built upon the Zapatista Revolutionary Women's Law to make her own voice and the voices of other women heard. As a feminist anthropologist I have sought ways to assist Antonia and other women in her community to bring their words and unique perspectives to the attention of those in Mexico and outside the country who are ignorant of the legacy of disregard for the rights of indigenous women.

After more than twenty years of friendship and collaboration, I am still an outsider to the poverty, racism, and male dominance that Antonia has endured. This reality has created challenges for me and Antonia in working together, which we have tried to meet by talking about our differences. As a white woman I have not known racism, only sexism, and for a time, poverty. However, I did not grow up poor; I was raised in a small college town in Michigan where my parents were both teachers.

I took a circuitous route to becoming an anthropologist, spending thirteen years working as an illustrator, often bartering my work for things I needed. I was poor, but buoyed up by friendships with people working for social change. I was also single and didn't have to worry about supporting anyone else. Things changed when I was thirty-five and just starting graduate school. I met a man and his two children, and we began living together. The next ten years were challenging as Mike and I struggled to overcome our limited economic resources, and I tried to find my place in an already existing family.

At forty-five, I obtained my first full-time tenure track teaching position. In part I was able to obtain that position because Antonia and many others in her community made it possible for me to complete my Ph.D. by welcoming me into their community. I am indebted in ways that I can never repay. My indebtedness informs the dramatic economic inequalities between Antonia and me. In this book we explore how we have dealt with the inequality between us in our personal and work relationships. We hope that our story will give moral support to others involved in similar relationships.

The Politics of Representing Antonia's Life

Antonia is a wife, mother, weaver, Catholic, community organizer, and supporter of the Ejército Zapatista Liberación Nacional, or EZLN (the Zapatista Army of National Liberation). The EZLN rose up in 1994 to protest the exclusion and oppression of the indigenous people of Chiapas by the Mexican state. Soon after the uprising Antonia joined a support base in her community, one of hundreds of community-based civilian groups that support the EZLN.

From the beginning, we intended this book to bear Antonia's real name, even though we recognized risks in doing so. In the 1990s, paramilitary troops, backed by the military, committed heinous acts of violence against Zapatista supporters in San Pedro Chenalhó (see Part 2, Chapter 2).

While writing the first draft of this book in the summer of 2009, I reached a turning point in my concern for Antonia's welfare if the book were to carry her real name. Human rights abuses against social activists perpetrated by police, the military, paramilitaries, and security forces are rife throughout the nation. For example, on July 10, 2009, members of the Zapatista-inspired "The Other Campaign" and participants of the "Civil Resistance and No Payment of High Electricity Rates Movement" in Candelaria, Campeche, were beaten and detained. Antonia and thousands of others in Chiapas also protest high electric charges by the federal Electricity Commission. Members of Zapatista bases have not paid electric fees since 1994 as part of their resistance against the government. Zapatista supporters defend their actions based on the Mexican government's exploitation of the natural resources of Chiapas without regard for the basic needs of poor people. Many indigenous communities there, including Antonia's, had to wait until just a couple years before the Zapatista uprising to receive electricity, while hydroelectric dams in Chiapas were providing more than 50 percent of the hydroelectric energy in Mexico.[2]

So far state officials have tended to look the other way regarding nonpayment of electric bills. But the EZLN remains in hiding, and civilian support bases stand ready to mobilize when needed in response to a stalemate between the government and the EZLN over the government's failure to implement the peace accords signed in 1995. In the context of the current repression and ongoing labeling of the Zapatistas by the Mexican and U.S. governments as subversives—and even terrorists—it seems paramount to protect Antonia's true identity.

In addition to the broader-scale repression, Antonia has been the target of envy within her community. In Tzotzil-Maya communities it is considered socially destabilizing for individuals to bring attention to themselves or to acquire more possessions or power than others. As this book evolved, Antonia accepted that its publication might fan already existing resentment of her by envious neighbors. But where envy mixes with political repression in Chiapas, personal and social suffering are likely to intensify, and I feared for Antonia's and others' welfare if her name were to be used.

When I shared my concerns with Antonia about whether to use her real name or not, she left the decision up to me. I decided not to use it, with deep regrets about not giving her the recognition that she deserves.[3]

LANGUAGE ISSUES

Antonia's first language is Tzotzil, a Mayan language spoken by close to 300,000 people living in the state of Chiapas.[4] Antonia learned to speak Spanish in primary school and speaks it well. While living with her, I studied Tzotzil, but we depended on Spanish to talk about our lives. When it came to recording conversations specifically for this book, we discussed whether to work in Tzotzil or Spanish. I thought that it would be ideal to use Tzotzil in order to add to the growing body of literature in Tzotzil about Tzotzil-Maya culture and history. Two drawbacks to this option were my lack of fluency in the language and the substantial funds required to pay someone to transcribe and translate Antonia's words, as Antonia didn't have time to do this herself. Antonia concluded that we should talk in Spanish. Her decision reflects a major thread in her life since childhood—a desire and capacity to reach across cultural and language barriers to increase intercultural understanding and collaboration.

Despite our decision to have Antonia tell her story mainly in Spanish, we are aware that Tzotzil has many qualities that convey experiences of life different from what can be conveyed in other languages. For example, Tzotzil speakers use a lot of repetition and joking. Antonia often jokes around and laughs with her children and others. I am confident that the sense of humor that leavens the difficulties of life for Antonia would have come out more strongly had we spoken about her life mostly in Tzotzil. However, reflecting on her life seemed to bring out a more somber tone in Antonia's voice, regardless of which language she used.

For those interested in the Tzotzil language and issues of translation and interpretation, Appendix A provides a transcription in Tzotzil, Spanish, and English of the message Antonia asked me to carry to her son when he was working in Alabama (see pages 209 and 210). This message reflects the more formal character of Tzotzil speech used on special occasions or for specific purposes.[5]

Gathering the Material

In 2003 Antonia and I compiled a list of the important topics and events in her life. During the course of working on this book, we transitioned from a more traditional interviewing style in which I posed topics from the list for Antonia to talk about, to recording less focused conversations about both our lives. We found the latter approach more enjoyable and equitable, as it required me, as well as Antonia, to do the difficult work of reflecting on my life.

During two recording sessions in the summers of 2005 and 2006, we shared our conversations with Heather Sinclair, a mutual friend. Heather was a human rights observer in a peace camp in Chiapas in 1996 and is currently a Ph.D. candidate in Border History at the University of Texas at El Paso. We recorded our three-way conversations in Heather's home in El Paso and at a Buddhist retreat center in Tularosa, New Mexico. Private conversations between Antonia and me took place in Antonia's home in Chenalhó, my home in Radium Springs, New Mexico, or in a room where I stayed in San Cristóbal de las Casas, the urban center of highland Chiapas.[6]

Published sources that I consulted for my narrative portions include my own and others' ethnographic writings. While the scholarship on Tzotzil-Mayas of Chiapas is rich, I place this material mostly in endnotes because I want readers to pay close attention to how Antonia describes the dynamic and complex process through which she takes aspects of diverse cultural influences into her hands and shapes her life. My sense from knowing Antonia for twenty-four years is that Tzotzil-Maya cultural beliefs and practices are the warp upon which she weaves the threads of her life from the variety of cultural influences with which she has come into contact.

My intent is to enable readers to appreciate Antonia's integration into a global society and the broader humanity that they share with her. In recent decades anthropologists have tried to correct an earlier tendency to treat cultures as homogenous and bounded bodies of beliefs and practices (Rus 2004). Today they strive to show how cultural beliefs and practices are internally contested and constantly in flux. This correction is nowhere more critical than in the study of women's lives.

As a woman in Chenalhó, Antonia has not had much power. Traditional Mayan gender ideology restricts women's place to the house and hamlet, and associates women with upholding traditions. Since political opposition to state control began to intensify in the 1980s and '90s, men have stressed their right to defend and conserve their cultures and traditions. Not unlike earlier ethnographers, indigenous leaders tend to present their traditions in mono-lithic and harmonious terms. Today, as more and more women are gaining a voice in how their cultures are presented and defended, a more complex picture of indigenous cultures and traditions is emerging. This picture reveals men's complicity in binding women to traditions that do not respect their rights in order to bolster claims of ethnic sovereignty.

Nevertheless, I try in this book to show how Antonia acts in the world on the basis of many traditional Tzotzil-Maya conceptions of human nature. She defends her native language and many of her people's beliefs and practices, even the traditional bride petition process in which a girl does not have boyfriends, but waits until a boy comes to her house to ask her parents' permission to marry her (see Chapters 4 and 5).

Organizing the Material

In this book I hope to carry the gift of Antonia's life to the world, but I don't want to deliver it in a package with a neatly tied bow. I want to allow for the assumption that people overflow boundaries and that appearances often deceive; what one sees may not be all that there is, and what one reads on these pages is only a partial, biased image. Writing about mourning his wife's passing, C. S. Lewis said, "I mistook a cloud of atoms for a person" (1961, p. 78). Lewis went on to say that we continually construct images of others, and that they have to depart pretty widely from our image of them for us to notice. Yet in real life, they are rarely "in character." They always have a card in their hands that we don't know about, that they might not even know about until they find it.

Although I want to allow for readers to meet Antonia on their own terms, to find the card in her hand, I have searched for a thread while organizing her words, to tie her life to my own and others' lives. I haven't asked Antonia's help to find this thread when I am with her. We stay focused on the stories themselves and how she feels about all the things that have happened in her life, leaving the work of stringing this all together to me. But early in our relationship, Antonia gave me a key to doing this work that respects our distinct cultural worlds while placing us on common ground.

During one of our Tzotzil lessons in 1987, I asked, "How do you say 'life' in Tzotzil?"

Antonia looked up from her weaving with one of her "You're not going to like this" looks, laughed a little nervously, and said, "How about *banamil*?"

Okay, I thought. I already know what *banamil* means. It means "Earth." It doesn't mean "life."

Antonia went back to her weaving, and I went back to biting my fingernails. How, I asked myself, could "Earth" take the place of "life"?

Later that day Antonia offered me some of her thoughts about "life," perhaps realizing that *la vida* is a significant concept for Ladinos and gringos. "Look, Cristina, when I think of my life I think of how I am passing over the Earth from year to year and with whom. Well, I think of a few years, like three or five. These are like chapters in the books you read. I'm changing in each chapter, different things interest me. But it's not important what happens just to me. What matters is that I follow the traditions and serve my people, that I show respect to people and God, that I pass well over the Earth."[7]

Years later I learn that Tzotzil does have a word for life, *k'uxlejal*. Nevertheless, the fact that Antonia, whose mother tongue is Tzotzil, didn't immediately think of this word suggests that it is not a common one.

By uniting "Earth" and "life," Antonia forewarned me of the danger of drawing the thread of her life too far outside the larger fabric of which it is a part: her family, community, Earth (a sacred being in Maya culture), and the generations of Tzotzil-Maya men and women who have passed this way before her. The collective ethos of Antonia's life accounts for much of its distinctiveness, as well as its relevance to the lives of women in other times and places who have struggled together for justice for themselves and the social groups to which they belong.

In addition to trying to convey Antonia's integration into a broader social whole, I also wanted the book's organization to convey the ebb and flow of her life—its many cycles of light and dark. Based on my understanding of these cycles, I have organized her story into three parts.

Part 1, "Becoming a *Batz'i Antz* (True Woman)," describes the important role that Tzotzil-Maya beliefs and practices played in shaping Antonia's understandings of how to be a respectful person and a proper wife, mother, and member of a household and community.

Part 2, "Contesting the Status Quo, Creating a Different World," explores Antonia's experiences in the weaving cooperative and Zapatista movements, and how they helped her find a way to express her more assertive personal style. This part also shows Antonia's struggles to be a good mother to her sons and daughters in rapidly changing times.

Part 3, "Gains and Losses, Lessons Learned," recounts Antonia's reflections on the challenges, setbacks, and suffering that stem from trying to honor her cultural beliefs and traditions while also being a Zapatista and a member of the Word of God, the local name of the progressive Catholic movement in highland Chiapas (known also as "liberation theology"), which began in the 1960s, soon after Antonia was born. Part 3 builds on previous chapters to show the conflicts that Antonia faces as she tries to balance her life as a wife and mother with her work in cooperatives and her collaborations with outsiders.

Most chapters begin with introductions placing Antonia's words within broader historical, cultural, and social contexts. At times these "introductions" precede a part of Antonia's narrative within a chapter. Sometimes my words relate Antonia's experiences to my own in hopes of deepening readers' appreciation of the commonalities and differences between Antonia's life and the lives of women in other societies.

Notes on the Book's Two Voices and Key Terms

The two voices in this book, mine and Antonia's, have been differentiated by the typesetter in order to help readers keep them separate. Where needed for context, I provide details of where and when Antonia talked about a specific topic, or the time period in which I wrote portions of my narrative. At points in her narrative Antonia addresses me as "you" or "Cristina."

Antonia uses *mestizos* and *ladinos* interchangeably to refer to non-indigenous people living in and outside of her township. These people tend not to speak Tzotzil (although many living in the township center do) nor to live in the rural hamlets of Chenalhó. Antonia and I use "Pedranos" or "Pedranas," meaning "sons and daughters of Saint Peter," to refer to Tzotzil-speaking indigenous men and women of San Pedro Chenalhó. Mestizos living in the township center of San Pedro Chenalhó, known as Chenalhó, are typically not included in this term. We also use "Pedranos" or "Pedranas" to refer to the indigenous people of the territory of Chenalhó who no longer consider themselves a part of the officially recognized township and instead belong to the Zapatista autonomous township, with its headquarters in Polhó, founded in 1995. Occasionally Antonia uses "Chiapanecos" to refer to people from Chiapas.

To pronounce Tzotzil words in this book, it is necessary to know that Tzotzil has glottalized consonants and glottal stops between two vowels and in a final position. The glottalized consonants appear with an apostrophe after the letter. Among these are: p', t', tz', ch', k', and b'. English speakers make a similar glottal stop when stopping the air between "u'uh" to mean "no." To Tzotzil speakers glottal stops distinguish vastly different words. For example, *takin* = "dry," while *tak'in* = "money." Also, "x" in Tzotzil is pronounced like "sh" in English. For example, *pox*, sugarcane alcohol, is pronounced "posh."

Maya and non-Maya linguists and anthropologists differ over how to write Tzotzil. In this book I use *k* in place of *c* or *q'u*, *j* in place of *h*, and *tz* in place of *ts* in order to facilitate comparison with other Mayan languages that use *tz*.

People in Antonia's Life

Domingo, her husband
María, her mother
Hilario, her father, deceased
Francisco, her older brother
Marta, Francisco's wife
Margarita, her eldest half sister (from her mother's first marriage)
Angélica, her youngest half sister (from her mother's first marriage)
Anita, her younger sister
Marcela, her youngest sister
Moises, Marcela's husband
Felipe, her first son
Magdalena, Felipe's wife
Sebastian, her second son
Juana, Sebastian's wife
Mariano, her third son
Alberto, her fourth son
Paulina, her first daughter
Antonio, Paulina's husband
Rosalva, her second daughter
Guadalupe, her best friend
Christine Eber, her *comadre* from the United States
Carol-Jean McGreevy-Morales, her *comadre* from the United States
Sally Meisenhelder, a friend from the United States
Nancy Modiano, a friend in Chiapas, deceased
Heather Sinclair, a friend from the United States

Time Line of Key Events Mentioned in the Book

1962   Antonia is born in a small community in the rural township of San Pedro Chenalhó, Chiapas.

1974   First indigenous congress held in San Cristóbal de las Casas. Domingo, Antonia's husband, attends at age eighteen.

1975   First diocesan assembly in San Cristóbal de las Casas makes official commitment to work "with and for the poor."

1978   Sna Jolobil weaving cooperative founded in San Cristóbal.

1989   Coffee prices fall to record low.

1992   Sociedad Civil las Abejas (Civil Society the Bees) forms in Chenalhó.

1994   Zapatista Army of National Liberation seizes four towns (January 1).
North American Free Trade Agreement is implemented (January 1).
PRI's Ernesto Zedillo is elected president (August 21).

1995   Zapatista supporters form San Pedro Polhó, an autonomous township within San Pedro Chenalhó, with headquarters in Polhó.

1996   The San Andrés Peace Accords on Indian Rights and Culture are signed by Zapatista and government representatives (February 16). Antonia joins the "peace belt" of people surrounding the building in San Andrés Sakem Chen where the talks take place.
Intercontinental or Intergalactic Encounter is held at Oventik Aguascalientes (July 27). Antonia and Domingo attend.
Four young men accused of being "head-cutters" are killed by an angry mob in Chenalhó (August 19).
Paramilitary troop buildup in Chenalhó and other parts of Chiapas; refugee camps begin to form.

1997   Forty-five members of Las Abejas are massacred at Acteal, Chenalhó (December 22). Antonia helps refugees organize a weaving co-op and writes a song for International Women's Day in Oventik.

1998   Padre Miguel Chanteau, a Catholic priest in Chenalhó for thirty-three years, is expelled from Mexico.

1999   Antonia joins 5,000 civilian Zapatistas who travel throughout Mexico to consult with fellow Mexicans on the San Andrés Peace Accords.

2000   Vicente Fox is elected president of Mexico, ending forty-five years of monopoly of power by the PRI (Partido Revolucionario Institucional).

2002   Antonia visits the United States for the first time (and returned again in 2005, 2006, and 2008).

2006   Chiapas ranks first among Mexican states in the number of migrants leaving each year for the United States.

2008   Antonia's youngest son leaves Chiapas to find work in the United States.

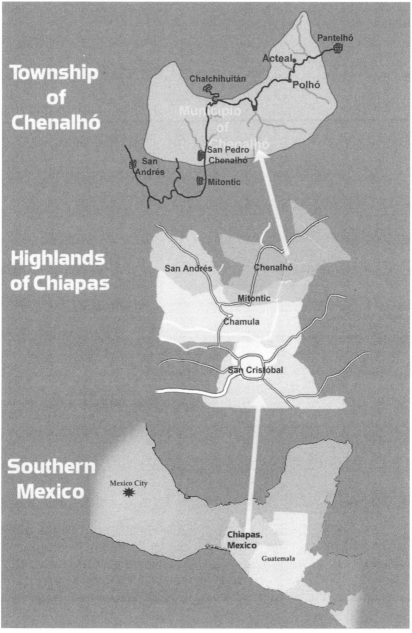

Copyright Bill Jungels, 2010.

The Journey of a Tzotzil-Maya Woman of Chiapas, Mexico

PART I

Becoming a *Batz'i Antz* (True Woman)

(FACING PAGE): A woman design, woven by Antonia in 2005. Collection of Christine Eber. Photo courtesy of Michael O'Malley, 2010.

In the 1980s I saw women weave images of men with four fingers and toes, symbolizing the four corners of the *milpa*. The four digits didn't surprise me because the ancient Mayan number for men was 4. But it did surprise me that I never saw a woman symbol on any weaving. After several years of asking women if they knew of a woman symbol, a box arrived with weavings to sell that contained a cloth with a woman symbol. I knew right away the figure's gender was female because of its three fingers and toes, and the three lines descending from its vagina. As with the Mayan number for men, the number for women corresponds with a pivotal aspect of their identities: preparing food for their families. The number 3 stands for the three rocks that hold up the *comal*, the clay griddle upon which women make tortillas.

Antonia recalls how the women in her cooperative rediscovered the design:

I didn't know that there was a woman design when I was younger. When you [Cristina] asked me why we didn't have a woman symbol, I asked the women in Tsobol Antzetik about it during one of our meetings. "How can we have a woman design?" My cousin replied, "Ah, it seems that my mother has one on a ceremonial cloth called *b'ut korision* [sacrificial victim] that she has stored away." "Can you show us so that we can learn the design?" we asked.

My cousin brought it to the next meeting to show us that this cloth has designs of a woman, a man, and other designs. When I first saw the design, I liked her braid. As we looked at the design, we joked about it. "Ah, look at her skirt! Look at her hand!" But we were happy when we saw this design. After that we began to learn how to make the woman design.

Chapter 1

A Childhood Memory

This memory, this thing that happened, it's very difficult for me. I can't forget it. I always tell my children and my husband, "You haven't had happen to you what happened to me."

Antonia

When I was a little girl I got sick with an illness. I don't know what they call it. I don't know if I was six or eight years old. My whole body swelled up. I was going to die from swelling. My hair fell out, and when it began to grow back it was coarse and thick.

Each morning I felt so cold from my sickness. My feet couldn't get warm in the bed. I didn't have a blanket, just a thin one that didn't warm me. My legs were swollen—my feet, too. I could hardly sleep in my bed in the morning.

When my mother woke up to make the fire, she would have to bring me to the edge of the fire to lie down on two blocks of wood. In the day I had to go outside to warm myself in the sun. Although the sun was strong, it didn't warm me. I had to take off my clothes so my skin would warm. I even went as far as to take off my blouse to warm my skin. I was a little girl, I didn't know what to do.

I felt so much like eating things. I wanted to eat fruit, pears, *elotes* [fresh ears of corn]. I couldn't bear to wait for the time when the *elotes* came out. I was desperate. But where was I going to find them? In the past, they didn't sell *elotes* like today. Now they're selling them all over the place. But in Chenalhó at this time there weren't any. I wanted to eat everything, but there wasn't anything to eat. No way to get it. My parents didn't have any money or maybe they didn't sell these things in Chenalhó. At that time there weren't markets or stores like today.

I had an old blouse that I hung in a tree so that it would rot. It was made out of an old bag that they put sugar or flour in. Each time I came to the tree,

(FACING PAGE): Photo courtesy of Bill Jungels, 2009.

the cloth would be more torn and rotted from being outside in the rain. I would tear off pieces to chew. I went to the tree to eat.

I also chewed on newspaper. It tasted good to me. In the past if we bought a kilo of sugar, they wrapped it in a newspaper. Afterward the newspapers were in the house, and they smelled as if they still had food in them. I ate these things because I felt as if I was going to die of hunger.

My illness lasted for many months, perhaps a year. My parents took me to the Health Center in Chenalhó. But they treated me very badly. "*Una chamulita*" [a little Chamula girl],[1] they called me! I don't know how I looked when I was sick. Maybe I looked worthless. But they acted racist toward me. They gave me medicine, but with the medicine I didn't get better.

My parents looked for *j'iloletik* [healers]. Although many healers came to me, my mother saw that I wasn't getting better. She looked for another and another. She would wait a few days to get some more money and then ask another healer to come. I don't remember who came first. But each healer when he came held my hand to listen to my pulse. He had to listen to my blood to know what sickness I had. Then he began to pray to ask that my sickness leave me. The healers asked my parents for rum, a chicken, candles, incense, and branches of *ocote, tsots te', lotsob chix,* and *valak xik.*[2] Those are the main plants that healers use. And with the rum they began to do a cleansing in the form of a cross. As I lay in bed they did this with four witnesses. Each time they cleansed me with rum and also with the chicken, three times in front of my heart and three times on each side.[3]

The healers said that mutton is good for illness. So I ate mutton. It took a long time to cure me. Eventually I got better, probably because of the healers. After, when I was a little better, I wanted to eat all kinds of things. I yearned for food. I couldn't wait to give my body what it craved.

Chapter 2

Parents

My mother could endure very hard things.

Antonia

Over the years I had heard bits and pieces about Antonia's childhood, especially about her father's drinking and the lack of food. None of what I heard was remarkable, not even the story of her illness. Most everyone in Chenalhó remembers some illness that almost killed them. Everyone has experienced hunger. Far too many recall their fathers drinking up any cash that the family managed to acquire. Adults remember being afraid, as children, of their fathers, and sometimes their mothers, when they came home drunk on market days. Their parents would demand food, and if it wasn't fast enough in coming, they'd lash out with harsh words—or a piece of cow hide if it was handy.

Antonia's father, Hilario, was a drinker until he contracted chronic bronchitis and entered the Word of God, the Bible-based progressive Catholic movement that began in Chiapas in the 1960s. When I knew Hilario in the late 1980s, he was a gentle, kind man. It hardly seemed possible that he had once been cruel and controlling.

Although he drank a lot when Antonia was growing up, Hilario worked hard in the fields and taught his children to respect the food he brought home from there. Antonia recalls, "When my father was alive, he didn't want to see even one grain of corn on the floor inside the house. We always had to pick it up. If it was a bit of corn dough, or a little bit of tortilla, my father always scolded us because it took a lot of work to bring the food to us."[1]

It didn't matter where my father drank, in the pueblo or in some house. In the past there was a lot of rum sold in houses. There were two or three families living near us where he went to drink.

My father drank a lot and the family didn't matter to him. He kept his money, the little that he earned. He always went to work for the mestizos. He carried wood, made corrals, cleaned patios in Chenalhó. There he could

make a little money. What he earned he spent on *pox* [rum made from distilled sugar cane]. He just spent what he had.

In the past my mother didn't weave, although she knew how. She didn't make many weavings because there was no place to sell them. She sold a little to people who wanted them in the community. For money my mother and I went out to work in other people's fields. Everything that my mother earned she used to buy our clothes and our food. My mother supported our family. That's why my mom couldn't save any money.

She suffered a lot on account of my father because he was very jealous. He always said, "Ah, you have another man. You have a lover." And many other things. He yelled at her a lot.

He didn't let her go places. He didn't let her laugh. He just wanted her to stay shut up in the house, with her head bowed, without looking around, without laughing. If there were people other than family in the house, if we lifted our heads to laugh, to talk, he got angry at us.

My dad always scolded my mom when he was drunk, and she had to leave the house and hide in the mountains. We had to go with her, too. When my father drank, no one slept. We stayed up all night, but my brother and my two little sisters and I couldn't take it. We would go to sleep, and my mother would stay up alone. If my father was in the house, my mother had to sit up all night taking care of him. And when my dad began to hit her, she woke us up to go hide. I wanted to die when my dad was hitting my mother. I asked God to strike me with an illness that would kill me.

My mother suffered a lot with my father. It was very difficult for her. She wanted to separate from him and went to her sister's house because she no longer had parents by that time. My mom was very little when her mother died. I don't think that she remembers her mother. She only remembers that a stepmother came to take care of her and that she didn't treat her very well. My mother was the youngest of four sisters, and after they married and went to live with their husbands, she was the only one left in the house. My mother had to take care of her father when he was very sick. He had an illness in which his feet became infected, and his wounds would never heal. My mother had to wash his wounds every day, and there were even worms in them.

Each time when my mother couldn't take it any longer with my father, she left him for a few weeks. But my dad always asked her to come home. "I'm not going to do that again. Forgive me," he would say each time when he came, crying. Since my mom believed that it was tradition to stay with him, and she felt sorry for him, she would forgive him and go back to him.

(FACING PAGE): Photo courtesy of Bill Jungels, 2009.

But the same thing would happen again! That's how it was for years and years from the beginning when they got married until I was pretty big. My mother could endure very hard things. If this were to happen to me, honestly, I couldn't take it.

When my father got sick, he gave up drinking and joined the Word of God. He asked God's forgiveness for everything bad that he had done in the past. He was sick for fourteen or fifteen years, I think. He changed a lot in those years. By the time he died, he was a very good man. He wasn't jealous any more. He let my mom do things. He stayed home alone when she went to San Cristóbal to sell weavings and to visit my brother and do errands, like when my sister Marcela needed a companion to deliver weavings to the co-op store [the store of Sna Jolobil (House of the Weaver)].

My mother's life changed a lot, a lot. After many years of bearing up with my father, she was finally happy.

Chapter 3

Learning to Work

*When my life was very sad was when my parents took me to another
family's fields to earn money or get corn for our family to survive. I had
to work with a spade alongside my mother. I didn't know how to work
well, but I made the effort. That's when I didn't like my life.*

Antonia

Since I was a little girl, the only chore that I liked in my life was to carry
water and wash clothes at the waterhole. But to work in the *milpa*, carry
firewood, I didn't like that.

When I first learned to wash clothes, I really didn't know how. The
dirt didn't come out and my clothes didn't look white. But little by little I
learned. At that time my mother used soap made from a plant called *chupak'*
(*amale*).[1] To make soap they removed the root of *chupak'* and then took off
the skinlike part and a stick would be left. Then they would crush the stick
with a stone until it foamed. They would put *chupak'* on clothes and also
on their heads. *Chupak'* was used especially to wash hair. That's what my
mother used on her hair.

But when I was growing up, I used soap from the store. I don't know
what kind of soap it was. It didn't work very well. We had to buy it. That's
why we always went to work in others' *milpas*. Some paid with cash, others
with corn. I remember that we usually received corn. I think that we went
out to work on Saturdays or Sundays, or sometimes I would skip school.
Whatever day my father wanted to work I went with him.

I also had to learn to sweep. When I swept the kitchen sometimes my
mother told me that I didn't do it well. "You missed all this. You can sweep
better. Watch how I do it," she would say. Little by little I learned how to do
it well. It's not difficult to sweep. What was hard for me to learn was to make
tortillas. That was really hard.

In my mother's time they ground *nixtamal* [cooked corn] on a metate [a
trough-shaped stone] using their own strength. I could never manage the
metate. It took strength and I didn't have much. When I was about seven or

eight [late 1960s] the manual grinder appeared. We didn't use the stone to make tortillas after that. Then later, when I was a woman, the electric grinder arrived. It made grinding a little easier. Little by little the manual grinder went out of fashion, and now many people use electric grinders. Even though the grinders are easier, older women are accustomed to the stone. My mother always made *matz* [a staple drink made of coarsely ground corn mixed with water] on the stone, but I didn't learn to do it very well.

My mother taught me to make tortillas by hand, with just my fingers, not on a piece of plastic. In the past, my mother always did it with her fingers.[2] Margarita, my mother's daughter from her first marriage, didn't know how to do it that way. But my mother tried to teach me so that I could carry on the tradition. I remember that I couldn't do it. I wanted to do it on the plastic because it's easier. But my mother told me, "You have to learn because when you marry you aren't going to carry a piece of plastic to make tortillas to your mother-in-law's house!" My mother thought that it was disgraceful to carry a piece of plastic to another person's house to make tortillas.

"But how am I going to be able to do it?" I asked her. I got angry and cried because I couldn't make tortillas with my fingers. One time she tried something to make me do it. She took a piece of dough, hot off the griddle, and wrapped it around my fingers. "This is your punishment so that you will learn how to do it," she said. When she wrapped the hot tortilla around my fingers, I cried. But even with that I couldn't learn!

Later, after I was married and went to my mother-in-law's house, it wasn't a problem for me to make tortillas on plastic, even though my mother thought it would be a big problem! Now women make tortillas on a piece of plastic. My mother doesn't do it with her fingers anymore either. Her tradition has been lost. We won!

My mother also taught me to weave. My half sister, Margarita, taught me a little, too. I learned from watching my mother, how she did it. First I made a toy loom. I just put some sticks together and began to weave. I tied together my mother's leftover pieces of yarn and played with the threads. Sometimes it worked, other times it didn't. When my weaving didn't turn out right, I threw it away. When it turned out better, I showed it to my mother, and she said, "Ah, that's good. Continue with that." That's how I learned little by little, watching how my mom did it. I would say to myself, "Ah, I think that's how it's done!"

Then, when I was about six or seven, I began to make something small like a napkin. But it didn't turn out well. When I was doing a little better—

(FACING PAGE): Photo by Christine Eber, 2010.

I think I was twelve years old—my mother told me that I should make a blouse. I don't know why I was afraid to make something big. Perhaps I thought that I wouldn't be able to do it. My mother told me that I could make it in two parts. In the past girls did it like that, but not anymore. When both halves were ready, I sewed them together. It took me months to make the blouse because I was in school.

We didn't use a lot of colors then, not like today. When I was born, the majority of women used only two colors—red and blue . . . and white. Yes, let's say three colors were used at first. In the past women called the threads *rabia*. I heard them say, "Ah, I have to buy my *rabia*." *Rabia* is like *ilera* [a very fine thread]. The design on my blouse was an ancient one that my mother taught me. It's called *batz'i luch* [the true design].[3] We still have it today.

When I finished that blouse, I thought, "Ah, how pretty my blouse is!" Now I remember how it looked, and it wasn't pretty! But at that time I liked it a lot. When it was finished, I put it away because I felt that it was a major accomplishment. I kept it for many years and only wore it during fiestas. During the week I would just wear a blouse of plain cloth without any designs. I will never forget the first blouse I wove because it was hard brocading[4] on the loom, and it took a long time to make.

Chapter 4

School

When I was really happy was when I was in school. I played and had fun there.

Antonia

Primary school was a time of exhilaration for Antonia. School, more than anything else in her early life, fueled her desire to find her own way of being in the world, different from that of her mother and other women in the community.

Schooling in highland Chiapas in the 1960s and '70s, when Antonia was in primary school, was a nation-building project aimed at assimilating "backward" Indian children into mestizo culture. Mexican educators saw "defective" cultures, not poverty and racism, as the major obstacles keeping indigenous people in their backward state. Teachers were young indigenous men, and a few women, who had left their communities to seek their way in the urban world. Sometimes that journey led them to turn their backs on their native communities and languages. At best they were always straddling different cultural worlds, and were often ambivalent about their little charges, who reminded them of what they had left behind.[1]

Indigenous parents saw schooling for what it was and put up some resistance to its expansion. But eventually primary schools existed in every indigenous community, and children were required to attend. Still, some parents didn't send their children to primary school if they didn't want to go—or if their labor was needed at home. Today mothers still keep children at home for their own welfare when it is raining heavily or the child is feeling poorly. Schools have no source of heat, and children caught in the rain on their way to school spend the day shivering in the cold.

Antonia didn't learn as much as she deserved to in school, nor in a way that respected her people's language, history, and culture, but by the time she graduated sixth grade, she could speak, read, and write Spanish, a tool that has helped her move outside the confines of a traditional Pedrana's life.

Since I was a child I always wanted to speak Spanish. I enjoyed speaking it. I had a teacher who didn't speak Tzotzil, and I wanted to talk with her. My Spanish wasn't correct in the beginning. For example, I wanted to say *enojada* [angry] and instead I said *mojada* [wet].

In school we hardly spoke any Spanish. If we spoke a few words, our *compañeros* [companions] laughed at us. We felt very embarrassed. That's why we didn't speak it. But I never felt as embarrassed as others to speak Spanish from the beginning.

I don't remember the names of my first teachers, but they didn't teach well. Later, when I was in third or fourth grade, a teacher came from Zinacantán called Mariano Conde. He was my favorite teacher. He taught us mathematics and also art education and other things that I liked. We danced, sang, and did exercises. I liked participating in dances a lot. When I finished primary school, he left too.

When I was in school, my parents couldn't buy my clothes or school supplies. I wore clothes made of something called a lona, a bag that they put sugar or flour in, with pictures on it. My mother bought these because they were cheap. She opened them up to make my blouse and shawl, but I don't remember very well if we embroidered on it or if we just made a border around the neck.

I just had one woven blouse that I made, but I put it away to use at each school celebration. I couldn't make more because I didn't have money to buy thread. In the past, if I bought a skirt, I could only wear it to school. I only had two skirts, one that I wore to school and one for changing into at my house. They were quite torn but they covered me. I still remember when I returned from school I had to change my clothes and wear my torn skirt. In the afternoon I went to the well to get water, and there I'd find my friends from school. I was ashamed for them to see me in my torn clothes.

We never had shoes back then. I began to use shoes after I left school because a teacher gave me a pair of sandals. I think I was about fifteen.[2] From then on I began to wear shoes. But it was strange for the people to see them. Sometimes they made fun of women who wore sandals. But years later they began to use them, too.

When I was about twelve years old I wore ribbons so I could participate in a school program. I had to perform in a dance, and the teacher asked me to wear a blue ribbon. I asked my mother to buy it, and she bought it for me because it was a requirement. She told me, "I'm going to buy this ribbon, but you have to keep it for other programs." I had to obey her, so I kept the ribbon for a few years.

(FACING PAGE): Little girls from the neighboring township of San Juan Chamula lining up for the beginning of a school day. Photo by Christine Eber, 1988.

When I was fourteen or fifteen years old, I could buy my own ribbons because I was making woven cloths and selling them to the teachers. There was a cooking teacher in the school, and she ordered a tortilla cloth from me. That was the first weaving I sold. Then another teacher named Angelina ordered many tortilla cloths from me. They kept ordering my weavings. I made them with fine thread in stripes of many colors. I think the teachers paid me 5 pesos for a weaving, or less. I don't remember.

When I was still in school, I began to sell gum, candy, and cookies in order to make some money to buy my school supplies. Each week I had to go to the center of Chenalhó to buy my gum and cookies. At that time there wasn't a store near the school, so I sold my gum and cookies at school.

It didn't take much effort to sell. It was easy, strolling around with my friends, selling gum and cookies to the students and the teachers, too. My teacher bought my gum, too. He liked to chew it. He bought my gum so that I could earn a little to buy my pencil and notebook, and threads for my weaving.

I also asked the teachers if they had clothes that I could wash to earn a little money. After school let out at 4 p.m. I went to the waterhole to wash the diapers that I carried home with me. I didn't like it so much when the diapers were really dirty. When I got back home, it was nearly nighttime. In those days, one part of my life was happiness, one part was sadness.

When Antonia graduated primary school in 1977, sixth grade was the social equivalent of twelfth grade in the United States. Even in 1996, when I was godmother for her son Sebastian's sixth-grade graduation, the feeling in the air that day was that the dozen twelve-year-olds, heads held high, standing in formation on the basketball court, were now adults. Sebastian was selected to read the graduation poem, the last line of which read: "Now we say goodbye to our childhoods."

I was also godmother for Antonia's third son, Mariano, when he graduated from middle school in the municipal center of Chenalhó. During mass before the ceremony, Padre Carmelo exhorted the young people to go on in school, not to resign themselves to being "masters of the machete and mistresses of the spoon." I cringed at the priest's words, but shared some of his fears. It hurt to see intelligent and bright-eyed youngsters unable to continue their schooling because of lack of money, or parents who fear that if they let their children leave the protection of their communities, they will lose their souls—not to mention their virginity.

Hilario and María saw no need for Antonia to further her schooling beyond sixth grade. She had learned the basics of arithmetic and to read and write in

Spanish, the main skills that school could give their daughter to hold her own in the mestizo world. In the 1970s it was rare for a young woman to continue past sixth grade or to leave her community in search of work. Antonia's parents weren't about to put their daughter's future at risk by sending her off to the city, where she would live independently and be unlikely to marry according to tradition. But Antonia had other plans.

After I finished primary school, I didn't want to stay in the house or keep working in the fields. I never liked that kind of work. I wanted to continue studying. In school I enjoyed myself. I had learned Spanish better than most of the children. I wanted to keep learning and to use my Spanish.

If I couldn't go to school, I wanted to find work as a teacher or cook. In that year there were opportunities to find work, but my parents wouldn't let me go on in school or look for work. They wanted me to stay and help them in the house. My mom always said, "Why are you thinking those things? Why don't you just stay here living like me?"

"I don't want to do that. I want to learn more. I want to make a person out of myself," I told her. But she never helped me with that.

The only one who supported me to go on in school was my older brother, Francisco. He always helped me. But he didn't have any power over my parents.

Once I went so far as to run away from home. My brother was already living in San Cristóbal. He came to live there when he was about twelve years old. He knew a teacher, the aunt of one of his friends. His friend invited Francisco to come to San Cristóbal to study and stay with his aunt.

I was only in San Cristóbal with my brother three or four days when my parents came to take me home. During those days I took care of the little girl of a woman who was staying in the house where my brother was living.

When my mom arrived, she was crying. I didn't want to return with my parents because I was afraid they'd hit me for running away. The mother of the little girl saw that my parents were really upset. She told me, "You'd better go back with them. Just ask permission from your parents to return here to find work." Then she explained this to my father. "She's going to return to the house, but you have to let her come back here to look for work."

"Well, that's fine," he said.

But when I got back to the house, he began to pray that I would forget all the things that were in my head, so that I would think only about the Word of God and working in the house. He prayed in the middle of the night because they say that people who want to make another person do something pray in the night. When I was deep asleep, he began to pray. He tied some branches together as a sign that I would stay tied to the house. After that I didn't want to leave the house to find work so much. "It's better to go with the Word of God," I told myself.

For a few years after that I still tried to leave home. In 1976 and 1977 my life was really difficult. I was always crying. I wanted to go to school or get a job to make some money. My brother Francisco helped me a little. He asked my parents' permission for me to leave home.

"Why don't you let her leave so she can continue studying and find work? My sister could be a teacher because she's very intelligent. One can see that she has a lot of talent."

But my father was very hard. At times my mom thought about letting me continue my studies, but my dad wouldn't budge. I felt very sad that my father wouldn't let me. I still remember how I was always crying, regretting that I couldn't go to school or find work. When I finally found a job as a married woman, I thought, "Why are they offering me a job now when I have a husband and a child, and not before, when I really wanted a job?" That's what I was thinking, with anger at times. I blamed my parents because they didn't let me find work when I was young.

I don't know if it was a blessing or a curse when my father prayed for me to stay at home and listen to the Word of God. When I'm not worried about anything and comfortable in my house, it seems that it was my father's blessing. If I had gone off to find work, perhaps I wouldn't have been in the Word of God, just working, worried about my papers, my salary, I don't know what else. But when things are just too much for me, when I meet some sadness, or some worry comes into my head, I think, "Ah, why didn't my father let me go? I wanted to be a teacher. I wanted to earn a lot of money."

Chapter 5

Making One's Soul Arrive

[E]ducation is a long process that starts when a child is born and lasts until reaching the summit of his life. It is conceived of as a slow but constant acquisition, bit by bit, of the "soul" (ch'ulel).

Jacinto Arias (1973: 28)

In 2006, when we were working on this book at Heather Sinclair's home in El Paso, Antonia quietly announced, "Since I was a little girl, I always knew I had value." Antonia's affirmation of her own worth didn't seem strange to me in that moment, but later I thought about how odd those words would sound coming from the mouths of most Pedranas—and many women in the United States.

Heather and I told Antonia that we couldn't say the same thing about ourselves. Although we had felt self-confident as little girls, puberty brought a barrage of messages about what makes a woman worthy, including being thin, trying to please others, and putting others' needs before her own.

Young women in Chenalhó also get many messages about how to be a *batz'i antz* (true woman). True women transform corn into food for humans, and they help in the fields if their labor is needed. They serve food to their fathers, brothers, and husbands whenever they are hungry. They make sure that there is water for drinking and cooking, and that their kinsmen have clean clothes. They are industrious and hard-working.

In complementary fashion, *batz'i viniketik* (true men) plant and harvest corn. They cut, carry, and stack firewood. Good husbands also help with household chores. They shuck and grind corn, feed chickens and other animals, collect fruit from nearby trees, comfort children in the night and care for them at times in the day, and buy items of food or other things the family needs.

Elders say that men and women should treat one another with respect because their work complements each other. They say that young men and women should not raise their voices in anger for fear of destabilizing household relations, which can lead to illness or death. But elders also say that young

women should not question their fathers' and husbands' authority, that they should stay close to home and not deal with strangers.

Ch'ulelal vulesal (making your soul arrive) is the Tzotzil phrase for the life-long process of becoming a true woman or true man. Ch'ulelal vulesal involves learning to act respectfully toward other humans and to fulfill one's complementary and reciprocal duties to family and community. It is premised on the belief that the ch'ulel (soul) is not affixed to the body at birth. The main human task is to behave in such as way as to firmly affix one's soul. Respecting, reciprocating, complementing, and serving one's community and the Mayan deities and Catholic saints are the main ways to accomplish this task.

Antonia moved gradually into womanhood through paying proper respect, working hard, and eventually marrying and having children. No coming-of-age ritual marked her becoming a batz'i antz. The onset of menses was a private affair. She recalls:

When I grew up my mother didn't tell me anything about menstruation. Mothers don't usually teach their daughters about it. I think that we didn't talk about it because we were embarrassed. I don't remember how I found out that my menstruation was going to come in time. When I started to menstruate, it wasn't a surprise to me, but I didn't like it. Nobody likes it. In the past nobody used anything to absorb the blood. We just let it be.

To make her soul arrive, Antonia has had to put her heart, head, and body into proper relation with others. Beginning when she was a little girl, Antonia learned to move and speak in ways that convey a respectful relation with those to whom she is subordinate, such as elders. For example, she learned to greet elders by stepping off the path, bowing her head, and bringing her right hand to her forehead, all the while saying "Juntot!" (uncle) or "Junme'!" (aunt). She learned to set chairs near the fire for elders and to sit on a tsomol, a wooden block.

Antonia would say that she hasn't done as well as many Pedranas in learning to make her soul arrive. I don't agree, but knowing how important respect is in Chenalhó, I empathize with her concern about falling short of the ideal. Antonia often contrasts herself with her respectful younger sisters, who speak with soft voices and don't leave home often or seek contact with strangers.

The clothing part of showing respect was easiest for Antonia to learn because as a weaver she took pride in clothing herself and her family in traditional

(FACING PAGE): Women preparing chenkulvaj for the Feast of Saint Peter. Photo by Christine Eber, 1987.

apparel. Knowing this, when I lived with Antonia, I wanted to show my respect by wearing Pedrana clothes. The day that I finally acquired all the clothes I needed to dress traditionally, Antonia helped me pleat my skirt and secure it in place with a wide woven belt. When all the pleats were straightened, she pulled my blouse out from the belt just enough so that the colorful tassels cascaded down my hip in a graceful way. When I entered the kitchen house where Domingo was seated by the fire, I expected him to nod in approval, but I didn't expect him to say, "Le' xa uni batz'i antzot" (Now you're a true woman.)

At the core of acquiring one's soul and behaving like a *batz'i antz* is learning to work in a habitual way that makes the actions and thoughts involved in each task a part of one's sense of self and way of being. *Nael* ("to know" in Tzotzil) conveys a different sense of knowing from what English speakers mean when they say "I know how to weave" or "I know how to speak Spanish." For Pedranos it's the dailiness of actions that makes one "know" something. Merely being able to perform the mechanics doesn't constitute knowing. One must weave or speak Spanish on a regular basis, make it part of one's identity, in order to know it.[1]

Antonia would say that she didn't know how to speak Spanish or weave during her adolescent years because she wasn't doing these things on a daily basis. At the time there weren't many markets for weavings, and she didn't have much interaction with monolingual Spanish speakers. But there was no doubt in her mind that she knew how to cook traditional foods. This knowledge is an essential part of Antonia's identity. It was, and still is, pivotal to becoming a true woman in Chenalhó.

Below are Antonia's recipes for corn-based foods and drinks that she learned to make helping her mother. *Takivaj*, the first food, is the only one prepared exclusively for saints' fiestas. Women who hold *cargos*, positions of leadership in saints' fiestas, must choose many helpers to assist them with food preparation and other duties, but their most important helper is *me' pan vaj*, the head cook.[2] She decides how much corn, beans, and other foods the cargo-holding couple need to have on hand, and directs the transformation of these foods into special meals served at allotted times. During rituals Pedranos refer to corn as "*sbek'tal xojobal kajvaltik*, the Body and Emanation of our Lord" (Arias 1973: 19).

All the traditional foods that I learned to make from my mother are foods that I must remember because I have to pass them on to my daughters. We can't forget these because our ancestors always made them, and we believe that we should continue conserving our culture, our inheritance.

The most important foods are the ones we make for fiestas. It's enjoyable to prepare these with many other women. For example, when we prepare food for the graduation ceremony for our children we [mothers] make it together. We donate money to buy the rice, tomatoes, onions, and ingredients for making mole. We make chicken with mole sauce.[3] There's a lot of talking and laughing, sharing it with other women.

Well, it's a little different making food for just the family. One doesn't feel as much happiness because there isn't as much talking and laughing.

TRADITIONAL FOODS MADE WITH CORN

Takivaj

Eating *takivaj* is the most important part of a fiesta. When I was about fifteen, I helped my parents serve a *cargo* in November for the Feast of the New Virgin. I didn't know how to help my mother very well that year because I was only fifteen and it was my first fiesta. I just went to eat, I think.

First my mother and her helpers had to put out a lot of corn. They had to make lots of tortillas for the helpers and also to give to the authorities. They also killed a pig and made *takivaj*.

Takivaj doesn't have any flavor. It's just corn dough. Nothing else is added, not even salt. The women place twelve little balls of corn in a leaf and then wrap them up and steam them. It's like a gift for each helper. My mother and the wife of the leader who would take her *cargo* the next year made a lot of *takivaj* to give to their helpers and also to the township authorities. Although it's not tasty, *takivaj* is very important in fiestas.

Chenkulvaj

Chenkulvaj is a major traditional food at fiestas and also at *sk'in ch'ulelal* [Day of the Dead]. It's a tamale prepared from corn dough. You put ground beans in it and wrap it up in a leaf called *ch'uch* [from a type of banana tree that doesn't give fruit]. Then we put it on to cook in a big pot. Everybody makes *chenkulvaj* for Day of the Dead when we exchange food with other families in the cemetery. We make *chenkulvaj* and buy fruit to give to our *compañeros* and relatives in the cemetery and also when they come to visit in our homes.

Memunalvaj

Memunalvaj is the same as *chenkulvaj*, except we put the tamale inside a *mumu* leaf. We wrap it first with the *mumu* leaf and later cover it with *ch'uch*. It comes out tasty.

Pitubil

Pitubil is like *chenkulvaj* except instead of putting ground beans on top of the corn dough, we use whole tender beans and mix them into the dough. Then we wrap it in *ch'uch* and put it on to cook.

Patz

I don't know if everyone knows about *patz*. My mother taught me to make this type of tamale. It's just dough with salt. We mix the corn well with salt and water. Then when it's mixed, we wrap it up in a leaf and put it on to cook. Nothing more, it just cooks and then we eat. At times we eat it with beans, like a tortilla. But we call this *patz*, a tamale without beans.

Machitavaj

Machitavaj is called this because it looks like a machete. We just put ground beans inside the tortilla and double it over while we are cooking the tortilla, and it comes out looking like a machete. It has the same taste as *chenkulvaj*.

Koxox vaj

Koxox vaj is a toasted tortilla. To toast it we lay the tortilla on the coals beside the fire. When it's a golden color, it's done. One can eat *koxox vaj* without beans because it's very tasty by itself. Also, one can keep toasted tortillas for many days. Mainly men carry *koxox vaj* when they go far to work because the tortilla lasts a while. For example, those who cross over the border to the United States carry only *koxox vaj* in little pieces. That's what Alberto carried in a little bag when he crossed the border.

Vokich

Vokich is a traditional food eaten at harvest time with beans or with shrimp. In the past, each year when people planted the milpa, they gave *vokich* with an egg inside to each helper. Right now it seems that this tradition is disappearing because most people eat chicken when they plant. But those who don't have chickens give *vokich* to their helpers. Also, *vokich* can be eaten any time.

Vokich is made like *atole*. First the corn is ground, and then it's mixed with water and put on to cook. Then when it's boiling you put in chile, onions, tomatoes, and cilantro, especially cilantro. It isn't flavorful without that. After it's cooked, we serve it with a boiled egg in the middle of the bowl.

TRADITIONAL DRINKS MADE WITH CORN

Matz or uch'umo

The majority of indigenous people drink a lot of *matz*. Drinking *matz* symbolizes being a corn planter. *Matz* is very important for men who go out to work in the fields.

To make *matz* first you put the corn on to cook with a piece of limestone. After it's boiling, you take out the limestone and wash it. Then you put it on to cook more so that it doesn't taste of limestone. After it's cooked, you take it off the fire, grind it, and mix it with hot water. We don't grind the dough for *matz* very fine, like for tortillas. In the past I ground my *matz* more coarsely, but right now I'm not preparing dough just for *matz* because I don't grind the corn in my house anymore. We use the electric grinder at our neighbor's house. Most of the time we use the same corn dough for tortillas and *matz*.

Pajal ul

There's another drink called *pajal ul*. It's made with young corn. When the corn is tender, we take it off the cob and grind it. Then when it's ground, we beat it. When it's well-beaten, we put it in a pot and leave it there overnight to sour. In the morning we add sugar and put it on to cook. It's necessary to use a net bag that we call a *moraleta* to strain it so that it's smooth. *Pajal ul* is a special drink for the Day of the Dead.

Chilim

Chilim is a bit different from *pajal ul*. First we put the corn on the *comal* to roast. Then when it's done toasting, we grind it. When it's ground, we mix it with water and put in some sugar. Then we heat it and a very delicious drink results! In the past they used *chilim* to marry. When the moment comes when the boy and girl get together, the boy's parents always bring the ground roasted corn to the girl's parents' house. The girl's mother and her helpers have to prepare the *chilim* to give to the son-in-law's family. When my son Sebastian married, I didn't have to carry *chilim* to his wife's house because her parents didn't want it.

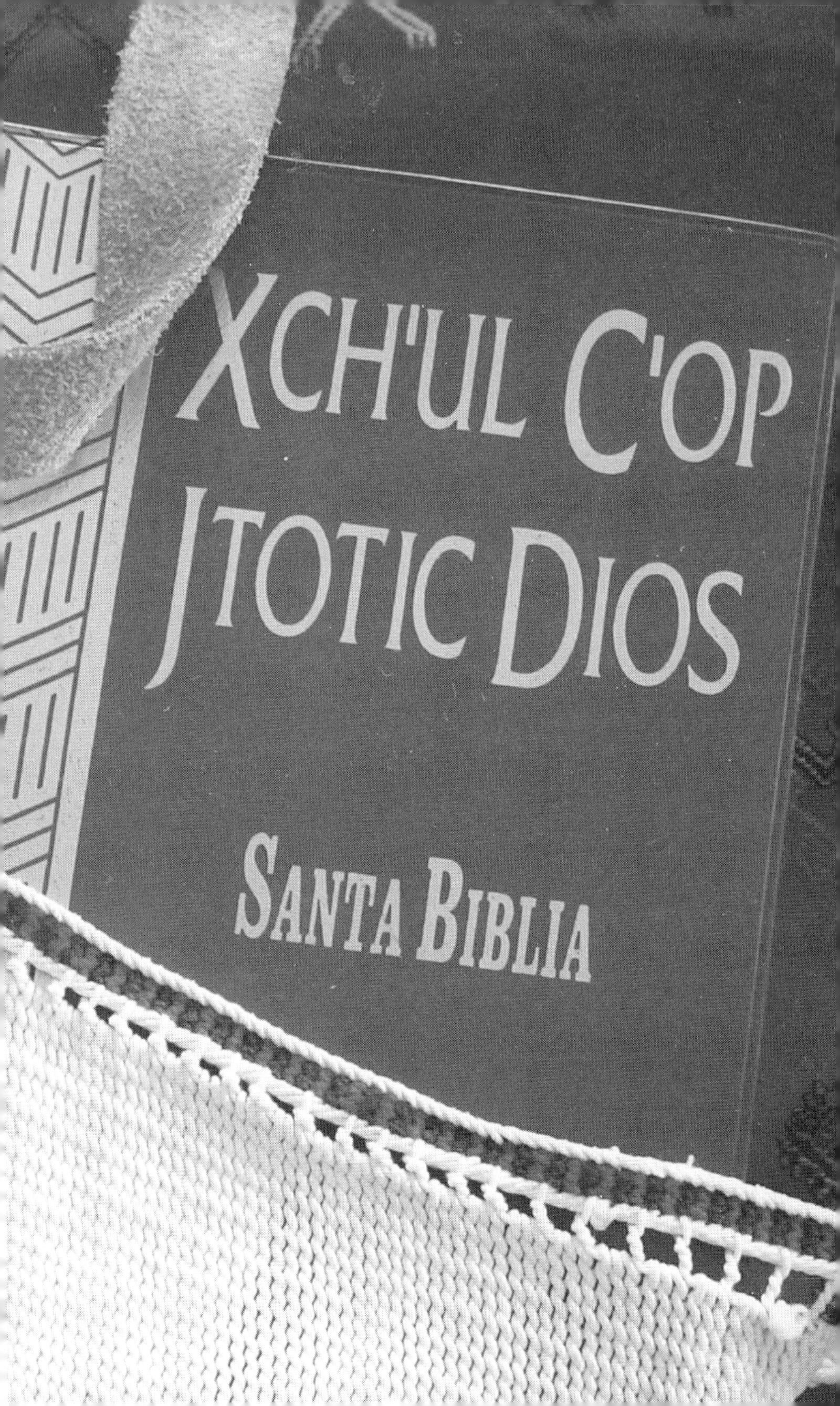
XCH'UL C'OP
JTOTIC DIOS
SANTA BIBLIA

Listening to the Word of God

Everyone has faith, since birth, just in different ways. My faith didn't change when I entered the Word of God. It just grew.

Antonia

Antonia didn't read the Bible or learn about the life of Jesus Christ until later in her teens. "Making her soul arrive" before that time involved respecting people, working hard, and reciprocating with the Maya deities and Catholic saints in a variety of household and communal rituals. The aim of these rituals was to maintain harmony with the natural world and beings-other-than-humans with whom traditional Pedranos considered themselves to share the world.

In traditional Pedrano cosmology, Mother Earth is a principal deity, along with *totik* (Sun, Our Father), *me'tik* (Moon, Our Mother), *jpetum-jkuchum* (supporters-protectors), and *totil me'il* (father-mother-ancestor-protectors) (Arias 1973; Guiteras-Holmes 1961). The protectors guard the invisible order, the other world, and prevent wrongdoing by threatening to send *vokol* (trouble or misfortune). All things are thought to have two aspects, the visible and invisible. Just as humans have souls, so do all that surrounds them (Arias 1973: 44). According to the ancestors, bringing one's soul firmly into one's being and maintaining harmony and balance between one's soul and other souls is the main human task.

In the past, people acted according to our ancestors' traditions. I only know about these because I saw what my father did when he was alive. My father didn't have religion. He would just pray to ask for forgiveness, because he was walking on Mother Earth, because he made her dirty. He also asked Mother Earth to give us food.

I also watched other elders. My half-sister Angélica's grandfather always made the sign of the cross when he was walking, wherever he wanted to go. He always had a lot of respect for God.

(FACING PAGE): *Holy Word of Father God/Holy Bible*, the Tzotzil translation of the Bible. Photo courtesy of Michael O'Malley, 2010.

In the past the people would go to the *milpa* to pray when they wanted to ask for more corn. They would kneel with a candle and ask for blessing. Paulina's father-in-law still prays each morning when he works in the fields. It doesn't matter if he's in the *milpa* or in the coffee fields. Three times a day people would make the sign of the cross to ask for help or to give thanks. In the morning when they woke up they thanked God that nothing happened in the night. Then in the middle of the day they asked to be protected from harm during the day. And in the late afternoon or early evening they gave thanks that all went well that day.

Now we are thinking that we should revive this tradition, because God provides all things. I think that we should thank God for everything. Like they say, it's necessary to be grateful for the good and the bad. For example, this day went well, so we need to say, "Thank you, God, that the day went well for me." But if we made mistakes, we also need to say, "Well, thank you Lord for this day, but forgive me for everything bad that I did."

Word of God Catholicism began in highland Chiapas in the 1960s under the leadership of Bishop Samuel Ruíz García. Don Samuel, as he is affectionately called, was influenced by the historic meetings of the Second Vatican Council (1962–1965) and the Second General Council of Latin American Bishops in Medellín, Colombia, in 1968. At these meetings bishops committed themselves to being involved in the realities and problems of poor people (Early 2012; Kovic 2005). Their commitment, along with the economic and political upheaval in Latin America, led to what has come to be called "liberation theology," a "rereading of the Bible from the perspective of the oppressed" (Kovic 2005). Ruíz is commonly associated with liberation theology, but he declined to use this label to describe the work of the Catholic Church in Chiapas, maintaining that to do so implies that theology can be other than liberating.[1]

Prior to Ruíz's arrival in Chiapas, it was a rare priest who showed an interest in learning native languages.[2] Under Ruíz's direction, pastoral workers studied native languages and explored the cultural and social strengths in indigenous communities. Eventually priests and nuns began to break down the traditionally hierarchical relationships between indigenous people and religious workers by empowering laypeople to carry "the Word of God" to others in their communities. Women's participation in lay roles increased with these changes.[3]

In workshops and retreats, nuns and catechists (lay leaders) encouraged people to see God in local spiritual terms, but also to see Jesus Christ as the son of God, to whom they could pray for guidance and whose life they could study for wisdom about their struggle for justice. These workshops helped people grow in their understanding of structural inequalities and gain courage to confront oppression. Together people read and reflected on scriptural passages and connected theory to practice. A popular song at workshops evokes this process:

> Ver, ver, ver (See, see, see)
> Pensar, pensar, pensar (Think, think, think)
> Actuar, actuar, actuar (Act, act, act)
> Todo en comunidad (All of this in community)
> Todo en comunidad (All of this in community)

My father and I entered the Word of God together when I was seventeen or eighteen years old. It started when a little girl asked me to be her godmother for her confirmation. To become a godmother I had to go with my parents to listen to the preparation. There the catechists asked me to join the Word of God.

But my father didn't just want me to listen to the preparations for three weeks. He wanted me to listen for the whole year, for my whole life, no? That's why he began to pray to God that I become a believer in the Word of God. He asked Saint Peter the Apostle to make me a preacher, like the apostle. I don't know if it was because of his prayers that I began to listen to the Word of God.

From then on, after many months of listening to the Word of God, I met Domingo. He was a preacher in the church in Chenalhó. I didn't know the man there preaching the Word of God, but later they told me, "That's Domingo." He looked strange because he was very happy and moved a lot when he preached. He always talked with a lot of people. It's his character, his way of being.

Later Domingo asked my father, "Does your daughter want to attend a course? There's a course in La Primavera."

"Ah, good, yes, that's fine. I think she'll go," my father said.

"Good, I'm going to go," I said, because I wanted to go!

I went for one or two months to hear the Word of God in La Primavera in San Cristóbal.[4] They gave a course about the Word of God, and those who took the course had to teach other believers afterward.

"Yes, that's fine. I'll agree to that," I said. I was very open back then. It seems that I wanted to do everything! Although I didn't know how, I wanted to do it!

After returning to Chenalhó, I began to teach the other believers how to make the sign of the cross. I became involved, singing hymns in the church choir. Later, when groups of believers began to form in other communities, we went to visit them. Because Domingo was a preacher, he got the believers together to visit the other brothers and sisters. I always went along every afternoon to visit a brother or sister. I liked the Word of God. I stopped thinking about other things and only thought about the Word of God. At times I wanted to preach a few words, too! From then on I continued knowing Domingo.

Chapter 7

Courtship and Marriage

When I was fifteen or sixteen I thought about marrying. "Ah, to be happy, to have a companion." I didn't want to live alone. I thought that one day when my parents die, if I don't marry, no one will be there to support me. But now I know that's not true, since I've seen that I can earn money.

Antonia

Antonia married Domingo when she was eighteen in the traditional bride-petition process, *joyol*, with a few new twists influenced by Domingo's involvement in the Word of God. The ceremony included reading some verses from the Bible and inviting a group of men to play their guitars and sing hymns.[1]

Domingo was very poor, but he had earned Hilario's and Maria's respect, and they weren't surprised when he came to visit one day in the company of his mother and two respected elders. Domingo brought soft drinks and food to his future in-laws as a symbol of their daughter's value to them. According to tradition, Antonia received only a few small gifts from her mother-in-law that symbolized her union with her husband-to-be: a drinking bowl, a striped tortilla cloth, and two net bags, one for carrying produce from the market on one's back with a tump line (*kuchum nutil*) and a smaller one (*chuchum nutil*) for carrying small or fragile items, like eggs, by hand. Antonia recalls that her tortilla cloth had only a few stripes, perhaps because her mother-in-law wasn't a weaver and had to pay someone to make it for her. Also, instead of the traditional drinking gourd, her mother-in-law gave her a plastic bowl. Antonia remembers her sister Anita giggling as she squeezed the sides of the bowl together.

At first I didn't think about having children, just to marry a man and be happy. Now I think that marriage is not just to be happy, but to have one moment of happiness and one of sadness, that's all.

I asked God to find me a man who would turn out good. It didn't happen in the beginning. After only a few days problems began. We made mistakes,

and there were always problems. At times I thought, "I wasn't lucky." But in comparison to other women, I was lucky.

I think that my destiny is in God's hands. Through God's blessing, Domingo and I are still together, and right now we don't have many problems. I don't know if it's going to continue this way forever, because at times we're tempted. Things come to break us apart, no?

After I met Domingo, we dreamt about each other. Our dreams told us that we were destined for one another. Domingo dreamt that he had my earring in his hand. In my dream I was walking on the path in the dark, and I saw Domingo's hat ahead of me. A light appeared around the hat, and I grabbed the hat fast. But when I started carrying it, darkness came. I walked in the dark about twenty or thirty minutes, and then the light returned. I didn't know the meaning of my dream right away. But after we married and had problems, I think that the darkness symbolized our problems. Although Domingo was my good fortune, problems came along with him.

I don't know how many months later Domingo came to ask to marry me. He always came to visit in my parents' house. It was as if he lived in our house. When Domingo didn't come in the afternoon, my parents would ask, "Ah, why isn't Domingo coming to visit us?"

That's why when he came to ask for me, I decided to marry him. But before that I didn't want to. In the beginning my mother asked me, "What are you going to say if Domingo asks to marry you?"

"I don't want to marry him! My husband isn't like that!" I said. I almost made fun of him because at first I didn't want to marry him. But later I decided to.

When he came to ask for me, he arrived in the afternoon with two helpers that he had asked to accompany his mother to petition for me. They spent about an hour and a half talking with my parents.

After talking with my parents, they didn't say a prayer according to tradition. They read a part of the Word of God about how a man and a woman come together. After that they left and returned another time in the morning. But we still didn't give an answer.

Domingo and his helpers brought soft drinks each visit. But they only left them in the house. We didn't drink them. They made four visits, first to read the Bible and leave soft drinks, the second and third to talk more with my parents and leave soft drinks, and on the fourth visit we gave the answer if I would accept him.

After they left the third time, my parents asked me, "What do you think

(FACING PAGE): Photo by Christine Eber, 2010.

about this young man who is asking for you? Do you want to accept him or not?"

"Yes," I said. I don't know why I said yes—because it was time for me to marry, I think. Since my father never let me go find work, I decided to marry and stay in the house. I thought that Domingo was a good man to marry. It didn't matter to me that he was older than me. He was twenty-five years, I think.

Finally, on the fourth visit, we said, "Yes, she will marry." Then they opened the soft drinks, and over drinks they talked about when to deliver the gifts, when Domingo would finally come to live in my father's house so we could be together.

On the fifth visit, the wedding, Domingo had to bring meat, corn, beans, bread, chile, salt, sugar, pineapple, bananas, oranges, *ocote* [pitch pine for lighting fires], *chilim* and twenty-four bottles of beer for my brother, the teacher. Maybe my father asked for that. I don't remember.

My godfather came to the fiesta, my brother, my half sister Angélica's husband, and another stepbrother. I think those were all the relatives. Also, Domingo invited his friends in the Word of God and a group of musicians from Polhó. Since many people stayed the night, they had to sleep on the ground on a straw mat with a little bit of blanket to cover them.

Chapter 8

Learning to Be a Wife

It's necessary for a man to respect his wife, and also for a wife to respect
her husband. They must be equal. A man must not mistreat a woman.
He must not beat her. Not only men should have the right to leave the
house. Women should have this right, too, in order to do good things.
We have the same blood, men and women. That's why it's necessary to
respect each other.

Antonia

1989

This evening Antonia comes as close as I have ever seen her to slamming the lids on the pots on the fire. She and Domingo have just had a fight about money. I sit as small as I can on my little chair near the fire, trying not to make any more problems for her. Memories of similar scenarios involving pots on my stove and fights over money flood my thoughts. I sigh, thinking of the common bond that Antonia and I share. We are both married to men who are struggling to overcome addictions and keep their emotions on an even keel.

Antonia says that Domingo had a small heart before he stopped drinking, when he became involved in the Word of God, but through many years of service to his people his heart has grown.

By the time I was living with Antonia and Domingo, they had developed a deep friendship and a large support network that they could turn to in times of need. Although problems come with being in daily contact with kin, living a great distance from relatives and friends has its drawbacks. Comparing their togetherness with my more cloistered life as a college professor made me keenly aware of the losses that come with emphasizing independence over cooperation. For *campesinos* in Chenalhó it would be disastrous to work in solitary labor. Survival depends on bartering, borrowing, cooperating, organizing, and connecting in all manner of ways. My culture's myth of the self-made man or woman is no more accurate than the Pedrano myth of the proud corn farmer living in harmony with others. But these myths help us rationalize our lives.

After we married, Domingo and I didn't sleep together the first night. In the past, couples slept in the same house but on opposite sides of the room for about eight days, until they finally slept together in the same bed. I think that this was so that couples could get used to being together slowly. Each morning during those eight days the husband had to get up at dawn to go and find firewood to give to his father-in-law and then go help him in the *milpa*. But Domingo didn't get up early to help my father.

Only a few weeks after we married, Domingo had to go to the plantation because he didn't have any money. The plantation where he went was called Plátanos. He had to go out very early in the morning to work. After he woke up, he got into a long line to eat. They gave the workers beans, but they didn't sort them well. At times there were rat turds in the beans. And they didn't give many tortillas.

When he left my parents' house, Domingo was healthy, but after about five weeks on the plantation, he got sick. He returned one night around 11 p.m. to my parents' house with a fever and headache.

His sickness lasted several years. At the beginning he had a fever and a lot of pain in his head. Although he made the effort to go to work in the *milpa*, he always came home in a lot of pain. At times my parents didn't like it that Domingo stayed in the house when he couldn't go out to work. Also, Domingo became very nervous with his illness. He said things that created problems with my parents.

I think that Domingo went one more time to the plantation after he got sick, but he didn't stay long. He also went to Villahermosa, Tabasco, to construct houses. He suffered from the heat and fell on a rod, hit his nose, and almost died. After that he didn't want to stay there. I didn't like it either when he returned without money. It was better for him to stay at home. It came out almost the same. He only went away to suffer.

Only a handful of foreign anthropologists have chosen to live full-time in highland Chiapas after completing their Ph.D. fieldwork. Nancy Modiano, an anthropologist from Brooklyn, was one of those. Nancy made a rich life for herself in San Cristóbal, befriending graduate students like me, and many indigenous children and adults who found a mentor in her, as did Antonia's brother, Francisco.

Nancy, more than any other person, is responsible for connecting Antonia and her family to mestizos in San Cristóbal and foreigners from other countries. Antonia first met Nancy on a visit that she made to Antonia's primary school in the 1970s. Antonia recalls being frightened of her as she had not seen a woman with such white skin. When Antonia's elder brother Francisco went

(FACING PAGE): Photo by Christine Eber, 1987.

to work with her as a gardener, Nancy took him under her wing and helped him become a bilingual teacher.

Nancy was one of the first people I sought out for advice when I came to highland Chiapas to look for a community where I could conduct research. Before me, Nancy had helped another graduate student from the United States, Carol-Jean McGreevy. After Carol-Jean contacted her in 1981, Nancy approached Antonia's parents to see if they would be willing to let Carol-Jean (Carolina) live with them for about six months while she learned Tzotzil and observed the children in school. It was decided that Antonia would be Carol-Jean's Tzotzil teacher.

In 1982 and 1983 my life was especially hard because Domingo was very sick. When Felipe was a baby, we didn't have any money. We couldn't buy soap or clothes. I lived with problems during those times, but sometimes I couldn't bear it any longer.

After we were married a year, we met Carolina. My first child, Felipe, was only one day old when Carolina came to our house. I was sick the day she arrived and stayed in bed with the baby. I don't know how many weeks passed while Carolina was in the house with Domingo so sick. She saw how much he was suffering and took him to a doctor. I don't know about these things, but they said that he had an epileptic attack. When he became very nervous, he fell on the ground and stayed there like a drunk man.

We saw many doctors in the time of Carolina, because she helped with all the expenses. First we went to the Health Center, to Clínica del Campo [the clinic for indigenous people], and also to Tuxtla [the state capital]. But they could never cure Domingo. They only gave him things to calm the illness. His sickness was very hard. I think that he lived with more than one illness during those fifteen years. Some days he could go out to work, but other days no. I don't remember what year the epilepsy illness left him. I think that it left him because the pills they gave him calmed it.

Carolina helped us with money for our expenses by buying our weavings. She also asked me to teach her Tzotzil. She paid me each hour, and this helped me to earn a little money. I did a lot of work with her, first transcribing from the cassette and then translating into Spanish. Transcribing was my way to earn money during those years. There wasn't any market to sell weavings at that time. I think that paying us to transcribe and translate was a way foreigners could help us, no? I was lucky. With God's help we came to know foreigners.

Nancy found out that Domingo couldn't work anymore and found me work in the Indigenous Woman's Program. She came all the way to my community to get my birth certificate. Someone told me that I had to go down to the school to give her my certificate, because she always came by car in those years. She didn't walk on the paths anymore.

After I agreed to take the job, I cried because I didn't want to leave my house. It was too late for me. I already had a child. I said to myself, "It's sad to leave my husband, because he doesn't have any schooling." I was very sad to leave my husband alone in my mother's house with my two little sisters. Domingo knew that I could earn money. "Yes, you should go earn a little, because I can't earn anything. I can't work because of my illness," he said.

I don't know what month it was that they came to get my birth certificate, my employment certificate, and other papers. Then in February they told me, "We're going to tell you which township you're going to work in."

"Good," I said.

"It's Mitontik."

A few weeks later I went to Mitontik to stay. Domingo went to drop me off one afternoon. Because there wasn't any transportation then, we walked about ten kilometers. The rain caught us, and I arrived really wet, with Felipe on my back. We didn't know where we would stay the night. There was no house or room where we could stay, so we slept on the floor in the town hall where the authorities meet. The following day Domingo returned, and I stayed alone with my son.

I didn't like the work. I was afraid and embarrassed because at first they didn't give me respect and a kitchen or my own room to sleep in. I had to sleep in the town hall right next to the room where the authorities met each morning at 6 a.m. I had to carry my toasted tortillas from home because I didn't have a kitchen. That's how I started working. Later they gave me a little house without a kitchen.

My work was with adults, teaching them to read and write, and also teaching women to weave and make embroidered things. I also went on home visits to show women how to take care of the house. The people from Mitontik didn't respect me very much because I didn't wear mestizo clothes, and they thought that I wasn't a real teacher. Also, it was necessary to teach this and that and that—too many things! Besides, I didn't have any training. Much later I went to a course of two or three days with my son. But before I came to Mitontik I only worked in the house.

I don't know how many months I put up with the job. I didn't like it, but it was something with which I could earn a little money. I remember one time when Felipe was with me, we were sleeping and a strong wind came up. I was terrified that the roof would fall on his head. I didn't sleep the whole night trying to protect my son's head with my arm. Pieces of cement fell on us, but I was so glad that our whole roof didn't fall. Roofs fell on many other houses. Many people went out into the street in the night. But I didn't go out.

I also suffered trying to get paid. My check arrived in Ocosingo. I had to go all the way to Ocosingo, two or three hours, to get my check. When I got there, they didn't give it to me because I had replaced another woman in Mitontik, and the check came in her name. With much difficulty, going back and forth to Ocosingo, they finally gave me the check. I think that I went first to Ocosingo in February, and they finally paid me in December.

By the time I received my check, I already had another baby. Sebastian was born when I was working there. I went to my house to give birth, but when I went back to work, I had Sebastian with me. Felipe didn't always come with me. At times I left him with my little sisters and mother because it was difficult to care for two children in Mitontik. The children knew how to walk, and there wasn't a good place for them to play. I didn't have a real house, nor a kitchen. There was only a little one-room house where I could sleep in a space on the floor.

I suffered a lot when I was working there. I didn't receive my salary, and then when I had another baby, there was no one to care for him. I was nursing Sebastian, and I couldn't leave him with someone. I paid a young girl to take care of him when I was teaching, but he always cried because he wanted to nurse.

Eventually I decided that it would be better not to work because it was too difficult for me with children, and it was so hard to get paid. After finishing my contract, I left. My supervisor didn't want me to leave. "You should keep working because you'll be promoted and you can continue your studies," she said.

But it was hard for me, because I didn't want to leave my husband alone. He was sad without me, and I was sad without him. I thought that if I leave my husband, I might end up with another man, and it would come out very bad for me! That's what I thought.

While Antonia was working in Mitontik, Antonia's younger sisters Anita and Marcela married, also according to tradition. The household was brimming with sons-in-law, and eventually Antonia's parents decided that it was time for Antonia and Domingo to make their own home. They felt justified in asking Antonia to leave because Domingo was not as sick as before. This was not the kind of move that Antonia had in mind when she was a single woman dreaming about finding her own way in the world. Leaving behind all that she had known in order to live with Domingo on his land in another community meant being dependent on a man with whom she didn't feel that secure.

When Domingo and I went to live apart from my parents, we began to construct our own house with the money I had earned as a teacher. But I didn't want to leave my parents' house. My sisters were already married, and my parents said that it wasn't good for us to stay and live with the other sons-in-law. But I didn't want to live alone with my children because Domingo always scolded me, and he was sick a lot. I suffered a lot with him.

"Who will take care of me if I go to live alone with Domingo? Who will bring me food if Domingo is sick?" I thought. I didn't want to live anymore. I wanted to separate from Domingo. I cried a lot and told my mother, "I'm not going to go. If you don't want me here anymore, I'm going to go to San Cristóbal because I always wanted to live there."

"That's not a good idea," she said. "Don't do it that way."

Finally I decided to go with Domingo and build our own house on his land. We made our house with adobe walls and a cardboard roof. But each afternoon I was sad alone in my house. There were many banana trees, and in the afternoon the darkness from the shade made me sad. We were accustomed to being around our relatives and friends, but I didn't have any nearby, except my mother-in-law. I wanted to be with my parents and my sisters. Every two or three days I went to visit my mother and spent the whole day at her house.

It took a long time to console me, about three or four years. Afterward I became accustomed to my new home. Now after many years of living away from my parents' home, I'm not used to things in my mother's house! But it took many years to feel that way. The majority of women in my township want to live apart from their parents. It seems that I'm different from the rest.

When I was in our home, I didn't want to separate from Domingo anymore except when he would scold or yell at me and disrespect me. He would say, "You aren't a good woman. You don't know how to do things. You don't take care of the children. You're a woman who gets angry easily." He said many things, and at times he didn't make any sense. One time I couldn't put up with it anymore, and I went back to my father's house for three days.[1]

Domingo couldn't bear it. He was alone in the house, thinking that it wasn't good to be separated. On the third day he came to ask my forgiveness. "I won't do that anymore. What I did was sad. I did it because I'm sick. I want you to forgive me," he said when he repented. He blamed his sickness nearly all the time. But during this time I didn't believe him. I just thought that when he scolded me, it was his way of doing things. To this day I don't know. I'm thinking now that it was because of his sickness, because I've seen how sick people become very sensitive. Perhaps that's why he scolded me, because now that he isn't sick, he isn't like that anymore.

Domingo talked in a good way, and because my parents didn't want me to separate from him, they advised us how to be good spouses. Moises, Marcela's husband, advised Domingo, too. Although Moises is younger than Domingo, he behaves well, which is why he could give good advice.

Although I never separated from Domingo again, we always had problems. We lived together with difficulty for many years. I believe that's because we're both sensitive, and neither of us knows how to calm the situation. But for three years now we've been getting along very well. Neither of us has gotten angry. We just get angry a little bit. Before we would get angry with each other, and I would stay that way for one or two days. I could hold a lot of anger. But not now. Now we're happy, thankfully.

Chapter 9

Learning to Be a Mother

Children bring happiness at times and sadness other times. When children have problems, that's when the sadness starts. But when they do good things or begin to talk with us, tell us good stories, that's when happiness comes. When it's just the two of us in the house, without children, it's almost silent and we go to bed early. But when we're together with our children we stay up relaxing and talking. One says something, another says something and then we begin to laugh and keep talking on and on. We don't realize when it gets very late.

Antonia

Antonia has six children, and none of them has died. While living with her, I never took this fact for granted. Among forty-five women I interviewed in a household survey in a neighboring community in 1988, twenty-five had lost seventy-five children between them. Antonia attributes her children's survival to luck and God's grace.

Although none of her children were gravely ill in childhood, Sebastian, Mariano, and Paulina each had operations when they were young adults. Antonia went into considerable debt to pay the clinic bills. One factor contributing to her children surviving childhood may be the relative equality in her relationship with Domingo. In Antonia's community men tend to have authority over their wives in decisions about health care. They may decide not to take a child to see a doctor or to purchase medicines, even if their wives want to. Another factor influencing her children's survival is the greater contact that Antonia has had with mestizo society and its health services, and her ability to negotiate with doctors in Spanish, due in part to having completed sixth grade.

Like most women in her community, Antonia values having children, but not more than she can provide for. Her eldest daughter, Paulina, now married with one child, says that she only wants one or two children. Other young women seem to feel the same as Paulina. In general, women have fewer children today than in the past.

Antonia didn't want to put our conversations about contraceptives and

abortion in this book. Although these topics are of interest to many readers, she feels that others don't need to know her thoughts on these topics.
Antonia just wants to say that although some women in her community talk
about plants to prevent pregnancy, they don't often work, which accounts for
"mountains of children in each family." As for contraceptive pills and IUDs, she
says that doctors and nurses talk about them, but that many women are afraid
to use them because they hear other women say that they bring pain or dizzi-
ness. While readers may wish Antonia would share more about her ideas and
experiences with birth control and reproductive practices, for Antonia these
topics are private matters.[1]

I had all my six children in the house. I didn't like to go to the doctor or
leave the house. It's very difficult to have a baby in another person's house.
At times a lot of blood comes out. Most indigenous women stay in the house
to give birth. We think that those who go to the doctor don't know very well
how to give birth.

When I was pregnant, I didn't tell anyone except my mother and Domingo. When I had my first pregnancy, I didn't talk about it with my mother
until I was about seven months pregnant. I didn't want people asking me,
"When are you going to have the baby? What are you going to have? Is it
a boy or a girl?" My sister Marcela still doesn't want to say anything when
she's pregnant. We aren't talking much about her pregnancy right now. But
other families have other ways. And right now with my daughter and my
daughters-in-law we begin to talk about their pregnancies at two or three
months.

I got very embarrassed when I gave birth. I didn't want anyone to see me.
I'm not a person who gets easily embarrassed, but when it comes to giving
birth, I don't think that anyone should see me. That's why always when I had
a baby, the children went to bed. I didn't say anything to them. When the
baby was born, it was a surprise for them.

I remember the night when Paulina was born. Mariano was five years
old. In the morning when he woke up, I was lying on a simple bed on the
floor near the fire. He came in with his eyes wide open and asked, "What are
you doing?" I was there with Paulina in my arms, and I said, "Look, a baby
was born." I showed him her head. "I don't think so," he said. He said that
it wasn't a baby, that it was a doll, and he hit her on the head! "Ah, why did
you hit her?" I asked. Later, he accepted that Paulina was real, but with a lot
of effort.

Now it seems that my children are changing. For example, my three-

(FACING PAGE): Photo by Christine Eber, 1987.

year-old granddaughter knows very well how her little sister was born. Each time when we asked her, "Where's the baby?" she would say, "Here," and point to her mother's belly. "Come out!" she would say.

We were only three people at most of my children's births—me, Domingo and my mother. My mother was like a midwife. God knows everything that happens in life. He has taken care of me. That's why no one else took care of me, except my mother and a midwife sometimes. When I asked a midwife for help, I gave her tortillas and *matz*. Each time when I went to her house, I brought a gift. If she came to my house, I gave her something to eat.

It's normal for the first birth to be difficult. When Felipe was born, it lasted many hours. The pain began around ten at night and lasted until eight in the morning. The following births didn't take that long. Sebastian's birth took from ten in the morning until four in the afternoon, about five hours. The others only took from two to four hours. I remember with the last birth, that was Rosalva, it was only two hours. My births weren't very difficult, except for the first one.

Since Felipe was my first child, my mother found a midwife who began to help me when I was seven or eight months pregnant. The midwife looked to see if the baby was in a good position. She made three visits to the house, and then when there was just a little time left, when the pain started, she came to the house to wait for the baby to be born. But my midwife wasn't with me when Felipe was born because it was the day that her son graduated from sixth grade. That's why I didn't have a midwife, only my mother, Domingo, and my older sister, Angélica.

It was a difficult birth. I couldn't bear the pain. I thought that I wasn't going to be able to give birth. When Felipe was finally born, all covered in a sack, it didn't matter to me. What mattered was saving myself!

Felipe had a sack over his body, and he didn't look like a baby. I still remember my sister saying, "Ah, this isn't a baby that was born!" Domingo just said, "It's not a baby." Angélica lifted his sack, and after a few seconds Domingo saw that he was moving his mouth under the sack. "It's moving its mouth!" Domingo said. Then he tried to rip Felipe's sack off, but he couldn't because it was very tough. He grabbed the ax nearby and carefully cut off the sack. When they took off the cover, Felipe began to cry.

They covered him with a cloth, took out the placenta, and cut the umbilical chord. We kept the cord for many years. It's our tradition to tie it in a tree if it's a boy so that he will know how to climb a tree. If it's a girl, the cord stays in the house. We bury the placenta under the earth in the kitchen near the door. I saw my mother do this and learned from her.

Men always help their wives give birth. During labor they sit on a little chair, and their wives kneel in front of them and put their hands on their husbands' shoulders while the men grab their wives around the waist in order to give them strength. That's how we did it when my children were born, and also when my sons married, they helped their wives this way.

Two of my children were born in my mother's house. That's why my mom helped me a lot. She also came to my house to take care of me with my other births. She made the meals for three days. Before she went home she left me a lot of tortillas. At times other women give tortillas to mothers after they give birth. My sister brought me some, too.

After the tortillas ran out, Domingo ground the corn and went to fetch water. Each morning he went to bring water so that when he went to work I would have water. That's how we managed. I don't think that Domingo was embarrassed to carry water. Perhaps a little bit, because each morning he would go very early.

It's our tradition to warm the baby by a separate fire. The main fire is in the middle of the kitchen. We separate the baby and the mother by their own fire near the wall because when there's a lot of people, the baby and mother can't enter around the main fire.

After I gave birth, I rested three days. At the end of three days I bathed myself and washed my clothes. My mother didn't help me wash clothes much, but with my daughters-in-law I have helped them wash. Then, after that, I began to walk around. I didn't grind corn or carry anything heavy, just wash clothes.

The number of days women rest depends on how each woman feels. Some women rest two, three, or four weeks. They stay in bed during that whole time. When they get up, they feel very weak. Many women tell me that I'm a very strong person. Yes, many people tell me that.

1989

Antonia and I walk up the last stretch of the trail to her mother's house, trying to make it there before the rain begins. I follow close behind, returning Alberto's smiles as he bounces up and down on his mother's back, wrapped in her red and blue striped shawl.

We reach the familiar fork in the path where I often pause when I'm alone to make sure I take the right path. Today Antonia pauses, too, to cut some branches from a nearby bush and lay them across the path that we won't take. I'm surprised to see her do this because of her Catholic beliefs. I have to ask her, "Antonia, do you really believe that Alberto's soul might leave him and wander down the wrong path if you don't block it?"

"Yes, it could," she replied. "But even if it can't, it doesn't take me any effort to do this. These practices have worked for our ancestors. Who am I to say that we should stop doing them just because I learn something new? We need all the help we can get to keep our children from getting sick and dying. I continue with the traditions, too."

In the beginning when babies go out with their mothers, at times they can't be calmed from crying and they won't sleep. We say it's because they've lost their soul. When a baby leaves the house, it doesn't know where its soul is going. That's why when we come to a fork in the path, we block off the path that we aren't going on with three branches so that the child's soul doesn't go down the wrong path. We can also make a sign by tying a black thread, a branch, or a piece of hide around the baby's wrist. When we do these things, it means that the baby's soul is fixed—that it can't leave the body.

If a woman rests with her baby for a few minutes, when she stands up she has to retrieve the baby's soul. For example, when I pick up my grandson rapidly, I brush my shawl over the earth to pick up his soul. I say to his soul, "Batik! Mu xa kom." [Let's go! Don't stay here.] When a baby falls, we quickly lift him up and put him back down on the ground three times, saying, "Likantal! Likantal! Likantal! Mu xa xi." [Get up! Get up! Get up! Don't be afraid.]

Although I do this with my grandson, my daughter isn't doing it with him. That's how the tradition is being lost. When the traditions don't take much effort, I do them. At times I don't believe very much in the traditions, and I don't want to follow them. That's why they don't work.

Chapter 10

Learning to Manage a Household

That's how it is, the life of an indigenous woman.

Antonia

By the time I came to live with Antonia in 1987, she was a married woman with three children. She was an experienced cook and household manager whose competence with the tasks of daily life often made me envious. Her movements around the fire reminded me of a dancer making each outstretched hand mean something, each bend of the knee a graceful bow to Earth. Despite the hard and repetitive work involved in cooking, Antonia seemed to care about the task at hand, to value it as an important action.

Antonia might find my movements just as graceful in my own kitchen with its strange gadgets, but I have no doubt that she saw me as awkward in her kitchen. There my movements were tentative and clumsy, like the morning I tried to remove the pot of beans from the fire with the edge of my sweater. To my horror the beans spilled into the fire, producing a muddy puddle of beans and ashes. Antonia's attention was elsewhere at the time, and I hurriedly tried to get rid of the evidence of my clumsiness. She must have heard the beans sizzling in the ashes because she came running over to me, exclaiming, "No! Don't throw them out the door!" For the next twenty minutes or so Antonia helped me extricate each bean from the muddy ashes, wash it, and return it to the pot.

Learning how to value beans, corn, and other foods and transform them into tasty meals has been deeply important to Antonia's sense of self, purpose, and belonging. Antonia finds self-respect and dignity in food preparation, in part because Domingo has worked hard to fulfill his responsibility to provide corn and beans as well as firewood. This gender division of labor shaped Antonia's parents' relationship and continues to provide the context for her relationship with Domingo, although each year they become more dependent on cash to buy the corn and beans they cannot produce. Despite these realities, Domingo continues to see himself as a corn farmer, a role he inherited from his father and other paternal ancestors.

I recall one day after the corn harvest in 1987 when Antonia and I were visiting her parents. The corn was high, and I couldn't resist stroking the silky tassels as we made our way through her parents' *milpa*. The tassels looked so much like human hair, an analogy that made sense to me when I learned that many of the Tzotzil words for parts of the corn plant are the same as for parts of the human body. Hair and corn silk share the same word: *sjol*.

We were arriving with a special gift of *ajan*, fresh corn, from Antonia's fields. As we said our hellos to the family, Hilario began to roast a few ears in the fire. Fresh corn, then and now, is a special treat, as the bulk of the corn harvest has to be dried and stored for grinding to make tortillas and *matz* for the rest of the year.

After a couple ears were slightly golden, Hilario handed me one and took another for himself. I thanked him and brought the cob to my mouth, the only way I knew to eat corn. In contrast, Hilario began to remove each kernel from the cob and pop it into his mouth. It was something like a sacrament to watch him separate each juicy kernel from the cob, savoring it before moving on to the next.[1]

Although raising food and transforming it into meals nourishes both bodies and souls, it is also a time-consuming and burdensome process. When I lived with Antonia, she had three small boys who weren't able to help her much with food preparation. Eventually, as a mother of six, it seemed that Antonia was always involved in some stage of preparing food, often with her daughters by her side.

In 1987 Antonia only had to manage one house and feed a small family. By 2005 Antonia and Domingo had six children and grandchildren, and a second one-room house closer to the road where their *milpa* had been. Antonia's plan was to use the new house to sell used clothing and for the two younger boys to sleep in. As often happens with a new idea, many people began to sell used clothes around that time, and Antonia found that she could barely recover her investment. But she had become accustomed to the new house and decided to build a little kitchen next to it so the family could spend more time there. Later Domingo and the boys built a store next to the house to sell food and household items. By 2009 the store had replaced weaving and selling used clothes as Antonia's principal cash-generating activity. The store and new house were also where the family spent most of their time.

Housework takes a lot of time. For example, to make tortillas for a family of eight is a lot of work. It's not the same as in the United States. When you

(FACING PAGE): Photo by Christine Eber, 2002.

have money, you can go out and buy food. In contrast, we have to prepare our meals.

We always make tortillas in the house. To make tortillas, first we have to take the kernels off the cob, and after that we put the corn on to cook with a piece of limestone. After the corn is cooked, it's necessary to take out the limestone and wash the corn and leave it until the morning to grind with a manual grinder. Today there are electric grinders, but we don't have one in each house. Only some families have them, and we carry our *nixtamal* to grind it at their houses. For one plastic bucket it costs 2 pesos, not much.

We grind in the morning, and after the corn is ground, we mix it well with water until it makes a ball of dough. Then we begin to make tortillas and put them on the clay griddle on the fire with a lot of wood. We lay the griddle on an iron stand. In the past we used three stones to hold the griddle.

We don't have a fixed time to begin. I begin at 5 or 6 a.m. When I lived with my mother, we began at 4:30. She always got up early. I finish about 8:30 or 9:00, depending on how many tortillas I have to make.

We have a gourd called a *jay* or *tsoljay* that we put the tortillas in, and that's where the tortillas stay. When we want a tortilla, we just take it out of there.

After making tortillas, we begin to make the meal of beans and some vegetables. If we fry beans or make soup, that takes extra time. Most days I don't make a meal with fried beans because I don't have time. We lose a lot of time making tortillas. Then when we're done making breakfast, we begin to eat fast.

After eating I go to wash clothes. After washing I have to sweep. In your country you never sweep. You don't know how. I've seen the sweeper in your house that picks up all the dirt. The majority of indigenous people where I live sweep with a broom. In the past we cut a bunch of branches in the forest and swept the floor with that. Two kinds of branches are good for sweeping—*mes te'* and *sak mes*.[2] I still like to use *mes te'*, but I can't find it near my house. I have to go to my mother's house to find it. If I don't wash clothes, I begin to weave, but there are other things to do, too, like feed the pig or chickens. We get interrupted to take care of a baby, to change his diapers. There are many interruptions all day. That's how it is, the life of an indigenous woman.

My new house lacks a lot to be nice. Oh, I need a lot of things! I'll never get everything I want or need. What I'd like to have is a cement floor.[3] My two houses have floors of pure earth. I want to have a floor inside and a patio outside the house. But who knows if I'm going to get it. Because each time when I earn a little bit, I have to spend the money on something else. That's how the money goes. I don't know, we'll see if I get one. Because this year I know that I won't be able to do it. The money that we make in the coffee season I won't be able to use for my floor because I have a lot of debts.

Chapter 11

Animals

Animals Are an integral part of Antonia's life and household economy. Before Antonia first came to my home in New Mexico in 2002, I worried about how She would feel about how we treat our cats and dogs like members of the family. I shouldn't have been surprised that she became a cultural relativist par excellence in relation to our pets. About the second day into her visit, she was sitting in the kitchen in a big chair with armrests, the chair where Memur, our old and deaf cat, spent most of his time. When I realized that Antonia was sitting on the edge of the chair to accommodate Memur, I told her to nudge him off the chair. But she didn't want to. From then on, it was Memur and Antonia in the big chair.

One of the first photos that Antonia took in our home was of our dog, Angélica, looking out our living room window. I had already thought about how Angélica would have had a better life than other dogs in Antonia's community because elders say that black dogs carry deceased Pedranos across a river into *katibak* (paradise). Angélica could have done this job well, being part Great Dane and Black Lab. In gratitude, still today many Pedranos hand tortillas to black dogs (but throw them at others).

Eventually I asked Antonia what she thought about Angélica being in the house and our cats sitting on chairs.

I don't mind your animals being in the house. We don't let animals in our house because they're dirty and carry diseases. Yours are clean and aren't sick because you take care of them. Also, they have their own food, so you don't have to worry about them eating your children's food.

FEBRUARY 2009, CHENALHÓ

Since I came to live with Domingo on his land, I have had my hens—just hens. I haven't raised turkeys. I've had a lot of chickens, but now I don't have

(FACING PAGE): Photo by Christine Eber, 1996.

any. They all died of cholera. When I had my hens, they always helped me a lot. Right now I miss them.

Cats are a big help because they keep the rats out of the house. Also my dogs, I've always had them to protect the house and the chickens. They make sure that no foxes, weasels, or *tlacuahche* [opossums] eat the chickens. The dogs bark and frighten these animals away. They also warn us when people come. Kutin, the dog without a tail, barks more than the rest.

Our horse is a great help for Domingo to carry firewood. Hopefully our horse won't die, because three or four of our horses have died. The last horse's stomach swelled up. We put some *pox* in his mouth because we say that it's medicine. He had to drink it even though he got drunk! But it saved him.

We had a pig when you [Cristina] were living with us, but we stopped raising pigs for a while after you left. We raised about six or seven pigs, but pigs eat a lot and don't yield much money. When Rosalva was nine years old, she began asking for a pig to raise. "I want to raise a pig. I'd like to do that," she said. I bought a pig for her and she cared for it. When it got big, we sold it. We decided to kill it at home because we could make more selling it by the kilo. We got about 1,000 pesos for the pig. When Domingo and the boys kill the pigs, I don't like to watch. It makes me sad. When they stick the knife in, Rosalva covers her face.

The money that came from selling the pig was for Rosalva to buy clothes and whatever else she needed. The last pig we sold she used to help with her sixth grade graduation expenses. With earnings from her pig she bought a slip, sash, blouse, belt, and shoes. The teacher asked the children to buy new clothes.

Chapter 12

Water

Our pump stopped working today. No water. I've only been back from Chiapas a month, and already I'm so dependent on running water that I can't imagine going a day without it. It's Saturday, and we worry that no one will come to fix our pump on the weekend, especially in the rural area where we live.

I find the section in the yellow pages under "pumps" and make some calls. Finally we try Hooper Pump Service, and a young man answers. He sounds as if he's out and about, I hope fixing pumps. "Sure, I can come," he says. "I'll be there in an hour."

Although it's a complicated job requiring a trip to the hardware store and a return trip to tighten some critical screws, Hooper's son fixes our pump. When we thank him profusely for his trouble, he tells us, "No problem. In the water business we work round the clock because we know that people need water."

The water source for Antonia and her family is a hole in the ground about a fifth of a mile from their house up a steep trail. To collect the coffee-colored water, Antonia and her daughters—and before they were born, her sons—walk the steep trail several times a day with twenty-liter containers on their backs and two buckets in their hands. In highland communities, providing water is women's and children's work.

A few years ago the state government began constructing pipes to carry water from a holding tank near the school in Antonia's community to individual homes. Most of Antonia's neighbors now obtain water from spigots outside their houses. Those who are Zapatista supporters did not formally request the water, but their land lies in the path of the pipes, so they took advantage of the situation. Antonia and her family have not received the water because their land does not lie in the path of the pipes. Also, as members of the resistance movement, they reject government handouts, believing that the government uses such aid to buy their submission and votes. They also reject other government aid in the form of cement floors and tin roofs.

After the Zapatista uprising, the first noticeable government handouts were pieces of tin to replace cardboard and thatch roofs. On one of my visits during this time, Antonia and I stood outside her house looking at the glimmering roofs dotting the hillside across the river. The abundance of tin roofs told Antonia that most of the people in this community supported the PRI, the Revolutionary Institutional Party, which dominated politics in Mexico for most of the twentieth century. One of Antonia's sons made a drawing during my visit depicting a huddle of houses with tin roofs. Above one of the houses Mariano wrote, "Casa de Don Pablo, de PRI" (House of Don Pablo, the PRI supporter).

On my most recent visit to Chiapas, I saw large billboards throughout the highlands advertising the government's program of *piso firme* (cement floors). At the home of a family who had received this aid, I took a photo of the plaque in the corner of their kitchen proclaiming, "Piso firme, 2001–2006, contigo es posible." (With you it's possible.)

2007, San Cristóbal de las Casas

In my community there's a scarcity of water. When I came to your house, it was different. In your house, everything is inside! I don't have to go outside to get firewood to cook tortillas, to get water, to drink, or to wash. I don't have to go outside to go to the bathroom. I don't have to go outside for anything. Everything is in the house! But at my house I have to walk outside in the mud. There's no mud outside your house when it rains. In the rainy season at my house, there's so much mud that we don't want to go out.

Now in the rainy season, there are waterholes. But we always have to leave our houses to go to the waterhole, like a distance of a hundred to two hundred meters or more. At times, when I don't cook a lot of things—because now there aren't that many of us—I only go once a day to carry a twenty-liter jug, with two buckets in my hands. One time is enough. But at times we need more water. During the coffee harvest I go to the waterhole seven to eight times a day to wash the coffee.

When I go to wash clothes, I take a pail to draw water from the waterhole. I start to wash on a stone, bending over or squatting. There's no stone that you can use standing up.

It's difficult to wash a weaving to prepare it for sale. When we're in a hurry to wash it, we still have to go to the waterhole. At times it rains while we're washing. The weaving quickly gets dirty with mud. At times we slip in the mud on the trail, and all the clothes fall in the mud—everything that we've just washed! And we have to go back and wash it all over again.

(FACING PAGE): Photo by Christine Eber, 1987.

In dry times there's no place to wash clothes. There's no water in the waterhole. When the waterhole is running low, the water looks yellow. In the dry season we have to go all the way to the river to wash. We go by truck to Chenalhó, but it costs money, it takes time, and it's all very difficult. If I walk to the river, it's a very steep climb back!

One time it happened that I went to the river to wash. I think the rain wanted to bother us because it was the dry season, and it began to rain. I returned drenched, carrying all the washed clothes. The colors ran, and they got stained all over again because they were all piled up together.

When there's sun, we can dry clothes outside. When it's raining or drizzling, we have to dry them inside by the fire. But with a lot of smoke! Sometimes they get yellow. They get dirty from the smoke and ashes, and sometimes the children touch them. That's why sometimes the weavings that we send [to the US] are stained when they arrive. It's very difficult. We can't prevent the white from getting stained.

When there's water, everything is washed well. But even if it's washed, when it's stretched out to dry, the mud comes and everything happens! When we don't want something to get dirty, it gets dirty fast! That's what happens.

Sometimes the weaving gets dirty while ironing or also when it's folded. Yes, it happens easily to white weavings. I find it very difficult to keep the weavings white. Although we want to send white weavings, they arrive dirty. But I see that it's not good to sell them that way. The customers don't want to buy them stained. Although just a little part is stained, it's noticeable.

I've been thinking for a few years now that I would like to have piped water, or a *rotoplas* [a large polyethylene tank placed on the roof or beside the house to collect water]. For example, in the rainy season, one can collect water in a *rotoplas*. And from the waterhole near my house—not so near—one can lower a tube to the *rotoplas*. A *rotoplas* costs from 1,000 to 2,500 pesos.

Water comes off the roof, too, but what's lacking is a way to collect it. That's why each time the rain falls off the roof, I have to line up some buckets that I have in the kitchen to collect the water.

A woman design, woven by Antonia in 2005. Collection of Christine Eber. Photo courtesy of Michael O'Malle 2010.

A mother and daughter weaving. Photo courtesy of Rebecca Wiggins, 2005.

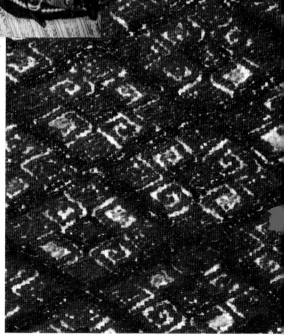

Sat k'u'il (ceremonial blouse). Photo courtesy of Michael O'Malley, 2010.

aders of the Feast of Saint Peter. Photo by Christine Eber, 1987.

Photo courtesy of Michael O'Malley, 2010.

Candles and incense lit for a service in a community chapel. Photo courtesy of Bill Jungels, 2009.

Celebrating Sk'in Ch'ulelal (Day of the Dead). Photo by Christine Eber, 1987.

Working with Coffee

I've worked a lot with coffee and everything that goes along with it.

Antonia

In the mid-1980s Antonia and Domingo began to plant coffee with hopes that it would provide a more stable source of cash than they had found selling animals or bananas and other produce. When the plants were still young, the couple had great hopes of selling their coffee at a good price, even though harvesting and lugging heavy bags down the mountainside was back-breaking work. Antonia felt confident that soon she wouldn't need to depend on selling her weavings to buy the food and other necessities that they didn't produce.

But the timing of their coffee venture couldn't have been worse. The era of neoliberalism had taken hold in Mexico in the early 1980s, and supports for the agricultural way of life that indigenous people had depended on for as long as they could remember were gradually eliminated. All farmers became vulnerable to drastic fluctuations in prices.

In 1988 Antonia and Domingo watched fearfully as the price of coffee fell from 2,500 a kilo in January to 2,000 in September, a harbinger of the 50 percent fall in the world coffee price in 1989. Still, the couple kept hoping that they could ride the waves as prices rose and fell. In 2002 the world coffee price fell to the lowest it had been in 116 years: 41 cents a pound. Although prices have not dropped that low again, during the 1990s Antonia found it necessary to weave to supplement coffee production. In recent years she has depended more on earnings from her general store.

March 2009, San Cristóbal de las Casas

In the 1980s I didn't think I would need to work hard with my weavings to support my family. I thought that I would give up weaving and we would make enough money selling our coffee. Unfortunately, the price fell a lot, so that now we don't earn very much from coffee. If there was a fair price we

could earn a little more with our coffee. But we still have coffee. It's something to help us.

Where I lived with my parents, we didn't have land where coffee can grow. Coffee needs a hot climate, and we lived in a cooler region. When I came to live in Domingo's region, he began to plant coffee so we would have a little crop.

It seems that coffee production is men's work, but I help Domingo. I don't know what year it was when we began to plant coffee, but I was weaving then, and with the money that I earned from my weaving I paid Domingo's helper to plant coffee. Domingo went to the land below us and took his helper with him. Since planting the coffee, Domingo has to weed it three times a year and pay someone to help him. Although I don't go to work in the field, I always pay Domingo's helper for the tasks that he does in the field. So I've worked a lot with coffee and everything that goes along with it.

When the coffee bears fruit, we have to pick it. I pick coffee, too, just not every day during the harvest. This year I didn't pick coffee because I felt weak. I think that's because of my sickness. I never had this happen to me before, but over this past year I have felt that I'm getting old and tired. That's why I didn't pick coffee.

The coffee harvesting process is first pick, second grind, third wash, and fourth dry. We pick the little red coffee cherries when they are mature. But one can't collect all the ripe beans alone. It's necessary to pay several people.

Then when the coffee is all picked, we have to grind it. When you grind, you separate the bean from the shell, the bean to one side, the shell to the other. But it's very tiring to grind. When you grind you get a lot of blisters.

When you're done grinding, you put the coffee in a burlap bag or in a wood box to sour. After two days, when the coffee beans are sour enough, you wash them. Since I don't have water near my house, I have to carry buckets from the well seven to eight times to wash the coffee. Then, when it's washed, we put it out on the patio to dry for three or four days. When there is a lot of sun, it dries in three or four days, but when there's no sun, it doesn't dry. It's worse when it rains. Then we have to quickly gather up all the beans and put them back in the bag so that they won't get wet. It's very difficult to prepare coffee for sale.

When the coffee is dry enough, it's ready to sell. We carry the coffee in *costales* [large bags] down the hill to the highway. I was sick when I had to carry the bags down the hill last week, but we have to bear all the pain that there is in our bodies. We have to put up with it, no matter how we feel.

We loaded the coffee onto a truck that we paid to take us to Pantelhó

(FACING PAGE): Photo courtesy of Bill Jungels, 2008.

to sell. We both went. One person can't do it alone. For four bags we made 4,500 pesos. With that I'm not going to pay off my whole debt because I had to borrow to pay the people who helped us. I have to take that out of the earnings. That's how the money goes. I believe that I may be able to pay off all my debt because we still have a little coffee yet to pick.

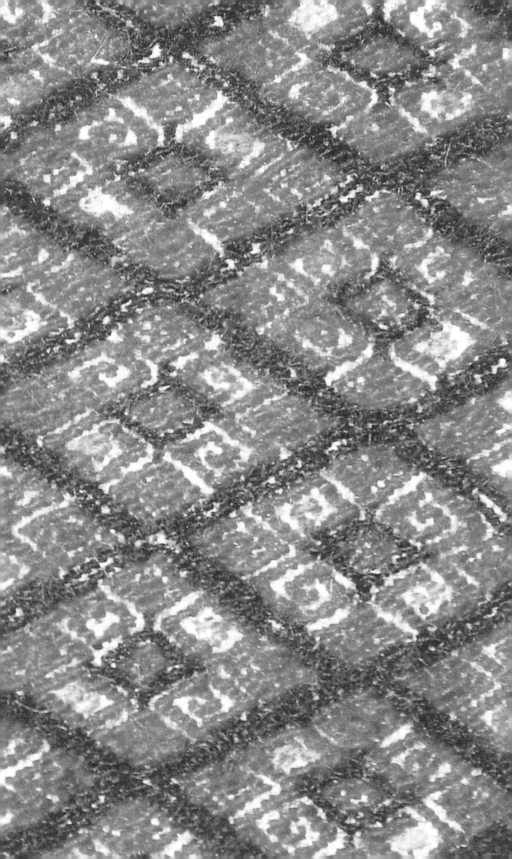

PART II

Contesting the Status Quo, Creating a Different World

(FACING PAGE): Design on the bodice of *sat k'u'il* (ceremonial blouse). Photo courtesy of Michael O'Malley, 2010.

This is the main blouse that the women wear when they're serving a *cargo* in a fiesta. They call the blouse *sat k'ui'l.* Why? Because it's as if it has eyes. Elderly women used to wear this blouse in the past. When I was a little girl, I saw an older woman wear this blouse around the house. Now not many women make this blouse because it takes a lot of effort and time to make. Women *cargo* holders borrow this blouse from a woman who lends it for fiestas.

I made the effort to make it because I wanted to learn this design. I was working in Sna Jolobil, and the director, Pedro Mesa, told us that it would be good if we would study the old designs so as not to forget them. He told us that we would receive a prize or a grant afterward if our work came out well. So I borrowed a blouse from the store to copy, and I earned a prize. I don't remember how much it was, perhaps about 50 or 100 pesos. But it was a lot in that year.

First I went to church to pray to the Virgin Mary to be able to learn to make the blouse and so that my work would come out well. Many women know how to weave with the help of the Virgin. I asked her for help because she wears brocaded blouses like this one. I asked her to give me her eyes, to give me her designs, to teach me so that I could be as good as the other women who know how to make this blouse.

I made the background in cotton and the designs in wool threads. I made it in three parts. First, I made the middle, because it's the biggest. It's called *sme'*, its mother. After that I made *sk'ob*, its arm. Then I made designs called *bakil choy*, fish bones, *be tsukum*, a worm that bites, *me' kumpok* [an old design whose significance Antonia doesn't know], and *batz'i luch*, the true design. I don't know how many months it took to make this blouse. I kept thinking, "Will I ever finish?"

Chapter 1

The Time of Fire

Since my childhood I've carried the government on my back. It's time I threw it off.

Antonia, 1995

By 1962, when Antonia was born, most indigenous people in highland Chiapas made a living by alternating between farming corn and beans on family-owned plots and working for wages for a few months at a time on Ladino or foreign-owned plantations. Leaving their home communities to pick coffee or cut sugarcane provided the cash needed to buy additional food as well as to purchase medicine, blankets, and other basic commodities (Rus and Collier 2003).

The Chiapanecan pattern of indigenous migratory labor had its roots in the expropriation of Indian land during the nineteenth and early twentieth centuries, which created both the large fincas and a labor force to work on them—a reserve labor force with scarcely any economic or political power. Although many indigenous communities in Mexico received communal land (*ejidos*) when the haciendas were broken up in the 1930s, the land reforms of the Mexican Revolution never took hold in highland Chiapas.

Over the next thirty years, several forces combined to make the system of wage labor combined with subsistence farming more difficult to maintain. Population increases meant that heirs received smaller plots of land. More consumer goods and services made their way into indigenous communities, competing for small amounts of cash income. And indigenous elites joined forces with the PRI (the only political party at the time) to maintain order and provide votes in exchange for the power to distribute governmental largess in the form of access to land, jobs, credit, monetary grants, or loans (Rus and Collier 2003).

In the late 1970s, Mexico experienced a repositioning in the global economic system and had to devalue its peso. This crisis, combined with the fall of world coffee prices in 1982, meant that the Mexican government could not make payments on its foreign debt. In order to pay back its debt and receive

(FACING PAGE): Soldiers in the streets of San Cristóbal de las Casas, Chiapas, 1994. Photo courtesy of Carol-Jean McGreevy-Morales, 1994.

funds for industrializing the economy, the Mexican government cut back its spending on public works projects, subsidies for food, and credit for farmers producing traditional crops. Small farmers in Chiapas were hit hard by these changes. Jobs in public works ended, and plantation work became scarcer without government support for cash crops. Cattle ranching intensified, putting more pressure on indigenous lands as ranchers fenced off and claimed community lands.

The crisis culminated with the passage of the North American Free Trade Agreement (NAFTA) in 1993. One of the first steps in implementing NAFTA was reforming Article 27 of the Mexican Constitution, thus paving the way for land appropriation by removing the possibility of formalizing ownership of *ejido* (communally held) land. NAFTA also opened Mexican markets to corn from the United States, subsidized and grown on a scale beyond anything possible in Mexico. Cheap US corn broke the backs of small farmers in Mexico, pushing them off their lands into cities and across borders to look for work. NAFTA's promise was that US manufacturers could take advantage of cheaper labor created by these changes, and that Mexico would move into a parity of prosperity with the United States. While factory work materialized along the border, few such jobs reached Chiapas. Eventually, it was clear that US manufacturers could find cheaper labor elsewhere, and factories in Mexico began to close.

The impact of all these changes made indigenous people more and more fearful and worried about options to support themselves and their families. Many joined protests against the government's policies during the 1980s and early 1990s, only to be met with repression. Meanwhile, government officials clung to the myth that a unified, cheerful Mexican peasantry would join in their new venture.[1]

A deepening sense of desperation was palpable during my visits to Chenalhó in the early 1990s. But nothing I saw during this time prepared me for the morning of January 2, 1994, when my husband handed me the *Hartford Courant* with a headline announcing, "Peasants Attack Mexican Towns."

I read on and discovered that the towns were in Chiapas and that the "peasants" were indigenous men and women. As the days unfolded, many articles were published showing photos of the rebels, who were said to belong to the Zapatista Army of National Liberation. One photo in particular has stayed with me since that day. It was of a woman rebel clad in a cap, pants, and ski mask, and carrying a rifle. The only thing about her that was familiar were her eyes, which were indisputably Mayan. Desperation had moved people in ways I never imagined.

I soon learned that on January 1, 1994, the same day that NAFTA went into effect, the Ejército Zapatista de Liberación Nacional (Zapatista Army of National Liberation) had seized four towns. The rebels were based in the lowlands of Chiapas, but their attacks took place in highland towns as well. The cry that went out from Chiapas on January 1 was "*¡Basta!*" (Enough is Enough!). With these words the EZLN called for land, housing, jobs, food, health care, democracy, and justice—and an end to the hundreds of years of exploitation and marginalization of the indigenous people and peasants of Chiapas.

Eventually the Zapatistas found their way into receptive communities in Chenalhó. Civilian support bases—unarmed community organizations that support the Zapatista agenda—began to form. Support bases in Chenalhó found common cause with another Pedrano social justice organization, Sociedad Civil Las Abejas (Civil Society [of] the Bees), which progressive Catholics created in 1992.[2] Following the Zapatista uprising, members of Las Abejas and Zapatista supporters struggled to unite for a larger cause: resisting domination by the PRI.

In 1994, when the Zapatistas rose up, we didn't know anything about them. We were only involved in the Word of God. We didn't know that there was going to be an armed uprising.

On the day of the uprising my mother went to San Cristóbal and was surprised not to see anyone in the streets. The city was silent. Eventually she found a few people who told her that there was a war. After that she was afraid and returned quickly to the house. On her way home she passed by my house to tell me, "They're killing people in San Cristóbal!" I was just about to give birth to Rosalva, and I wasn't thinking about anything but her.

After a few months in 1994, we began to learn that the Zapatistas were indigenous people struggling for justice and in support of the poor. Given that we, too, were poor, we began to make connections with them. Support groups began to form in Chenalhó. Many Catholics joined the Zapatista support base, but some didn't want to. The priests and nuns who came to our community to give courses said that what the Zapatistas were doing wasn't a just struggle. Some catechists listened to them, but later many catechists began to join the bases. That's when a split began among the Catholics, between those who wanted the Zapatistas and others who didn't want them.

The ones who didn't want to be Zapatistas chose the name Las Abejas and formed the Abejas group. With this, the religious ones in Chenalhó divided amongst themselves. Before this we were united just by being in the Word of God. But after the uprising, we began to divide because people didn't know which way to go—which was good, which was bad. We were confused.

Although we had learned about the Word of God, the Zapatistas and the Bees began to criticize each other. The Zapatistas said, "God doesn't like what you're doing," and the Bees said, "You're not acting like Jesus Christ would." The two groups didn't understand each other and criticized each other. I don't know how many years it took, but later the Bees understood that what the Zapatistas were doing came from the Word of God, too. The Zapatistas are liberating us now the same way that Moses liberated the Israelites in the past. Although the Zapatistas rose up in arms, it was like calling out with a trumpet so that the government would hear us. Using only our voices, the government didn't pay attention to us. That's why the Zapatistas rose up in arms. But not all the Zapatistas use arms. We in the bases support the army, but we don't use arms.

Little by little the Bees and the Zapatistas in Chenalhó began to combine their ideas so that now they are more united. When many in the Word of God were divided, I felt a little sad. It was unfair that *compañeros* in the Word of God were divided.

In the beginning I always participated in the meetings because I wanted to hear what the Zapatistas had to say. Although I was very excited at first, later, as the years passed and they were saying, "We're going to win! We're going to win a better life!" I didn't see any triumph. I began to think, "Ah, the triumph won't come soon. All we can do is to struggle and struggle more and not give up."

We struggle for our grandchildren, the children of the future, not for ourselves. Although I have seen that many have died, I see no gains. I could die in a week, or in a few months, so it's better that I not focus on triumph. It's better just to struggle so that something might change in the future. I no longer think that in a few months or years we're going to win, that we will have, as stated in the Zapatista demands, decent housing, schools, and other things. The government made an agreement in San Andrés with the Zapatistas, but they didn't fulfill the agreement. Who knows when we will see what the Zapatistas are demanding? That's why I don't think about triumph right now. I just want to continue to struggle. Change takes a long time. The government is only beginning to open its eyes and its ears. That's why it's necessary to remain calm.

Antonia's call for patience in the face of the government's efforts to dismantle the resistance movement in Chiapas illustrates an attitude in Zapatista communities that has made their autonomous projects possible. Zapatista supporters did not build their schools, clinics, cooperatives, and justice systems in the safety of secure and peaceful lives. They did so while being threatened daily by political parties and military and paramilitary troops aimed at isolating Zapatista supporters from the broader population.

In 1995 Zapatista supporters in Chenalhó decided to form a new township with a set of social and political institutions parallel to the formal township institutions, with their headquarters in Chenalhó. The creation of an autonomous township, San Pedro Polhó, located in the community of Polhó, was their first major effort to live free of government domination.[3]

Not long after the formation of San Pedro Polhó, I asked Antonia what had led to this.

The government got involved with its bad orientation, and people got used to that. The government still has its hands in things, and because of its control we formed a new township. We don't want to divide the people of Chenalhó, but we don't want to be in the government's hands anymore. We had to separate to find our own opinions, but we want all people here to be united and free to give their opinions.

Antonia often uses metaphors to describe life in her township. To help me appreciate how Zapatista supporters felt as they embarked upon creating an autonomous township, she evoked the image of a newborn child.

We're like a baby. When a baby is born, it doesn't do anything, just cry for its mother. So it is with us. We cry out to God because we're living with injustice. We're really oppressed. We are like a newborn child who doesn't know how to make money yet. It doesn't have a *milpa* yet, nor clothes. That's how it is with us. We don't know how to work well yet. We don't have economic resources to be autonomous. But even if a baby doesn't know how to create new things, we have our mind, our struggle, our imagination. We have these. We know what to do. It's not that we stay like a baby, waiting for his food. No. We can look for it. We know how to search for it.

Antonia went on to say that in time God would help them acquire economic resources, perhaps outside of their community. In fact, resources did come from outside of Chenalhó as a solidarity network spread throughout the world for the Zapatista movement. Students, professors, community activists, health promoters, church workers, and many other groups of people joined forces to show their support for the Zapatistas. I too joined the call, and together with colleagues, students, community members, and members of various churches in Las Cruces, New Mexico, and in other parts of the United States began to hold fundraisers, sell weavings from cooperatives, and speak to the public about the meaning of the Zapatista movement.

Observing the autonomous activities in Chenalhó over the past fifteen years, I have been interested in the strong linkage between the Word of God and the Zapatista movement. Many of the catechists who helped spread the Word of God in the 1980s became involved in the Zapatista movement, some even becoming commanders in the Zapatista Army. Bishop Ruíz recognized the justice demands of the Zapatistas and was a major voice in the peace talks in 1995 and 1996, but he was adamant about not condoning violence in any form. The nuns and priests whom Antonia mentions coming to her township were sympathetic to the Zapatistas but followed the bishop in their condemnation of violence. In contrast, on the local level many Word of God Catholics saw the Zapatistas' use of arms during the few days of the uprising as justified, and they joined unarmed groups in support of the EZLN in the following months.

Soon after she joined a Zapatista support base, Antonia told me that the Word of God is her flashlight that shows her where to walk. She went on to describe how the Word of God and the Zapatista movement relate to one another.

When I joined the Word of God, it was my way to learn about injustices. It was the light on the path so I could see where to walk. We learned how things are and what we can do in the future. But on our path we came to a big log, the government and powerful people, that blocked our way. We couldn't go any farther until the Zapatistas came and cut the log. After that we began to act on the teachings that we had learned in the Word of God. That's why we call what we are doing *ja lekil pas k'op* [the holy struggle], because our struggle comes from God. Words about fighting for justice don't come only from Marcos, Davíd, Javier, and the other Zapatista commanders [and subcommanders], but from the Word of God. The words from the Bible and the Zapatistas are very similar.[4]

The bishop showed the way toward justice, as Jesus did, but I don't think that he pulled the people, like Marcos.[5] In the time of the believers we demonstrated and went on pilgrimages to Tuxtla. I walked with Rosalva on my back in the heat. But the government didn't pay attention to us. It treated us like animals, like monkeys, like flies that fill up the streets. It never listened to us because it knew that the believers didn't have guns, and it wasn't afraid of us.

The government began to listen a little when Marcos arrived and the war began. Before Marcos and the Zapatistas, we were always standing at the door knocking, but we couldn't open the door. It was as if we didn't have the key. But it seems that Marcos had the key. When he opened the door, many people went walking with him.

According to what Marcos has said, it's not important the race, the blood, the intelligence of a person. It's not important. We are all human beings. We want there to be liberty and justice for everyone, not just for Mexico, not just for Chiapas. For the whole world. Because there's a lot of poverty in the world. We have to unite, organize ourselves—everyone, no?

Chapter 2

1997

Then those in Judea must flee into the mountains. The one on the house-
top must not go down to take what is in the house. The one in the field
must not turn back to get a coat. Woe to those who are pregnant and to
those who are nursing infants in those days.

Matthew 24:16–19

The violence that began in Chenalhó in 1996 and culminated in a massacre at
the end of 1997 was the direct result of the spread of a low-intensity war in
Chiapas. A major component of this war was the creation and maintenance of
paramilitary groups in communities such as Antonia's with large bases of support for the Zapatistas. During this time, paramilitary groups were supported
by funds channeled through municipal offices and development programs, and
protected by the police and the military. Members were mostly young indigenous men without land or hope of obtaining it. Time spent outside of their
communities in search of wage labor had alienated them from their families and
communities, making them vulnerable to groups offering camaraderie, some
measure of power, and the booty of war, including animals, trucks, land, and
coffee harvests. The PRI and military officials used these young men to create
confusion and dissent by fanning the fires of long-standing disagreements over
land and community resources (Arriaga Alarcón et al. 1998; Aubry and Inda
1998; Eber 2003a).

Chenalhó became home to thousands of internal refugees during this time.
Others fled to San Cristóbal. As the refugee camps in Chenalhó filled, Mexican soldiers set up checkpoints, maintaining that their presence was necessary
to restore peace and order. Several of my non-Pedrano, foreign friends were
stopped at these checkpoints and deported for coming to "help the Indians."
I didn't want to be deported for fear I would never again be able to see my
godsons, *compadres*, and friends, so for a couple years I didn't try to enter
Chenalhó. During those years Antonia's brother, Francisco, and his wife, Marta,
often let me stay with them in their home in San Cristóbal.

Fear and terror spread throughout Chenalhó as rumors circulated of men

dressed in black walking on trails in the night and cutting off the heads of anyone unfortunate enough to meet them on the path. The *cortacabezas* (head-cutters), as these men came to be known, were frightening to Antonia and her family, but they did their best to try to make sense of this horrible rumor.

One night in July 1996, Antonia's mother, María, was about to go outside when she saw a strange animal or person on a ledge above the house. It was black like a jaguar and springing from place to place. María watched in terror as the figure changed from a jaguar into a man and back again into a jaguar. Could this be a head-cutter? María concluded that it was, and others agreed with her when she told them what happened.

María's perception of a being that is capable of changing from a jaguar to a human reflects traditional Mesoamerican beliefs about the *nagual*, an animal that shares the soul of a human and can bring harm as well as good. For example, a jaguar may be the soul companion of either a powerful healer or a witch.[1]

Everyone I spoke to during this time asked me why someone would want a human head. I didn't know how to respond except to say that the head could serve as proof of a person being killed if the killer needed evidence that he had done the deed. Several friends to whom I spoke looked to their cultural practices and historical experiences to answer the question.

It is customary in Maya communities of highland Chiapas to place the heads of four chickens in the foundations of a new house, and the heads of four bulls in the foundations of a school or other public building to protect these structures from evil forces. In like manner, some Pedranos told me that they had heard that mestizos use human heads to build bridges. After the Panamerican Highway was built with indigenous labor, rumors also circulated that human heads were used in its construction. I took the idea of human heads being used to build bridges and highways as metaphors for the bodies and souls of the indigenous men who built these structures under slave labor conditions and sometimes died. I concluded that the head-cutters were probably paramilitaries, comparable to the white guards or labor contractors who make their living exploiting the labor of indigenous workers.[2]

Hysteria about the head-cutters led to the tragic lynching of seven young men by people living in the town center of Chenalhó. The angry mob dumped the boys' bodies into a crevice above the town center on August 19, 1996.[3] The young men were from different townships and were reported to have lived together on the outskirts of San Cristóbal, where they were studying. As with

(FACING PAGE): Pilgrim at the shrine in Acteal, Chenalhó, looking at the photographs commemorating the forty-five men, women, and children who died in the massacre on December 23, 1997. Photo courtesy of Bill Jungels, 2007.

most events during this time, Antonia could only say what others had told her about this event. She did not witness any violent acts herself, for which she feels deeply fortunate.

In 1997 life was very sad and difficult. Many things happened and we had to be very vigilant that year. The head-cutters came, and those boys died, and there was the massacre at Acteal.

In that year people talked about a lot of things—*cortacabezas* and *chupacabras* [goats who suck people's blood]. But I think that they didn't understand what a *chupacabra* is. In my opinion, the *chupacabra* is the bad government that just sucks the blood out of the indigenous people.

It was said that there were lots of head-cutters, men who cut people's heads off so they could sell them. I don't know if it was true, but we were afraid. They said that the head-cutters wandered along the paths and came into houses. They carried a rope to tie people up. That year people were talking about it a lot in all the communities. I didn't see or hear anything. But many people said, "Ah, I saw it. I heard it." "Ah, it's over there running, it's hiding!" they said. Sometimes I didn't believe it. It just came from fear, I think.

I don't know how people came to think that the young men in Chenalhó were head-cutters. There were six boys from different communities staying at Anabel's hotel. One came from Acteal. I don't know about the rest. I think that they came from around Pantelhó. One was a Zapatista, I think—or they were schoolmates, or they were with the government. They came there to Chenalhó to live, I think. I don't know what was happening in Chenalhó at that time, but they were in Chenalhó when they captured them.

They say that they acted like head-cutters. They said that they did exercises at night, that they jumped from the bridge. I don't know what they did in the river. I think they also used that thing you [Cristina] talk about—drugs. They behaved very badly, I think. That's why one day a group of people went to get them at the hotel where they were sleeping.

"Yes, the head-cutters, it's better to kill them," they said. They started to get many people together, I don't know how many people, and they took the boys to the top of a crevice, there where the highway passes near Chenalhó. They brought the boys tied up and threw them down the crevice. I was very sad when I heard what happened to the boys, because we didn't know if it's true or not that they were *cortacabezas*. No one said clearly.

DECEMBER 23, 1997, ACTEAL

Heather calls me at my office and asks if I have read my e-mail. There has been a massacre in Chiapas. I open my e-mail and frantically search for a message from the Chiapas list. I find one that must be what Heather read. It says:

New Alert—45 Zapatista Supporters Killed After Attack by PRI Gunmen
The Associated Press reported that gunmen attacked Zapatista support-ers in two small towns about twelve miles north of San Cristóbal, killing at least forty-two people. It is the bloodiest attack in Chiapas since the twelve days of fighting in January 1994 between the EZLN and the Mexi-can government troops.

Members of the campesino group Las Abejas said forty-two people were killed and six were missing in the massacre which took place Monday, according to Manuel Gómez Pérez, an official of the rebel local government for Chenalhó county. La Jornada newspaper has reported forty-five deaths, while National Public Radio has reported forty-seven killed.[4]

I soon learn that Acteal is a community in the north of Chenalhó that I had passed many times over the years on my way to Pantelhó. I just hadn't noticed it. Now it's on the front pages of US newspapers.

I don't return to highland Chiapas until summer 1998. Antonia agrees to speak in a film about the massacre and indigenous women's lives in the context of the low-intensity war. The film crew and I still can't enter Chenalhó, so we invite Antonia and the other members of the weaving co-op to gather in the courtyard of Antonia's brother's house to film. I haven't seen Antonia since the massacre, and that night we talk in my room in Francisco's house. We both cry. I tell her how powerless I have felt, and she tells me not to worry. I want to hear about her feelings, but she wants to talk about mine.

I'm a grandmother now, she says. When women grow older, they get weary from carrying around a lot of burdens. "We're all tired and sad," she says. "But God sees that you want to do good things. He'll give you the strength to con-tinue."

Later, remembering Antonia's words, I am comforted, but ashamed that I didn't offer her more. As so often happens in difficult times, Antonia offers me emotional support. I want to return it to her, but my efforts feel inadequate.

I felt very sad and worried when I heard what happened in Acteal. I began to cry when I heard that many people were dead. "Who could it be that died? Could it be someone I know?" Everyone was worried. We thought, "Is it go-ing to happen in our community?"

I knew two people who died. One was Alonzo, a catechist. We weren't friends, just acquaintances. Nine days after the massacre I went to Acteal to see where Alonzo and the other people died. There we saw their sandals and their necklaces thrown about on the ground.

"What fault did these people have who died there?" I asked. The people who died in Acteal were only asking God for liberation, for peace. The men and women at Acteal were struggling for the well-being of our children who aren't born yet. The paramilitaries who came to kill at Acteal don't understand peace. They took the lives of children. That's why at times we can't forgive them.

Although God says that we have to love and forgive our enemies, if I love you and you only want to kill me, what can I do? I have to defend my life, and others have to defend me. Because if we didn't defend our children, their lives would be taken and justice would end. That's why to love is to defend. Clearly, some people are going to die, as is happening now. Many have fallen in the struggle. But to live without defending, it's not possible.

God isn't angry at those who defend their rights. It's like David did in the time of Jehovah. Do you know that there was a prophet David who defended his rights? There was this soldier named Goliath. I don't know in what text of the Latin American Bible it tells about this, but David confronted the government soldier. David was poor and little, a soldier of the poor people. The same thing is happening right now. We are acting like David. What else can we do?

Chapter 3

International Encounters

"I'm not going to go," I thought to myself. "If only I could be together with my children, happy, at home. But now I have to leave my home to advance the struggle and abandon my kids. It's the government's fault that we're doing this. If there was justice, these people from different countries wouldn't be here. If this struggle didn't exist, I wouldn't have to leave my kids. We wouldn't have to have these meetings. The people struggling for justice suffer too much from all this work." All of this I was thinking as I sat by the side of the road waiting for the truck. I felt sorry for myself and began to cry.

Antonia, on leaving for Oventik to attend
the Zapatista Intercontinental Encounter in 1996

In the years right after the uprising in 1994, the Zapatistas organized several intercontinental gatherings that Antonia and Domingo attended as part of their participation in their local support base. Domingo was more enthusiastic about these meetings than Antonia. She almost didn't go to the meeting she describes below because it meant leaving her youngest child with her mother and the rest of the children at home alone. But in the end she went.

When Antonia told me about the experience, I was moved by her concern for the older women from different countries who attended the event. She empathized with them having to carry heavy backpacks, sleep on the ground, and deal with the rain and mud.

July 1996

When we began to organize for the Intercontinental Encounter, first the men prepared the things that they would need there in Aguascalientes II.[1] All the support bases collaborated, working with their hands, constructing little houses. Then, when the houses were ready, we contributed toasted tortillas and everything that would be needed. Even if a person didn't have something, he had to contribute. In this way we could help one another move the struggle forward. Some who are Zapatistas don't want to coop-

erate or collaborate. They leave the organization eventually because it's required to cooperate.

When we had gathered everything together, we brought it all to Aguascalientes. When everything arrived, people were appointed to be in charge of keeping order. There weren't enough buses to carry the people from our community who went. We had to stand up the whole way.

It was difficult after we arrived because it was raining and there was lots of mud. I remember that I couldn't find a place to sleep. Later a person offered us a piece of plastic where there were other pieces of plastic on the ground, and Domingo and I slept there.

Although there was mud and rain, the people didn't feel it because they came with high spirits. After the support bases had arrived, they got us all together to wait for the other countries to arrive. We ate and rested. Those who didn't have beans like us ate only toasted tortillas and salt. Those who had a little bit of money bought an avocado.

When the other countries began arriving, we got into formation. Many men, women, children. So many! We applauded the visitors and then we informed them about what the Zapatistas are doing.

First we showed how the war began in 1994 in a theater production. All the support bases got into formation in the dark. It was about 10:30 in the night. They lit torches of *ocote* [pitch pine] and began to walk, each one with his torch. The *ocote* was a symbol of how the war began in 1994. It showed how the support bases who helped the Zapatista soldiers and donated their tortillas were in darkness before the uprising. All the countries saw this when they did the play. It was beautiful, but at times sad.

When they finished showing how it was in '94, Commander Davíd began to speak. "Thanks for coming to see us here," he said. "The bad government doesn't have any respect. All the men and women who are present here have seen how injustice is."

After Commander Davíd, a woman named Hortense spoke. She said, "We began to rise up in arms because there's no respect. We didn't have freedom, the right to participate as women. Now we're making the effort to go as far as we can. I ask you to support the women who are advancing the struggle for their rights."

Next Ana María spoke. "It's been ten years since we prepared the war. As women, we are marginalized. No one respects us. They treat us like a rock, like a plant. We are forgotten women. Now there is no other way out. That's why in 1994 we began the war. Only with arms can the government hear women's voices."

(FACING PAGE): Mural at Oventik. Photo courtesy of Linda Laughlin, 1997.

Major Ana María and the others told about how they began the struggle and how they have seen that there's a lot of exploitation. They talked a lot, but I forgot all the words.

When each woman and man finished talking, the people were very happy and applauded loudly. All the people from the other countries chanted, "E-Z-L-N, E-Z-L-N, E-Z-L-N." We felt very content that we're continuing in our struggle, and we didn't feel afraid.

Then they showed how they make the fiesta in each township, how our cultures look. First they showed the township of San Andrés. They said, "In this way we're making each fiesta. We know how to carry out our traditions. We know how to do everything in order not to lose our culture. We don't want to lose our traditions."

Then some men from Chenalhó showed how we make the fiesta in Chenalhó. "We know how to do everything that is in our tradition. We don't want to forget our traditions. It's not true what the bad government says that the Zapatistas are losing the traditions in each township."

Then the popular dancing began. Mountains of people began to dance. Almost all night they danced in order to endure the cold, because it was pretty cold. Rain came. I danced, too. I danced with Domingo only for a little bit because he always has his *cargo* duties.

So the fiesta ended and we began to go to sleep. The people from other countries just slept in the places where they were seated. I think they were very tired from the trip.

In the morning, at eight or nine, we began to get into formation again to say goodbye to the visitors who were going to go to other Aguascalientes. We said goodbye, gave salutes, and applauded them. It took a long time. We began at nine, and it wasn't until noon that all the visitors finally left for other Aguascalientes. At the end of the goodbye, they continued the cultural festival. I returned to my house before it ended.

It's very difficult for those who came from other countries to suffer for two days with all the rain and mud. They are used to eating good foods, to sleeping in good beds. In contrast, we never have good food, good beds. We sleep on the floor. We're always with just our tortilla. That's why I thought, "Ah, how are they going to bear a night with these foods, with these beds? Perhaps it's going to be very difficult for them."

A lot of older women came. They had their things that weighed a lot, and they had to carry them. I know that they're not used to carrying these things. That's why I felt bad for them. But they felt bad for us, too. That's why they were moved to come here. If there wasn't poverty and injustice, the older people who came from other countries wouldn't be suffering with us here, and we would be content in our homes.

Yes, it was mutual. That's why at times I wanted to cry. I felt a lot of emotions. Besides, I see how Domingo suffers. Before he was in the struggle, he couldn't take such suffering. But now he always bears up under lack of sleep and hunger. It seems that he doesn't get sick much anymore. But how does he take it? At times I say, "How good that he's not sick!" But at times I can tell that he's very tired. Although he's not sick, he's tired. His eyes get red from lack of sleep. But through the struggle and his work in it, God heals him.

I think that Domingo has matured a lot. His heart is very strong, stronger than before. He's walking on a very beautiful path toward justice. With a lot of strength.

He likes to do it, too. "Although I'm suffering, I have to do it," he says. "I can't give up the struggle. I'm going to keep on with it until I can't anymore," he says. "If I die from the struggle, it's okay," he says, "because the struggle is my only path."

An important contribution of the Zapatista movement is its focus on gender equality, specifically enabling women to participate in decision making within the movement as well as in the political affairs of their communities. As an outgrowth of the focus on gender, meetings at the regional, state, and national levels have been organized by progressive and democratic groups in which women explore issues pertinent to their lives from their individual and collective perspectives (Speed et al. 2006).[2] It is common for these meetings to be very long due to the many languages spoken, as well as the commitment to finding consensus on important issues. Meetings are also long because translations are often in all languages of those present.

International Women's Day has become a major highlight of the year for Antonia and women in the resistance movement in her community. Antonia has attended several celebrations of International Women's Day, the most recent in Oventik in 2009. At the first celebration she attended in 1995, she learned about the New York City Triangle Shirtwaist Company factory fire in 1911 in which 146 women workers died because their managers kept the doors to the building locked. Although Antonia's memory of the fire is not factually accurate, her merging of facts from women's lives in Chiapas with the story of the women factory workers in New York speaks to the commonalities and solidarity she perceives between herself and other oppressed women.

I don't know what year it was that we went to San Cristóbal on the eighth of March, International Women's Day. There they told us what had happened in a city called Chicago. Women were working in a factory there, and they wanted fair conditions for their work. On March eighth, I believe it was, many soldiers came to kill the women who wanted a fair salary. That's what one of the women told us. She said that exploitation of workers still continues, that we don't have rights, that we don't have a fair salary, that the blood of the women of that time lives on in us as women today.

I learned from this demonstration that it's true that women don't have the right to defend our rights and that exploitation and injustice continue in every country. I felt a little sad to hear everything that has happened and how it's still going on.

The next year, 1997, there was an International Women's Day celebration in San Cristóbal and in Oventik, too. I decided to write a song in order to reflect on how the government acts. Sebastian and I practiced singing the song together because he was little and wanted to sing with me. That day that I sang with Sebastian, I was thinking, "With my words the government is going to hear us and perhaps, after a few years, it's going to give us justice." But it's been many years since I wrote this song, and with all the other things that the *compañeros* have done, things haven't changed that much. It's the truth what I wrote in my song, but after I sang it, I thought that if I do something or not, it seems to come out the same. The government still doesn't listen to us. I thought, "How is the government going to hear my song? Maybe it wasn't worth anything to sing it."

Then I thought that if Cristina found out about my song, it might be worth something. "It's good that there is a woman who can get the word out, tell other *compañeros* about it." That's what I thought that year. Even if the government didn't hear my voice, other people could listen, think about how life is in Chiapas, how life is for women, what women think. For that I think it was worth something.

It took a lot out of me to write my song. But that year I wanted to write a song with my own words, even if people made fun of me. Right now I don't know if I will write more songs or not. I don't think that I will write another. But I keep hoping that one day the government will listen to us.

> March 8th, 1908, many women died,
> because they asked for liberty, and justice.
> The bad government didn't like
> how the women protested.
>
> The bad government sent soldiers
> to burn their factories,
> where they worked,
> the oppressed women.

They aren't animals,
those the army was sent to kill.

The bad government was like a blood-thirsty animal,
like a buzzard that eats dead people.
The Zedillo government is the same,
it wants to be a buzzard, too.

The government doesn't say clearly
if it will give peace, liberty, and justice.
It only deceives us and doesn't fulfill
its promises in the dialogues of San Andrés.

But we will not surrender.
We will continue going forward,
asking for justice,
men, women, and children.

We are not cowards,
not like the government.
The government feels strong
because it has guns, tanks, and airplanes.
The government ignores the suffering of
the people holding hands to protect peace.

Chapter 4

Sons

I have a lot of faith and hope that my sons are going to become like their father.

Antonia

NOVEMBER 14, 2002, LAS CRUCES, NEW MEXICO

All the seats are filled in the University Museum at New Mexico State University as Antonia, on her first visit to the United States, narrates a slide show about life in her community. She didn't know what a slide was until we put the show together last night, and tonight she is giving her first public talk to a group of foreigners in their own country.

She's a natural. She seems to know what people need to hear. I show a slide of Antonia weaving, and she talks about how women must weave in between their other labors to make money to feed their children. Weaving is not a hobby for them, she explains. I click to a slide of the waterhole, and she tells about how women have to walk up the hill several times a day to collect water. Eventually we come to a slide of Alberto and Mariano in front of their newly painted house. When I took the photo, I didn't notice, or it didn't matter to me, that the boys were only wearing undershorts. Antonia is silent. She didn't say anything about the slide when we chose it last night. But now, in a packed lecture hall, she sees it with new eyes—the eyes of people who can afford to buy their children pants and shoes and to send them to camp instead of to the fields during summer vacation. The hall is silent as Antonia bows her head and weeps. I don't know what to do or say. Then a woman rises from the back of the hall and says what few of us in the room could say.

"Thank you for your courage to come here and talk to us. You are a brave woman, and we appreciate you very much. I am from Belize, and I know how you feel because we have a lot of poverty there, too. Most of the people here

(FACING PAGE): Photo by Christine Eber, 1993.

don't know what it is to be poor, to watch their children suffer. It hurts me to think of your children and children in my country suffering."

When they were little, my sons went out to the fields to work. I didn't want my children to go the fields when they were little, but Domingo needed their help. Domingo had to take them to work with him early in the morning. He always left the house about 5 a.m. He had to yell at the children because they didn't want to get out of bed very early. It made me feel so bad when he yelled at them. I cried a lot about my children.

It's such a shame that my children had to work. I think about the children who only go out of the house to walk around, have fun, go to parties, their own birthday parties, I don't know how many other parties. Each summer the children of the mestizos take trips to other cities. My children's vacations are spent going to work in the corn and bean field.

Right now, it doesn't hurt me so much to recall this, because my children are big now. Now they can take it. But from age seven they went in just their undershorts to work in the fields with spades and machetes. They didn't know any better. I think that I am to blame for having many children and not being able to provide for them.

FELIPE

Antonia's eldest son, Felipe, never liked to work in the *milpa*. Antonia and Domingo often contrasted him with his younger brother, Sebastian, who took to the hoe and spade with a passion. Throughout his childhood Felipe suffered from headaches, which made it hard for him to work. Even at night he didn't sleep as soundly as his brothers. He often broke the quiet of the night with a shout or scream. On those occasions Domingo would take him outside to urinate and then tell him to go back to sleep. Eventually Domingo placed a photo of Felipe that I had taken under the boy's head as he slept, because he complained that the devil tried to grab him in his dreams. Domingo hoped that the devil would mistake the photo for Felipe and take it instead of his son's soul.

When I was living with the family, Felipe was seven. Antonia sometimes kept him home from school to care for the younger children while she wove to earn cash. He was also too sickly to attend school many days. After Felipe graduated sixth grade, Antonia and Domingo agreed to let him live in San Cristóbal with Antonia's brother. There he could go to school in exchange for helping in Francisco's garden and running errands. On off hours, Felipe strolled through the streets of San Cristóbal with his cousins, coveting the products in the stores, from high-top sneakers to tape players and junk food. But he soon left his uncle's house to return home.

After another failed attempt at middle school in Chenalhó center and a vo-
cational program in San Cristóbal, Felipe eventually borrowed enough money
from his parents and others to pay a man in Chenalhó to teach him to drive.
After acquiring that skill, he realized his childhood dream of being a driver.
Driving a taxi enabled Felipe to explore the world outside his township, to
command a powerful machine, to develop his facility in Spanish, and to buy the
things he wanted. It also involved him with men who drank a lot and didn't follow traditional forms of respect for women.

I've learned that children don't come out the same. For example, since he
was a little boy, Felipe didn't obey us, although he helped me a lot with his
little brothers. I think that's why he thought he could take my money, because when he was grown up he said, "I suffered a lot taking care of my little
brothers."

I remember these years when he wanted to spend money. The year when
the price of coffee went up, we must have made about 2,000 or 5,000 pesos,
I don't remember. I put the money in a pot high in the rafters because we
didn't have a special chest for it. I thought that Felipe wouldn't see it, but he
found it. Each time when I counted my money, about 50 or 100 pesos would
be missing. I wondered, "Did I spend it? Where did I spend it? Did I forget
how much I have?" This happened two or three times. Later, Felipe said to
his little brother, "I took some money."

I felt a lot of shame for my son during those years. I didn't want him to
disobey us, to steal, to lie, to go out of the house a lot. I was very sad about
what he was doing, and I didn't want people to know about it. That's why
I began to pray. I don't know what year that was. I think it was 1996. I went
to the church to pray to ask God to teach Felipe to do good things. I didn't
know what to say when I prayed, but I tried really hard. Since I'm a woman
who cries easily, I began to cry when I was praying because I didn't know
what I was going to say. But I had to make the effort for my son. I went three
times to the church to pray for Felipe. I don't know if it was because of my
prayers or because he was maturing, but later he began to behave better.
When he was about eighteen or nineteen, he began to listen and learn what's
good to do.

When a child doesn't want to obey or behave well, we ask our parents'
help, too. Sometimes they advise us, even if we don't ask. They know that
their children need support. They begin to advise their grandchildren, to
give their words to them. When children marry, they also give their advice
to the couple. Our children only have grandmothers, but they have the right
to give their words to their grandchildren. It's our tradition here. Even another person, if he is very kind and wants to advise someone else's child,

he has that right, too. For example, my brother-in-law, Moises, he's a very respected person, and he has the right to advise our children.

Felipe's base of operations as a taxi driver was the *lum* or *cabecera* (headtown), the administrative center of Chenalhó. In between taking passengers where they needed to go, he had time on his hands, which he often used to check out the girls going to and coming from the middle school and high school. Felipe was handsome and hard to resist, and Magdalena fell in love with him.

At fourteen, Magdalena was one of the prettiest girls attending middle school in the headtown. She was also very intelligent and fluent in Tzotzil, Tzeltal, and Spanish. Her father was a retired teacher and wanted to give his daughter an opportunity to go to school past sixth grade, so the family made the sacrifice to board Magdalena in town and find money to pay the other expenses necessary for her to continue her education. Things went well for a while. Magdalena seemed to be dedicated to her studies, and on weekend visits to her parents she was a dutiful daughter, helping around the house.

For a couple years Felipe had been telling his parents that he wouldn't do *joyol*, the traditional bride petition process in which a young man asks to marry a girl of his choosing and then works for his father-in-law for a period of time. "I don't want to work for my father-in-law," Felipe told his parents. Felipe and Magdalena both knew that their parents wouldn't approve of their plan to circumvent *joyol*.

In 2000 what Felipe did was a surprise. I didn't have any idea that my son was going to marry. I only knew that he was in love with girls, but I didn't know which girl. He didn't want to tell us when he was going to marry, when he was going to bring a girl to our house.

It was late in the day when he brought Magdalena. I was away from the house visiting neighbors when Felipe arrived with her. Only Domingo was there.

"Tati [Dad], I've come," he said.

"Tati," the girl also said.

When I returned, we had a talk about what they were going to do. We decided that we had to go to Magdalena's house to find out what her parents wanted for the payment since we weren't going to do *joyol*. We had to go. We had to find the money.

Three days later we went to her father's house. He lives in a colonia, quite far from where we live. It took an hour to arrive there by car.

We arrived at the house with a case of soft drinks, but her parents were angry. They didn't want this kind of thing happening to their daughters.

They didn't want Magdalena to marry Felipe. They were very angry and didn't want to talk. The mother was especially angry.

We had to ask for their forgiveness. It took time to talk, to understand each other. Finally her father said, "You have to pay 10,000 pesos."[1]

No one asks that much. It was a lot for us. We said that he was asking a lot. "If you were asking for a cow, or a bull, something to eat, that would be okay," I told him. But it seemed that he only wanted so much money to punish us for stealing his daughter.

That's all we said because he wouldn't listen. Later he lowered the price to 7,000 pesos. We wanted him to lower it more, to 5,000, but he didn't want to. Finally we said, "Well, we're tired of talking about the money. Let the price stay there. But right now we don't have the money. We still have to find it."

We only had 2,500 pesos in our hands, so we left him a down payment. After two weeks we had to go back to deliver the rest of the money. We had to borrow from my mother to complete it, but we couldn't come up with the 7,000. We could only deliver another 2,500.

When we arrived for the second visit, he was very friendly, as if we were family. We were relieved that his anger had passed. We had a good conversation. "You don't have to pay the 7,000," he said. "Just pay me 5,000." He lowered it in half! So we only had to pay 5,000 in the end. It was good for us because we didn't have money, and neither did Felipe.

I felt very ashamed. I didn't want to be a mother-in-law at this time. I didn't feel like a mother-in-law. But what could I do? I had a grown son. I had to be a mother-in-law and later a grandmother.

SEBASTIAN

Since childhood Sebastian has been hardworking and interested in both farming and weaving. He accompanied his father to the fields without complaining, and asked his mother to help him learn to weave once he saw that she was making money selling her weaving.

Since he was a little boy, Sebastian was interested in learning to weave. He would ask me for a weaving that wasn't of use anymore, and he would play with the threads like a toy. Later, each time when I was making a little weaving, he began to touch it, to see if he could weave it. Later he asked me to start a weaving for him because he didn't know how to begin. He began to make the baby boy's tunic because it's not very long and wide. Now he likes to weave these. Although he doesn't know how to begin on the loom, he knows how to weave when the weaving is in process.

When he turned fourteen, Sebastian began to accompany his dad to meetings of the Zapatista base in his community. Young people fourteen or older were welcome at the meetings, and one girl in particular came often with her parents. Sebastian shot glances in her direction, but she was good at avoiding eye contact. Sometimes he thought he saw a little smile about to form on her lips, but then it would disappear. This girl didn't seem to take any nonsense from anyone. Once, at the end of a meeting, her mother said something to her as she knelt to pick up her net bag. She brushed a braid away from her face as she laughed. Two dimples creased the sides of each cheek, so big that Sebastian got lost in them. He had to marry this girl.

Juana was nineteen, the same age as Sebastian, and the only girl in a family of four brothers. Her family was poorer than Sebastian's, and her parents were elderly. She had spent her life caring for her parents and brothers. No wonder she was serious.

Sebastian wanted to do right by his parents, Juana, and his prospective in-laws and was willing to do bride-service. So he asked his parents for permission to help him do *joyol*.

About five months after Felipe married, Sebastian wanted to marry, too. Sebastian asked us if we would go with him to ask for his wife. He wanted to do *joyol*.

"I met a girl who I like and I want to marry her. I don't know if you would do me the favor of going and asking for her with me," he said.

"Have you given it thought, and are sure you want to marry her?" we asked.

"Yes," he said, "I want to marry her, and I think she likes me, too."

"Okay, then, we'll go and ask her parents what they think. Pick a day when we can go to Juana's house."

We said yes because Sebastian wanted his wife to become part of our family, and they were in love. They saw each other at meetings in the community and in other places, and they fell in love.

We began the process in June. I like to do it as it was done in the past. For me it's worth it, even though I don't really know how to do it well.

Juana's parents live nearby. When we went to their home to petition them, I was embarrassed to use the high voice.[2] Sebastian never talked much with the high voice and was embarrassed to do it, too. But my mother helped me by coming with us. I couldn't do it alone. The three of us talked to Juana's parents—Domingo, me, and my mother.

When we arrived it was late, seven in the evening. We had brought soft drinks. We stood outside the door and said, "Bankil! Vixin!" [Elder brother! Sister!]

"*La* [Come in]," they answered. "*Ochan* [Enter]," they said. Some don't let the parents enter, those who aren't good people.

We went inside. When we were inside, we asked, "Are you here?"

"Yes, we are here," they replied.

Then we began the petition by saying,

> "How good that you are here.
> I come to talk.
> I come to visit.
> Because I have my talk,
> my conversation
> with you,
> and with your daughter."

> "That's fine."

> "I come to visit with your daughter
> here in your house.
> I come to talk.
> It's that my son here,
> he fell in love with your daughter.
> That's why we want to appreciate your daughter.

> "Thanks to our Mother the Virgin of Guadalupe
> that you have a daughter,
> that my son's eyes fell on her.
> Let there be no lack of appreciation.
> Let our talk be accepted.
> It's our tradition that our children marry.
> That's how the ancestors started it."

We said this while we were still sitting. Then we went over to kneel by the father and mother. Domingo, my mother, and I each knelt. We began to speak in the high voice, with a sound like a prayer, "Thanks to God that you are here in the house. We came to visit you to ask your daughter to marry our son. It's that our son's eyes fell on your daughter. Our son wants to be a part of your daughter's family." We continued saying many things. Then they said to us, "Sit down. It isn't necessary to kneel. Let's just talk."

We only knelt twice. Some do it more than three times in the same visit so that the girl's parents will accept their son. We sat for a while, and then we began to say our petition again. After the second time they said, "That's okay." Then they started to say some things.

"It's true that your son has thought this out. So it's fine with us," they said. "But you need to accept what we tell you."

So we sat down and began to talk. We discussed what gifts they wanted, how much money they wanted, and if Sebastian would stay in Juana's home one or two years. They wanted two years of bride-service. That's how we began to talk.

"That's fine, if you just bring these gifts that we want," they said. They asked for money, bananas, pineapples, meat, and so on. They didn't want *chilim* because they don't know how to drink it. They asked for rice instead. This was easy for me, because it takes a lot of work to make *chilim*.

While we talked, Juana was there hiding because she was embarrassed. They didn't have a big house, so she was just sitting in a corner. She didn't have a shawl over her face, but she didn't show us her face.

The first visit we just brought sodas, but Juana's mother didn't want to drink them. When we knelt in front of them, they accepted what we came to say, but they didn't want to drink the sodas. "I don't want sodas because they give me stomach pain." She said this because sodas are very cold, but I think she was angry because we didn't bring *pox*. They wanted *pox*. But we didn't want to give alcohol. I told them, "It's not fair for us to drink it because we don't drink. It's not our tradition," I told them.

"Ah, but we want *pox*," they said.

Since we asked for their daughter, we had to provide what they asked for. That's why we had to return another day with beer and *pox*, which they drank. With that they accepted our petition, and we picked a day when we would return for the final visit, when we would bring the other gifts and eat together.

After that Sebastian had to work to earn money to pay his in-laws. I think it was 3,000 or 5,000 pesos. He went away for several months. I don't remember where. After that he worked at a very hard job here in the community. There are people who buy large rocks, and Sebastian had to move rocks for other people to sell. He also had to borrow a little money.

On the third visit we brought the fruit and other gifts. Moises came to the wedding, and my mother and my brother Francisco too. Juana also invited her relatives, and her godparents came. We ate together in Juana's house. They drank and got drunk, but we didn't drink anything.

That night Sebastian stayed at the house—sad, I think. When they married, Juana's parents asked that he stay two years with them. But it didn't end up being that long. After two weeks Sebastian got sick with a tumor and had to go to the doctor for an operation. After the operation he had to recuperate for a few months and he couldn't work. We decided that it wasn't fair for him to live in his in-laws' house without helping his father-in-law. We decided that he should stay in our house. So we went to ask that he no longer live with his in-laws. They didn't like it that he only lived three weeks in their house. But what could we do? It wasn't for pleasure that he left.

Mariano

Education took Mariano down a different path than that of his brothers. When Antonia talked about Mariano to me in 2006, he was still attending high school in the township center and struggling to balance mestizo and Pedrano world-views. Eventually, with financial aid from Antonia's *comadre*, Carol-Jean, and Kathy Scigliano and their students in Pittsburgh, Mariano left home to attend a college specializing in computing skills.

I have seen how it is for Mariano. He's in two worlds. It seems that he under-stands, but at times his mind goes to the other side because he's still study-ing. When they study in San Cristóbal, their minds get mixed up. When Mariano was in middle school, the teachers told him, "God doesn't exist. Hell doesn't exist. Nothing exists in the world."

We say, "Jesus Christ is with us. Hell exists, and everything else that it says in the Word of God we believe." For example, in the Word of God it says that it's not good to look for many girlfriends, to have many wives. But the teachers in the middle school teach the children how to have sexual relations without babies. The teaching of the Word of God says that it's not good to do that. That's why Mariano doesn't know which is good or bad. At times he agrees with his teachers, but then when he comes back to our house, he believes us. That's where the conflict lies. It's difficult to be in two worlds, to learn in two different ways.[3]

For my children in general, I want them to learn to do good things, and I don't want the boys to drink so much. Domingo and I have said to our sons not to drink and not to have friends who drink a lot. My sons have friends that they just go out to have a beer with in the streets. They travel around with their friends to basketball tournaments. They're away a lot, and when they return, they're drunk. We say to them, "You shouldn't do that. Stop be-ing basketball players. It's better to work to earn money, to get food."

Domingo and I have said various times that it's not good to have friends who drink a lot, who don't do good things. It's beautiful to have friends, but one has to see how the person is, if they act in a good way. It's good to have a friend to be happy with, but if it's just a friend that you drink with and do bad things with, that's no good.

I think that they're going to understand when they're more mature, because right now it's very difficult for the boys to understand our advice. But I think that later they're going to be like Domingo.

Hopefully, Domingo and I aren't to blame for the boys drinking a lot. Although Domingo didn't drink when they were growing up, he yelled at them sometimes.

Chapter 5

Daughters

If young people fall in love and they still respect their parents, they come to ask their parents if they can marry and then do joyol. *But the majority aren't doing that now. When they fall in love, they go off together, and the parents are saddened and ashamed. That's why my mom said, "Thank God that not one of my four daughters shamed me." Our husbands came to our home to ask our parents if they could marry us. But I doubt that a boy is going to come to ask for Paulina. I think that she's going to fall in love at school because she's outside of the house every day.*

Antonia, 2003

I'm advising my daughters about how to take care of the house and to weave so that in the future they can earn some money like me. My mother taught me to weave and embroider, and my daughters are learning what she taught me. I don't remember how old Paulina was when I began to teach her. But I think I'm different from my mother because I haven't been teaching Paulina and Rosalva very well. Rosalva just watches and begins to weave and then asks how it's done. That's how she does it. Sebastian's wife, Juana, has helped Rosalva a lot. It's that I don't have a lot of time.

We also advise our daughters not to do bad things—for example, scold people and steal from them. That's the advice I'm giving all my children. We also want them to go to church with us and not move far away from us. We want our sons and daughters to be united with us.

PAULINA

When Paulina was born in 1991, I was delighted that Antonia finally had a daughter to teach to weave and share household work with. A daughter was also important to Domingo, who had not yet had the chance to be guardian of one of his children's souls. In Chenalhó, fathers and mothers are said to have a special guardianship of the souls of children of the opposite sex.

But as the fifth child and eldest daughter, Paulina struggled to find her place

within the family. She was often sick, and when I came to visit, I felt that I needed to go to her defense when her brothers made fun of her or asked her to wait on them.

But Paulina didn't need help for long. By the time she was twelve, she was advocating for herself and outshining everyone in the family with her inquisitive mind and outgoing personality. It made sense that Paulina should go on in school after graduating from primary school. Mariano was in high school supported by donations from students in Pittsburgh, and Alberto had received a scholarship from my husband and me. Paulina wanted to keep studying, too, if someone could make that possible.

"Sure, Paulina," I told her. "If you really want to go to school, my *compañeros* in Las Cruces and I will help you."

For three years Las Cruces–Chiapas Connection raised money for Paulina to attend middle school. During my annual visits I would sit with Paulina around the fire while she showed me her homework and asked me English translations of Spanish words. Paulina handled the academic part of middle school well. The biggest challenge she faced was negotiating the confusing differences between her parents' ideas of respectful interaction between boys and girls, and the mestizos' ideas about courtship and mixing the sexes in school and extracurricular activities.

In 2006, when Antonia visited New Mexico, fourteen-year-old Paulina's marriage was the big news, but news that distressed Antonia. In a conversation with me and Heather, Antonia expressed regrets about Paulina quitting middle school when she had planned to go on to high school. Antonia knew that Heather and I wouldn't have allowed our daughters to marry at fourteen. We could understand the pressures that made it difficult for her to find a solution for Paulina that allowed her daughter to continue her education. But I wished that we could rerun Paulina's life like a film and stop it just before the wedding day.

We found out that Paulina was in love with a boy. When he was drinking one day with Felipe, he told him, "I'm in love with your little sister. I want her to be my wife." I don't know how many other things they talked about.

Later Felipe told us, "He says that he's in love with Paulina."

"Who is he?" I asked.

"A boy from Three Crosses."[1]

Then I asked Paulina, "Are you in love with this boy?"

"Yes, I can't deny it. It's true," she said clearly.

"But what are you thinking? You're studying, and you know that no boy

(FACING PAGE): A mother and daughter weaving. Photo courtesy of Rebecca Wiggins, 2005.

here wants to have a girlfriend who is in school. You'll probably quit school."

"Yes, I'm not going to continue studying," she said.

Later, when Domingo found out, he told her, "You've said many times that you weren't going to do this. It's not right for you because you're studying." I don't know what else he said. He became angry and hit her three times with his belt.

"You're not going to do that again," Domingo said.

A week later my sons found out that she was talking with the boy again.

"What are you thinking?" I asked her. "Are you still with the boy?"

"Yes, but I'll give him up," she said.

"What are you thinking about your studies? Are you going to continue?" I asked.

"I don't know. Perhaps I'll just quit after my last year of middle school," she said.

I got angry at these words because I didn't want her to quit her studies. "Why are you still going to school if you aren't going to continue? I let you study in order to go as far as you can, like Mariano. He's getting ahead a little, and I want you to do the same. If you leave school, you'll marry a farmer from here, and you'll suffer because you get sick a lot."

She's often sick. Her head, bones, and feet ache. She's not in good health.

I asked her, "How are you going to marry? You know how it is here. Although you don't work in the fields much, you will always have to carry water, you will always have to carry something that comes out of the fields, you will have to walk on the trails, and you don't like to walk in the mud. I let you study so that you could have a good job, so that you could walk in the streets like a teacher," I told her. "How are you going to bear it if you marry a boy from the country?"

I became angry because she wanted to get married. I hit her bottom three times. "This is so you'll leave him," I told her, "so you'll continue studying."

I left her crying and really angry with me. When I got sick a few weeks after that, she didn't show me any pity. I think I deserved it.

A few days later Felipe saw them talking again, and I don't know what else. He came quickly to tell us. "Your daughter isn't obeying you at all. She's always going around with this boy," he said.

As I was sick, I said, "Well, I don't know what to say." "Go see what your father says," I told him.

"Okay," he said, and he went to the store to tell Domingo. He told him, and they decided, "That's it. She has to marry. It's best to go tell the boy's parents."

When they came home, they told me, "We're going to tell the boy's parents."

"Okay," I said, because they wanted to do it, and I didn't know what else to do.

And so they went to tell his parents. It was a Monday when they left.

"This is what is happening with our daughter and your son," they told the parents.

"Ah," the parents said. "Well, that's fine. Let's take care of it. We'll see if they want to marry," they said.

Before he left, Domingo said, "On Wednesday, about five in the afternoon, we'll talk again." So we had to wait until Wednesday for them to talk with us. Together with Domingo and our sons we agreed about what we were going to do, if we were going to let her marry the boy, what gifts we wanted them to give us, and how much they would have to pay. Then when the boy's parents arrived, they were ready to ask for their son to marry Paulina. They brought two cases of soft drinks and two of beer.

After they arrived, we told them everything that had happened. We asked the boy if it's true that they were in love. "Yes," Antonio said. "Yes, it's that we fell in love. But we haven't done anything, just talk," he said.

"Well, are you going to marry my daughter?" Domingo asked.

"Yes, I will," he said.

Paulina was in the kitchen while we were talking in the main house. When we found out that Antonio wanted to marry her, we began to talk about how much they were going to pay and what they would bring. They asked our permission for one and a half weeks to acquire the money and buy the gifts. After we made the agreement, we drank our sodas, and that's how it ended.

We also began to invite our family, my brother and my sisters, to come to the wedding. Then when the time came, we were gathered together with my brothers and sisters, my mother and everyone. But about ten or fifteen minutes before they arrived with the gifts, my brother Francisco asked Paulina, "What do you think, Paulina? Are you ready to marry, or did your parents make you?"

"No," she said. "I'm not ready. I want to continue my studies," she said.

"If you don't want to marry, now is the time to break off the marriage," he said.

When we heard her words, we were very upset. Guests were already in the house. I began to think, "Could it end up like we've seen on television? That they break off the marriage at the last minute?"

"I don't like what you're saying," Domingo said. "Nobody obligated you. You decided on your own. You said that you loved the boy a lot. So I don't want to hear any more about it. If you keep it up, I'm going to hit you," Domingo said. He got very angry.

I began to explain calmly, "Yes, it's true that we told her she had to make a choice, but nobody forced her to marry. I don't know why she's changing her mind now, because yesterday, and the day before, and a week ago, since we made the agreement, she didn't say anything. Only now when we have to pay for the sodas that we've drunk is she saying something. But now it's impossible to break it off. Look how many people are here right now and more are coming. All the gifts have been bought. It's very difficult to call it off now," I told him.

"Yes, yes, it's true," my brother said. "It's true that you can't do anything else now that they're arriving," he said. "If you had said this yesterday, or the day before yesterday, like your mother said, it would have still been okay. But right now, it's difficult to change things. It's okay, Paulina, you decided to do it. You told your parents that you would be happy to wait for your husband. Now you don't need to think about anything else. We just hope that your husband will let you finish your third year of middle school. We'll talk about that," my brother said.

"Okay," Paulina said.

Then, at that moment, someone said, "They're arriving!" and we stopped talking. The boy and his parents were arriving with all their gifts. First they brought sodas. They made many round-trips to bring all the gifts on their backs.

When everyone had arrived, we gave advice to the couple. Her uncle said to the boy, "You're going to marry Paulina. You shouldn't scold her. Forgive her for what she doesn't know how to do yet, because she's still young. Little by little she'll learn things."

Then my brother explained a little about schooling. "Afterward you can talk about whether she wants to finish middle school. You can talk among yourselves and make an agreement."

But Antonio didn't respond! When we were talking, he only said, "Ahm-mmmmm, ahmmmmm."

Paulina's godfather also advised the boy that he should go to church because his wife grew up in the Word of God, and her parents are believers, and her father was a catechist. A lot of people talked about the Word of God at the wedding. Although his parents are in the Bees organization, Antonio said he doesn't go to meetings of the Word of God. Later, after the wedding, we said to him, "You have to be in the Word of God." One Sunday after they married they attended a service. We'll see if they keep going.

After the advice, we began to receive the gifts, to eat together with the families, all the brothers and sisters. And that's how it went.

They stayed with us three nights, and the fourth night they left. But Paulina had a cold and only stayed one night in her mother-in-law's house before returning to our house. She said she was very sick. I think that she was looking for an excuse to come home.

Antonio came with her, and I asked him, "How is it going with Paulina there in your house?"

"Well, she's sad," he said. "Crying."

"Ah," I said to him. "Try to console her. It happens like that when a young girl marries, because she's not used to being married yet."

I cried when I left my mother's house, and I was an old woman! That's why I told him, "Don't get angry with her because it always happens that way."

Antonio returned on Sunday and told us, "She's going to stay here two more nights. Later my little sister will come and take her back to my house. I'm going to go to work in San Cristóbal," Antonio said.

"Ah, good, that's fine," I told him. "If you're going to go to work, that's fine. Because you need that," I told him. "Just watch over your money and take care," I told him.

I'm very committed to my son-in-law. I want to advise him. I counseled him not to be a taxi driver, to work in something else. "It's better to find another kind of work. I've seen your brother-in-law, Felipe. He can't save his money, and he drinks a lot when he's in Chenalhó. It's not good to work as a driver," I told him.

I gave Paulina advice, too, to bear up under it, how it is at her mother-in-law's house. I didn't go right away to Domingo's house after I married because my parents asked us to stay at their house. "You have to bear it," I told her.

"I don't want to go. I want to be here," she cried.

Later, when I was about to leave to come to the United States, I asked her, "Are you going to come home to visit while I'm gone and stay until I return?"

"I'm going to come!" she said. "Although only my father will be here, it's something for me, to be with my father."

"Okay," I said. "But make an agreement with Antonio. Don't demand too much, in case he gets angry. Talk well with Antonio," I told her.

I want them to get along well together. I care about my son-in-law a lot. He's my first son-in-law. I've said to Antonio, "Come to agreements. Talk about what you want to do. I don't disrespect either you or Paulina. I appreciate all my children. And now that you are here with us, you're my son," I told him. "Although I only have four sons, I feel as if I have five sons," I told him. "I'll treat you as if you are my own son," I told him.

Later, after the wedding, I asked Paulina, "Did you talk about your studies?"

"Yes, but he didn't give me an answer."

Now she says she doesn't want to go. I think that it would be difficult for her to study now that she's living in her mother-in-law's house. Also, it seems that Antonio doesn't want to let his wife go off alone, but I think that's normal for young husbands.[2] Other young men make fun of him and say bad things to him. I think that he's going to let her go to weaving co-op meetings because she's going there for her work. I'm sure about that.

MARCH 2009

"But this zipper is too long!" With an exasperated look, Paulina holds out in my direction the pencil case that she has just finished. The maroon zipper is the perfect color for the striped case, but it's about an inch too long. Eleven more zippers of the same length adorn a nearby rock, ready to be sewn into eleven too-short pencil cases.

"Do you think that people will still buy these?" she asked. There was no way that we could sell the pencil cases in the United States, and I had to tell her so. "Look, Paulina, people expect the zipper to be the same length as the bag, but let me help you sew up the sides of the pencil cases and make them into little bags that I can give away to my family with coffee inside."

Paulina's face brightened at the prospect of still making some money from her experiment, and we set to work making the bags.

Since she married, Paulina has been working hard to become a good weaver. She spends considerable time at her mother's house getting guidance with her weaving and help with her toddler. When I was visiting her mother in 2009, Paulina's husband, Antonio, was helping with the coffee harvest. While Antonio was in the fields with Domingo, Paulina worked on her weaving between tending her son and helping her mother prepare food. I was proud of Paulina when she won first prize at the weaving co-op competition for a large tortilla cloth with rows of chickens that she learned to make watching her mother.

Paulina is becoming a woman by following in her mother's footsteps. It seems that indigenous girls in Chenalhó must find their way along one of two divergent paths: staying at home and producing products to sell, or going on in school and working outside their communities. Paulina is following the first path, while Rosalva is pursuing the second.

ROSALVA

When it came time for Rosalva, Antonia's youngest child, to graduate from sixth grade, I feared that she would not receive support from her father and brothers to continue school in the headtown because of what had happened with Paulina. The boys and Domingo influenced Antonia in ways I found confusing, given her independent mind.

Many times Antonia and I had talked about the implications of Rosalva being her *kexol* (replacement). According to Tzotzil-Maya beliefs, people replace each other in *cargos* as well as in families. Rosalva not only looked like Antonia, but she shared her sense of humor and desire to try new things. Being Antonia's *kexol* might mean that Rosalva would follow her mother's path and be a weaver and household manager, or that she might follow her mother's spirit, which yearned for a broader life than those of other women in her community. No one could know the fate of Rosalva's soul, but Antonia had the ability to influence it. I hoped that Antonia would advocate for her daughter as she wished that her mother had advocated for her. I reminded her of how her own brother had supported her dreams to go on in school.

I made it clear to Antonia that the Las Cruces–Chiapas Connection was ready to raise funds for Rosalva to go to school, as we had done for Paulina.[3] But money was only half of the problem. An equally daunting obstacle was the family's doubt about Rosalva being able to manage the challenges of mixing with boys in middle school, and her brothers' resentment of their little sister having opportunities that they didn't take.

When I'm old, it's necessary for someone to replace me. Perhaps one of my daughters—for example, Rosalva—will be my replacement because it seems that she has the same way of acting as me. She talks clearly and isn't embarrassed either. Also, what I'm doing, she wants to do. For example, now I'm embroidering, and she wants to embroider. She always likes to do things in school, and that's the way I was. One time when I was thirteen or fourteen I went to San Cristóbal to play in a basketball game. Rosalva also likes to play basketball, run, dance, sing, everything that the teacher asks.[4]

One time Rosalva went to Chenalhó to run a race, and she won and she was barefoot! Since she only wore sandals, and we didn't think it would be good to race in sandals, we bought her tennis shoes. But they weighed too much, and that's why she decided to run barefoot.

Another time, during the graduation celebration, she sang a song and won. There wasn't a prize this time, but she won. Her teachers were very happy with her. They came over to congratulate Domingo. They thanked him for letting Rosalva keep going to school. They even sent a greeting to me through Rosalva.

Her teacher has talked a lot to his students, saying, "We'll see who is going to continue, and who are going to be housewives." One time Rosalva told me, "In the future when I see my teacher, I'll be ashamed if I don't go to middle school. Right now I'm putting in a lot of effort, but later as a housewife I'll feel a little ashamed around my teacher. I'll think, why did I put in a lot of effort if I quit?"

In the past Rosalva said she was going to go to middle school. Recently, she asked us, "Are you still going to let me go?"

"Well, I think not now," I told her, "because look what happened with your sister. It's better for you not to go to school anymore. Stay in the house and weave so you can earn a little. Also, your brothers and your father aren't going to let you. I think that it's better for you to stay in the house," I told her. "If you want to marry, you're free to do that. Boys are going to come to ask to marry you. It's not necessary for you to go to middle school to find a boy."

"Ummm," she said, and then she was quiet. She stayed very quiet after that. Later I asked her, "How are you feeling? Do you agree not to go to school?"

"I think so. It's okay. It seems that the store is like my little school. I will take care of it. That's what I'll do," she said.

"Good," I said.

It seems that she agrees to stay and take care of the house and the store. But I don't know if she agrees or she just can't say what she feels. I don't know if she says what's in her heart. I don't know what she thinks, because in the past she wanted to go [to school].

I felt very sad when my father wouldn't let me continue my studies, so much so that I still remember it. Also, when I wanted to leave home, there was work as a teacher and a cook, and now there aren't as many opportunities. If one starts studying, it's best to continue as far as one can. For example, Mariano is going to complete six years of studies after middle school, and he's still continuing, but we don't know if he can earn anything. He might just be losing money while his mind is expanding. Later he might not be able to find work. That's what I, we think. I want my children to earn something from their studies.

We say that for the boys, middle school and high school are valuable because men leave the community more than women. For example, boys go out to look for work. At times, if their employers ask for school papers, if they have a certificate from middle school or high school, they can find better work. Although the girls have certificates, they're not going to go in search of work like the boys. They stay in the house and marry. That's why we think that it's not important for the girls to go to school. It seems true because although Paulina completed her third year of secondary school, from her studies she can't earn anything. She can't earn money from her studies, and it's wasted on her. When Paulina wanted to complete middle school after she married, we said, "For what, since you don't want to continue studying? It's not worth anything because it's not necessary to have a certificate to raise a child. You don't need a certificate to have a husband."

Truthfully, it doesn't require a certificate to raise a child. Like me, I raised six children without a certificate. That's why I think that it's enough for my daughters to have primary school since they're going to be like me. And I'm doing fine.

That's what I think, at times because of anger. I wanted them to continue studying as far as they could. Now that they aren't advancing, I am thinking through my anger. As my *comadre* said, I felt terrible when my parents wouldn't let me go on in school.

We don't have support in my family for Rosalva to continue studying. My brother, yes, but Domingo and the boys won't let Rosalva go. My mother also says, "It's better not to let your daughter go to middle school. Just let her finish primary school, and then she can stay and take care of the house. If she goes to middle school, nobody will be with you. You need your helper in the house. And when you're sick, who's going to take care of you?" Domingo also said this, and the boys, too. I was sick at the time, and I think that's why my mother and Domingo said that.

When Paulina finished primary school, the boys asked us, "Are you going to let Paulina go to middle school?"

"Yes, we're going to let her," I told them.

"She'll just look for boyfriends. She'll only look for a husband," they said.

"Well, we'll see. If it happens, there's nothing we can do about it," we said. And it happened! It came true!

The boys don't want their sisters to study. They think, "Why should my sister get to go and I couldn't study?" But we didn't tell them they couldn't go on in school. They just didn't want to.

Domingo, the boys, and I think that the girls only go to school to find boyfriends or husbands. We don't like our children to fall in love and then leave one boy and go with another. If they fall in love with a boy, we think it's better for them to marry so that they won't just stay in love. At times it turns out very bad, like what happened with Paulina. She just wanted to be in love. But when we discovered it, she married the boy, although she hadn't thought about marrying him.

I don't want my daughters to go to school if they can't handle the pressures. Rosalva is going to be a young woman. What if she meets a boy and they fall in love, and we find out again and they get married?

Like Mariano said, "It's better if Rosalva doesn't go to middle school. She's just going to fall in love and maybe get pregnant. If your daughter gets pregnant, she's going to leave the child here in the house for you to take care of while she goes off with another man. You'll have to raise the child. I don't like that because one day when you're old and can't work hard any more, I'll have my job and can take care of you. But I won't take care of a child that doesn't have a father. I want to support my parents because they raised me since I was a little boy. But I don't want to support someone else's child."

We'll see how it goes. I change my mind a lot. Like in the beginning when Paulina married, I got angry. I said clearly, "It's better that my daughters don't go on in school." But if Rosalva wants to study, well, it's okay with me. I think that I'm going to talk more fully with her and see what we can do. Although at times I need Rosalva to help me take care of the house, I don't want to cut off her rights, no? If she wants to go, we'll see if we can convince her brothers and Domingo.

I don't know what they're going to say. If I'm the only one saying, "Go ahead, go ahead," if something bad happens, later they'll blame me. "You said she could go and look what happened!" they'll say. Afterward I'm going to feel very sad because I don't have my family's support.

I'm going to try to convince them with soft words, no? We'll see what they say. I'm just going to say, "What do you think? Do you think that Rosalva's going to do the same as Paulina, or can we let her see what she can do, so that later we don't blame ourselves because we cut off her right to go to middle school?" With a few words we'll see what they say.

I can't say that my daughter should go on in school, and you can't say that either. Although you and your *compañeros* are helping me make it possible for Rosalva to study, it's not the same as having support from my family. I feel bad because a scholarship came to my house for Paulina. It wasn't my money that paid for Paulina's education. I felt a lot of pain that we were only asking and asking for money and then not valuing it. I'm afraid that the same thing is going to happen with Rosalva, that she'll give up her scholarship in the middle of her studies.

You say that even if Rosalva stops studying in a few months or a few years, each day that she's studying, she's learning something. If you can give her the idea that education has value, I think that an education is going to be something beautiful for her in her life.

I don't know what more I'm going to say. I'll follow my family's agreement, what they say. We're waiting for my brother to say something. My brother gave me a lot of support in my life to go on in school, even though my father didn't let me go. Today not only the boys have rights. The world is different now.

Since our talk in 2006, Antonia has been able to defend Rosalva's right to go on in school. Rosalva finished middle school and entered high school in 2009. The grant that she receives from the Maya Educational Foundation makes it possible for her to attend school but isn't sufficient to cover renting a room in town. Rosalva continues to come home each day after classes and helps around the house and in the store in the evening, despite pleading with her parents to rent her a room in town. On a daily basis Rosalva straddles contradictory conceptions of being a woman and a human being, the price she pays for an education in Chenalhó.

Chapter 6

Daughters-in-Law and Grandchildren

*Sometimes I don't want to hear that I'm a grandmother because when
I think of grandparents, I think of people who are sixty or seventy years,
and I'm not fifty years old yet!*

Antonia

Becoming a mother-in-law increased the number of people under Antonia's guidance. For a couple years both Magdalena and Juana lived with her. Initially Antonia didn't look forward to being a mother-in-law, but becoming a grandmother soon followed, and Antonia embraced this role fully. Felipe and Magdalena had a boy and girl, Sebastian and Juana two girls, and Paulina and Antonio a son.

JUNE 2005

My two daughters-in-law didn't know how to weave when they married my sons. But when they came to live with us, they decided to learn. They asked me if I wanted to teach them, and I told them, "Yes." It didn't take long to teach them because they were adults. Just by watching, they started to weave. I only told them how it's done. "You do this like this," I told them. First they observed how I did it, and then they started to do it. My daughters-in-law's weavings turned out well, not very fine, but I don't weave that well either.

When my daughters-in-law were living with me, I took them to see a doctor when they became pregnant for the first time. They wanted to give birth at home, but when the time came, the babies wouldn't come out, and we had to take Juana to the Health Center in Chenalhó, and Magdalena to a nurse and some midwives. With Magdalena, they gave her an injection. After the baby was born, she lost a lot of blood and almost lost consciousness, but they gave her an IV and she was okay.

When Juana gave birth to her second daughter, she gave birth at home,

(FACING PAGE): Photo by Christine Eber, 1987.

but not inside the house! Her pains began in the early morning hours. Sebastian left before dawn to fetch his mother-in-law. I don't know how long he stayed at her house. I was with Juana, and the baby couldn't wait for her father. When Sebastian returned, his wife had already had her baby. He didn't see how she was born and how the placenta took a long time to come out.

When Juana was in labor, she had to go to the bathroom, but when she was outside, she realized that the baby was coming. We went outside to be with her, and the baby was born outside of the house—not very far from the house, because we told Juana not to go too far.

We waited a few minutes for the placenta to come out, but it didn't come out. We were really afraid. We had to walk together back to the house carrying the baby and mother without breaking the umbilical cord. One of us grabbed Juana and the baby, another held the cord, another brought some boards to make her bed. I told Paulina, "Go find some *valak xik*!"[1] But she wasn't familiar with this plant, and she brought another one instead. I yelled, "That's not it!" I scolded her because we were worried that the placenta wouldn't come out. Paulina got angry because she couldn't go to school that morning. It took her a lot of effort to bring me *valak xik*.

The placenta finally came out with difficulty. It stayed inside about an hour and a half. For my granddaughter's birth we were just Magdalena, Paulina, my friend Guadalupe, Guadalupe's mother, the midwife, and me.

I help my daughter and daughters-in-law with my grandchildren. My grandchildren love me, and I like to carry them around. I carry them in a shawl because we can move around and do things with them on our backs. In comparison, just holding a child, one can't do other things. Many women go out to work with their children on their back and spades in their hands. Also, one can weave when the child doesn't want to be in bed. We put them on our back, and they stay there sleeping while we weave. When children are a bit bigger, they weigh a lot, and it's very heavy to carry firewood and water with a child on your back. But God helps us carry the load.

My grandchildren say, "Ya me'! Ya me'!" [Grandmother! Grandmother!] each time when they see me or want to come to my house. When I see my grandchildren, I feel happy.

Chapter 7

Cargos

God chose me for this cargo. *He gave me the chance to be here and is guiding me and giving me strength. I couldn't do it without him.*
Antonia, on her first trip to the United States in 2002

As an academic, stepmother, and grandmother, my story is the story of most women in the United States who struggle to balance work and family. At times our struggle is so self-absorbing that it can come as a surprise when we learn that poor women in "developing countries" confront similar challenges. I came to Chenalhó valuing women's perspectives and viewing their household-based work as socially and economically valuable. I was also ready to appreciate women's collective work from studies I had done of women's participation in revolutionary movements in Latin America. But I did not anticipate that women would be as involved in collective work as they were in Chiapas, and struggling with some of the same issues as women activists in other parts of the Americas.

Soon after arriving at Antonia's home, I realized that the local women were involved in a couple of vibrant social movements, and that these movements were complicating their lives in myriad ways. In the early 1980s, Antonia and her mother and sisters became involved in the weaving cooperative movement and in the Word of God. Then, in the early 1990s, Las Abejas (the Bees) and Zapatista support bases formed, increasing greatly the number of hours that Antonia and other women were involved in community work each week.

I came to live with Antonia in 1987, when she was intensifying her participation in the Word of God and Sna Jolobil (House of the Weaver), a weaving cooperative based in San Cristóbal that she belonged to at that time. After the uprising in 1994, she became a Zapatista and attended meetings in the support base in her community. At one point she was nominated to be a leader of her support base but had to decline because of all the work she already had with six children and being a representative of the weaving co-op Tsobol Antzetik.[1] From her involvement in the Word of God and the Zapatista base, Antonia helped create many different cooperatives.

Prior to the Word of God and the Zapatista movement, only men attend-

ed community meetings. Women's *cargos* were limited to serving as *jnetume-tik* (midwives), *j'iloletik* (healers), or partners with their husbands in cargos in township governance (abtel patan) or in service to the saints and Mayan deities (*abtel nichimal* [flowery *cargos*]).

Since the 1980s Antonia has served many *cargos* in the different coopera-tives she has helped form, usually serving as president or secretary. She takes her duties seriously and imbues them with a spiritual significance akin to that used in the flowery *cargos* for the saints and Mayan deities.

Antonia has also spent countless hours meeting with others in her com-munity to discuss community problems and to carry out the collective work in which she is involved. This work has brought benefits and drawbacks. The major drawbacks are the added number of hours that she has to work and the stress of not being able to fulfill all her duties as well as she would like.[2]

When Antonia was younger, she enjoyed going to meetings, but as her child care and household responsibilities increased, the stress of fulfilling all her du-ties mounted. Although Domingo helps Antonia at times, he hasn't come close to sharing housework and child care with her. Antonia just tries to do it all as best she can.

There are a lot of different kinds of [traditional] *cargos*. There are special *cargos* for the whole township, for example, *alférez* [sponsor/leader of saints' fiestas], *presidente* [township mayor], and *regidor* [a civil officer, like a reg-istrar or magistrate]. After serving as *alférez* for a saint's fiesta, one can be elected to serve as an authority, for example as *regidor* or president. The men who fill these *cargos* must be respected men who know how to give good ad-vice. In the past the authorities weren't paid, but today they are. In contrast, the *cargos* for the saints are voluntary. In the autonomous Zapatista villages, the authorities who serve *cargos* don't receive any money, although they do important work.

There are also *cargos* in which one represents only the community or a group—for example, when I serve as president or treasurer of a cooperative. We don't receive as much respect in these kinds of *cargos* as people do who serve the *cargos* for the whole township. For example, when a woman is *me' alférez* [woman sponsor/leader of a saint's fiesta] she has to ask *me' ulubil* [preparer of atole for the fiesta] for help. She and her husband have to carry a bottle of *pox* when they go to ask *me' ulubil* to help them. In contrast, in the *cargos* that I serve, nobody offers me even a soft drink to ask for my help. In place of soft drinks, just criticism![3]

In the past women didn't have the right to hold *cargos* or participate in

(FACING PAGE): Leaders of the Feast of Saint Peter. Photo by Christine Eber, 1987.

meetings. They just stayed in the house. But now that's changing a little. It seems that the Zapatistas are acting to give women the right to participate. Now women can attend meetings. Sometimes they participate in the community, and at times they serve *cargos*. For example, Guadalupe has a *cargo* in the store cooperative. Also, two other women are working in the store. But most women don't go out to other places, only around the community. Many women still don't want to participate because they're embarrassed. This embarrassment is a problem that we women always struggle with.

When women go to meetings, they seem very quiet and don't open their mouths. I think that's because women's minds aren't very open yet. If there are meetings, topics that we need to resolve, not many women participate. Just me. I always participate and ask questions, "What do you think?"

"Well, whatever you say," they answer. "Yes, it's fine, we agree with what you say."

After participating a lot, I stopped attending the meetings in the support base. I went with the intention to participate in a positive way, but some people didn't like how I participated, and they got angry. Sometimes we would argue right there in the meeting. I didn't like that because we weren't there to argue. Little by little I became discouraged and didn't feel like going to the meetings anymore. But Sebastian always went to the meetings, and when he came back home, he would say, "They discussed such and such at the meeting." "Why wasn't I at the meeting?" I would say to myself. "I want to take part and give my opinions too." Domingo would say, "If you want to participate, go to the meeting and give your thoughts." So now I'm thinking about going back to the meetings. But I don't know if I have time. The truth is I don't have time. I have to work for myself. I have to take care of my store and go to meetings of the cooperative store. It seems that I have a lot of work to do now that Rosalva goes to school in Chenalhó, and Paulina went to live elsewhere.

At times Antonia has expressed regret about her efforts to care for her children while being intensely involved in the Word of God, the Zapatista movement, and a series of cooperatives. She accepts the challenges of combining activism and motherhood as part of the holy struggle, but at times she has felt that she is not a good mother. Because mothering is such a central aspect of women's identities in indigenous communities, sometimes Antonia even doubts her worth as a woman. At times her society's expectations for women overwhelm her self-evaluation. Working on this book seemed to be a mixture for Antonia of moments of feeling a renewed faith in her worth as a woman, a mother, and a defender of social justice, and at other moments doubting her personal worth in relation to others in her society.

It's very difficult to participate in the community because women have a lot of children. When a woman has a *cargo*, there's no one to take care of the children. That's the main problem that we have. It's not the same as here, where you have child care centers, where you can leave the children in someone else's care. In contrast, we always have a child stuck to our back or our breast. That's how children grow. When they're a little bigger, five or six years old, they still need someone in the house to give them their meals. Also, men don't earn much. They also need women to make money in order to maintain the house. But if the woman goes out of the house and also the man, no one cares for the children. It's difficult. Nobody can stay to care for the house because of lack of money. We lack a lot. If we had money, I think that it would be easier for the women who want to participate or have *cargos*. But even if they have money, they may not want to accept a *cargo*.

I have six children, and it's hard to participate and take care of them. Many times I have had to be away from them. When my first child was one or two years old, I had to carry him with me to Mitontik for my job. And later, when he was two and a half years old, I left him with my mother when I was living with her.

Later, when I had three boys—Felipe, Sebastian, and Mariano—the older two took care of their [three younger] siblings, the littlest ones. They carried them around on their backs. I left them alone in the house each time I went out, and they felt alone and desperate in the house. They knew that I would return in the afternoon, and they waited for me on a rock near our house. There was a little place with a rock where they could play. They always waited for me there, watching for me to come down the road.

To remember this right now is sad, to remember what my children and I have gone through. Looking back I feel that I owe my children. They didn't seem to gain anything from their suffering. At times they still think about how they suffered, how I left them alone.

Although they're grown up now, they still want to be together with us, as we're their parents. They can't be happy without us in the house. For example, on Easter I went with Domingo to church, and Mariano went to Chenalhó to buy food. But we were in church and couldn't eat with him when he returned. He became very sad and returned to Chenalhó because they show films there. In the church they don't show anything. But he became a little sad and later said, "Each time I want to be with you, I can't be with you."

Well, it's true what he said, because I don't just go to church. I also go to meetings in the store. For example, like I'm here [New Mexico], right? I've been away from my house two or three days already. Mariano must be sad. They're putting up with being alone in the house.

I explain to them why I'm here. I explain that I have to go sell weavings, that it's something to help my *compañeras*, that I want to be a person who helps her *compañeras*, that I don't want to work just for myself. It's good for both me and my *compañeras*, I tell them. Also, I make some money for me and my family from my weavings. I've seen that in order to sell my weavings, I have to make the effort to leave my home. I explain that it's good to attend church, to learn, to struggle and everything, and if one day we become righteous people, we will receive a prize in the end. I tell my children that I don't go out just for me or our family, and that I'm not looking for a reward here on Earth. But the children want a big reward here on Earth.

At times, when Mariano becomes discouraged, he says, "You don't have to go out so many times because it doesn't benefit you at all. For example, in the meetings, what money do you earn? What have you achieved from that? Or the co-op store, how does it benefit you to go to the meetings there? It doesn't benefit you at all," Mariano says. "You only go to waste time. You'd be better off in the house working and weaving," he says. "With your weaving you're going to make money. In the meetings, you don't make any money."

He doesn't agree with what Domingo is doing either. "Ah, my father goes to a lot of meetings. He doesn't want to work," he says. "He's used to going out. He wants to take walks for pleasure. My dad is just like us. We want to go play basketball. My dad is doing the same thing," he says. "From my point of view, we're always the same, suffering. Why do you go out a lot? You should stay with us, take care of us, be happy together as a family," Mariano says.

Each time when Mariano comes to the house, he wants me there. When I'm not there, he goes back to Chenalhó to find his friends. And sometimes they drink. "Although I want to be together with my parents, I never find them at home," he says. Sometimes it makes me feel bad, too, because my son loves me and I'm not there. He's very different. He always waits for me to eat. He wants to eat together with the family.

At times the other children complain, too, not just Mariano. "What importance do other things have? You don't earn money with them. I don't want to go to the meetings," they say. "Why should I go? Just to waste time, that's all."

I answer them, "I still have confidence in what I'm doing. I still have the desire to do it. That's why I have to do it, although you want me to stay in the house. Perhaps when I don't feel like going out, perhaps then I'll stay in the house. What I want to do, I can do, and what you want to do, you should do. Like when you want to do something, I can't tell you, 'Give it up.' You have to do it. And it's the same with us, because we're adults."

I don't think that all families are the same. We leave our children in peace. For example, although we want to take the children to church, if the children don't want to go, we don't force them. I don't think that it has much value to force them.

Not all our children go to church. For example, at times Felipe doesn't want to go. He just wants to play basketball instead. Since he was a little boy, we let him do what he wanted. In other families, what works for the parents also works for the children. I have seen families in which the children don't go out to play basketball. They just stay in the house, working, and going to church, too. But there aren't a lot of these families. Just a few.

Chapter 8

Cooperatives

It was like planting a tree. First we planted a seedling and tended it until it grew. We watered it and waited. Our tree grew a little bit each year. We didn't expect it to bear fruit for many years. Eventually we began to eat a little bit of the fruit from our tree, but only after many years of working hard to help it grow.

Antonia, on creating the weaving cooperative
Xojobal K'ak'al (Light of the Day)

In 1987 Antonia and Domingo worked with about twenty other members of the Word of God to start a general store cooperative in the headtown of Chenalhó. To my knowledge, this was the first cooperative in Chenalhó's history.

I enjoyed hanging out in the store with Antonia and other co-op members. Once I accompanied members as they held a special prayer session to counteract envy from people who opposed the creation of a cooperative store. Antonia matter-of-factly recalls problems with the store.

Domingo always went to the meetings there. I just went to support him. Sometimes he didn't have time to go and sell, and I sold in his place. Some members didn't like it that I took his place. There are always problems when we are in an association. Some said they couldn't continue because they weren't earning anything, that they were just wasting their time going there to sell. I don't know how many years this co-op lasted.

The first weaving cooperatives in Chiapas began in the 1950s and were administered by state and federal agencies such as the National Indigenous Institute (Instituto Nacional Indígena [INI]).[1] Women who joined cooperatives formed by INI benefited from higher prices and access to tourist markets, but they were not involved in the business or leadership aspects of these organizations.

(FACING PAGE): Women in the Sna Jolobil cooperative hanging blouses to be judged in a weaving competition. Photo by Christine Eber, 1987.

Although most women did not want to be leaders, many expressed concern about not having access to business records or a voice in financial decisions.

Antonia's first experience with these kinds of cooperatives was in 1981, with a group in the center of Chenalhó called Artesanas de Chiapas, sponsored by the PRI party. Antonia remembers that she made her first real friend in this group. Before community-based organizing began in midcentury, friendships were not common among indigenous women. Kinship relationships filled people's lives, leaving little room for relationships with non-kin, except *compadres*.

In the PRI artisan group we didn't sell very much, but I made a good friend, my first best friend. We worked together to organize the women. It seems my best friends are always women with whom I work. Like now, Guadalupe is my best friend. I've known her since I moved to Domingo's land. She's a preacher and a leader in our community. Later we worked together as representatives of Mujeres Marginadas [Marginalized Women], a Zapatista baking co-op and general store. That way we got to know each other more, and until today she continues to be my special friend.

Guadalupe helps me a lot. Although she's younger than me, she knows more than me and the other women. It seems as if she's my guide. For example, at times I can't bear the problems that come from working with people, and she offers me a word from God where he says that we can bear it, that we must suffer like Christ did. She tells me words that make me feel good. That's why I say that she's my guide. Truly, there's no one like her. If it weren't for Guadalupe, we might not still have the general store cooperative that we formed. She has the strength to handle the group, to uplift it. I'm also making an effort alongside her.

During the 1970s, non-governmental organizations began to work with indigenous women to create alternatives to state-run cooperatives. Although women had a greater voice in these groups, they still did not enjoy the level of representation and control that many desired.

In 1985 Antonia's mother, María, joined Sna Jolobil (House of the Weaver), one of the oldest non-governmental cooperatives in highland Chiapas, which is still in business. Antonia and her sisters soon followed. In the mid to late 1980s the Sna Jolobil headquarters and store provided Antonia and her relatives a place in San Cristóbal where they could speak their own language and feel respected. Although the co-op held annual meetings of its members, most of them did not have a strong voice in the organization. Members worked in small local groups in their communities and depended on a local representative to deliver their weavings to the co-op store and collect their pay. With her facility in Spanish, Antonia became the leader of her local group.

My mother entered Sna Jolobil first, and I followed later. At first I was very happy to earn money from my weavings, and I knew that it was safe selling at the store in San Cristóbal. It wasn't the same as waiting for someone to order a weaving from me. After that I was working steadily and I felt happy. I was excited to work, which is why I made larger, more elaborate weavings. Today I don't think I could make those weavings.

I was the representative of our local group of Sna Jolobil from the beginning. I did a lot of work for my group, and I bore a lot of suffering. I had to go every two weeks to the store in San Cristóbal because the women depended on me to collect their pay. I had to wait many hours inside the office, always carrying my child. It was a very small office, and I felt as if I was in jail, all closed up. After many hours of waiting, the store managers would say, "Ah, there's no money yet," or "I don't know if it has sold yet. Return another day." That's what they said, no more. I had to ask a percentage of each weaving from the women to pay my transportation and other expenses, and I had to go back without money, spending the women's money for nothing.

It lasted years that I was doing that. Later I said, "It's better to separate myself from Sna Jolobil and form our own cooperative," and I left.

When Antonia and her mother and sisters decided to leave Sna Jolobil in 1991, they formed their own cooperative, Tsobol Antzetik (Eber 2000). They hoped to gain greater control over the pricing and marketing of their weavings through working with me and others who could help them sell their weavings in the United States. Antonia was a representative for ten years, after which her sister Marcela took over for her. Marcela served the co-op with much dedication and good spirit until she finally resigned in 2008. The work had become too much for her while raising ten children. With Marcela's resignation, the co-op members decided that the job of representative was too much for one woman. In 2009 they elected Antonia's sister Anita and another unmarried co-op member to share the *cargo*.

When we were discussing options after Marcela resigned, I conveyed the suggestion from the Las Cruces-Chiapas Connection that we help them find a way to pay someone to do the representative's work. Tsobol Antzetik members did not want their representative to be paid for fear of the inequality it would create between members and the potential envy that could result. They also rejected the idea because paying representatives contradicts traditional conceptions of *cargos*.

In the beginning, when I was representative of Tsobol Antzetik, I liked it. But later, after I don't know how many years of being the representative, I didn't want to do it anymore because it took a lot of time, and I thought that it would be better to let others do this work. Also, I had to leave my home to sell, to arrange meetings, and lead the meetings for the women. It's necessary to have experience and to give it thought. It takes time to think what I'm going to say, what I'm going to do. Dividing up the money, compiling all the weavings to ship to the US, little by little I got tired of it all. I didn't want to be representative anymore. That's why I quit.

I also wanted to leave because I had *cargos* in other groups. I thought that I could leave Tsobol Antzetik because others knew how to do the work, too. My sister Marcela took my place, but I think that the same thing is happening with her that happened to me. It seems that she wants to quit being representative because she has a lot of children and not much time to weave. She says that it's very difficult to distribute the money, and assemble all the weavings, and make the list of the weavings. I think that's true.

My sister does it all. First she makes a list of each woman, how much work she brought, and then she makes the account of the money due each woman. Then she adds up the total due. Out of that she has to take out the cost of shipping. At times we pay the shipping ourselves. At times she charges us for her transportation to San Cristóbal to mail the weavings. Then she has to make an account of how much the weavers will receive. She says that she needs to work her brain, no? It takes time to think and everything else. That's why she doesn't want to be representative anymore. Also, other women want to join the group, and my sister doesn't want more women to enter because that will mean more work.

During the years of the military and paramilitary violence in Chenalhó, Antonia felt called to go to Polhó, the headquarters of San Pedro Polhó, the Zapatista autonomous township in Chenalhó, to assist refugees flooding into the community. There she helped women organize themselves into a cooperative so that they could sell their weavings to human rights workers posted there, or foreigners who visited Polhó on delegations.

I first went to Polhó to sell some weavings because foreigners came to visit Polhó. In 1997 many displaced people arrived in Polhó, and I wanted to be with them in order to support and help them, to form artisan groups there. I worked two years with the displaced women in Polhó.

In Polhó we began to form a group of women to help each other with their weavings, to sell them just in Polhó. We had a store of artisan work. I always went there to see how the work was going. I didn't go alone. We were five representatives in all. One *compañera* and I were the only ones who lived at a distance. But we made the effort to see the women and inspire them. I gave them ideas of what artisan work I knew how to make. The women learned how to make artisan work in order to earn a little bit of money, because they didn't have any. Many left their communities without clothes. They didn't have anything.

When the group began, they were just called "Artisanry." They didn't have a name. But after a few years, I think, a representative from Mujeres por la Dignidad came, and they began to form a local group of Women for Dignity in order to sell weavings in San Cristóbal at the co-op store. But we saw that in San Cristóbal they want fine work, work that is well done, and some of the women couldn't weave that well. The women became discouraged with their work because at times it didn't sell. When we began, more than eight hundred women were in the group, and we couldn't sell all their work. So little by little they became discouraged and left the group. Even me, I couldn't go any longer. That's how it dissolved. I think that there is still a group of women, but not as many as when it began.

While she was volunteering in Polhó, Antonia also started a small cooperative in her community with women in her local Zapatista support base. This group worked differently from Tsobol Antzetik. Instead of each member keeping the money she earned from selling a weaving, members pooled their earnings and used the money for joint projects.

In 1996 in my community we formed a group of Mujeres por la Dignidad called Xojobal K'ak'al [Light of the Day]. In the beginning we were fifteen women. We worked in collective, weaving and embroidering together, and saving the money that we earned. We didn't work together every day, only two days a week. The other days the women worked on their own work. We sold our weavings, and from there we saved our money in a fund for when we would need it for a project. We always combined the money that we earned from the weavings. It stayed in a box, and later, when we had a little bit saved, we divided it up, some money for each woman and some for the box. It was a bit difficult for the women. Some of them couldn't wait for the money, and they left the group. Only four women remained after the others left.

After two years we pulled together the money that we had earned from the weavings for our group and began to think about what we could do with it. I had the idea to start a store. I said to my *compañeras*, "Let's start a store." My three *compañeras* said, "Well, that's fine." So we borrowed land. Domingo and another *compañera*'s husband began to construct the store, and we women helped, too. We carried the earth to fill in the land, which was a little low. Then when it was ready, we began to buy some merchandise with the 600 pesos. That was our savings. We began small.

During the 1990s, members of the resistance movement in Chenalhó developed additional cooperatives focused on specific products such as coffee and bread. As I watched co-ops come and go, it seemed that when one died, another would spring from its ashes.

In 1996 members of Antonia's support base received a donation from a European group that enabled them to start a baking cooperative.

I had an idea to form a baking cooperative. It kept coming into my mind. I always talked about it. "If I had an oven, I would make bread!" I said back then.

After we received a donation, we had a meeting with the group so we could be in agreement. At the meeting we said, "Now we have this amount of money, and a proposal to build an oven and create a bakery collective."

"Yes, we agree," they said.

With the money the men set out to work. There were a lot of men, like fifty or sixty, who built the oven. We women began to learn to make bread. Since we didn't have any idea how to make bread, we invited a friend who knows a little to teach us.

We had to prepare the dough and everything that we needed to begin. But the bread didn't come out well. But we were making an effort to learn, and eventually we learned to make bread. About six or seven years later there was a problem with the wood to bake the bread. It's necessary to have a lot of wood to heat up the oven, and the men said that they didn't want to bring wood anymore because it was a lot of work and it was scarce. For example, we have trees, but they are far away. It takes a lot of time to collect the wood. When Domingo goes out to collect firewood at 9 a.m., he returns around 1 or 2 p.m.

We changed our idea to construct a general store instead of a bakery. When we saw that we had saved a little money, we began to construct a store. It's been two years since we built the store. When we began the store, we asked for a prayer in order to progress in our work. Our main prayer leader, Don Bartolo, prayed for us. He has since passed away. We continue to sell bread in our store, but we bring it from another bakery.

Chapter 9

Traveling

Before I came here, I didn't understand much. Although you [Cristina] always talked about things, sometimes I didn't feel like listening because it didn't seem to be worth anything to me. But now when I'm feeling it in my own body, I am beginning to understand. When I show the photos to the women in Chenalhó and tell them about everything that has happened to me here, they aren't going to understand very well or feel what it's like. They might just laugh. I think that's because they feel embarrassed or far away from what I'm talking about. The women weavers are just going to say, "Thank you for all the work you did." But they're not going to know how it was to be here, what happened to us, all the work that we did.

Antonia

In fall 2002 I had a sabbatical from teaching and was thrilled for the chance to bring Antonia to New Mexico and give her the opportunity to get to know people from a different nation in their own cultural and social contexts. Bringing Antonia to the United States was a project with many steps. The first was obtaining funding for her trip. At the time I was a member of Corazón a Corazón (the social justice committee of Saint Albert the Great Newman Center), which raised funds for her travel. The next step was obtaining her visa. I had never helped anyone apply for a visa before, so I began by looking for someone Antonia could travel with to Mexico City to ask for her visa at the US Embassy. In Mexico everyone must travel to Mexico City to apply for their visa prior to their departure. This is a costly trip from distant states, and as happened with Antonia, sometimes one must reapply and pay another $80 (in 2002), plus have the money to pay for room and board in Mexico City while waiting for the second appointment.

We were fortunate that Celerina, a weaver from Jolom Mayaetik, a weaving cooperative in San Cristóbal, needed to obtain a visa for a tour of the United States about the same time as Antonia's visa appointment. Barbara Schütz, who

worked with Kinal Antzetik, a sister organization of non-indigenous women, arranged for Antonia to share a visa appointment with Celerina.[1]

The second major challenge was determining whether Antonia could actually come to the United States, because Domingo was gravely ill prior to her scheduled departure. I was in Chenalhó at the time and accompanied the family through Domingo's illness, which he survived through the help of doctors, traditional healers, and many prayers. A few days before we were scheduled to leave, Domingo seemed strong enough, and Antonia decided to go. She wanted to fast for three days, as is custom before traveling, but felt too weak from the stress of caring for Domingo. Seeing Antonia's condition, three of her *compañeras* from the baking co-op volunteered to fast in her place, each one taking responsibility for a day.

Before I found out that the money was ready for my trip to the United States, I didn't know if it was really going to come true. Also, I didn't know how to get my papers and everything, until my brother told me that I had to go first to Tuxtla to get my passport. When I found this out, I made trip after trip in order to be able to get all my papers. First I came to San Cristóbal to find out what my brother had to tell me. He said, "You have to bring all your papers, your birth certificate, and your identification card." Right away I returned to Chenalhó to get them and came back to San Cristóbal the same day. The next morning I had to go to Tuxtla to get my passport. It was good that the people who give out the passports do it in one day. I just had to fill out the papers. But it was difficult for me, because I had never filled out papers before. Mariano helped me fill out the papers and do everything that I needed to do.

When I returned, I had to arrange an appointment with the US Embassy to ask for my visa. They gave me the date when I was supposed to be in Mexico City. It was in September. I went to Mexico City with Celerina, a young woman from San Andrés Larrainzar. We agreed that Celerina and I would buy tickets to go together. When I arrived at the bus terminal with my children, I looked around for the young woman called Celerina.

"Where is she? Where could she be?" I asked myself. I didn't know her face. I had only heard her name. Barbara told me that she was going to go to Mexico City to get her visa, and if I wanted to go with her, I could. She told me, "She's a young woman from San Andrés and quickly you'll recognize her by her clothes." I was looking for someone wearing clothes from San Andrés, but there was nobody. I was very worried.

(FACING PAGE): Photo by Christine Eber, 1987.

"Am I going to go alone or stay?" I wondered. So I wouldn't lose the money, since the ticket was already bought, I decided, "I'm going." That month Felipe was working in Mexico City, and I thought, "He'll help me."

So I left. The bus had me on it! I was really worried when the bus pulled out. I had never been to Mexico City. After we left the city, we were going and going along until we reached a fork in the road, and the bus stopped. I saw a woman from San Andrés get on the bus, and quickly I realized that it was Celerina. I signaled to her with my smile and asked, "Just now you've made it?"

"Yes, it's that I was late getting to the bus station. I didn't arrive on time so I got a taxi, and they took me to meet the bus." She said that she was embarrassed. At that point I cheered up a bit because I finally had a fellow traveler.

When we arrived in Mexico City, we went to a hotel to stay the night with another woman from Kinal Antzetik who wanted a visa, too.

At the embassy the next day we had to fill out papers and everything that was necessary. When we tried to enter, they wouldn't let us bring our backpacks. We had to leave them outside in the street. Luckily, Felipe was with us. He waited a few hours outside on the street taking care of our backpacks. I only carried a little purse with me. But with each step, they searched it. "What are you carrying? What do you have in there?" They didn't want any things to enter the embassy, just bodies!

I got through it with difficulties because they asked me questions and had me fill out papers. Not just a few, many! At the entrance to the office where you have the appointment, I was alone. I didn't go with the other two *compañeras* because they had already finished filling out their papers. I didn't know how to do it very well, and my helpers weren't with me. "No, you still need to fill them out," the workers at the embassy told me.

I got very nervous. I thought that since my *compañeras* had already entered, they were going to receive their visas. I thought that one receives a visa fast. But, nooooo! You have to wait! Two people were outside with me, and they were very kind. "Ah, don't be nervous. We're here to help you," they said. They showed me how to fill the papers out. When they were filled out and there wasn't anything more to do, they said, "You can go on," and they showed me where to go next.

So I made it to the place where people who are going to travel wait to speak to someone. An older man spoke to the three of us, but it was as if he didn't speak Spanish. He spoke a little bit of Spanish and a little bit of English. I couldn't hear what he said very well. He was behind a window, and we were outside. He just spoke from inside, and we listened from the outside. He had a microphone, but he didn't use it. He just said two or three words to us. "No, you can't have a visa. You have to go back." He rejected all of us together, and we returned with nothing!

The following day I didn't know what to do. I called Domingo and explained everything to him. I asked Domingo if it would be better for me to return or stay until I could get another appointment. "Since you don't have what you went there to get, you can stay while I'm not seriously ill," he told me.

So I stayed one week in Mexico City while you [Cristina] made calls to officials and supported me. Then at the second appointment, they gave us the visa. It was a different person who gave it to me, a very friendly woman. She asked me, "Are you married? Do you have a child? What is it that you're going to do? Are you going to work, or are you going to stay to work in the US?"

"No, I'm not going to work. I have a house. I have a husband. I have children. I'm a mother of six children," I explained to her. "I'm only staying for twelve or fifteen days, something like that," I told her.

So it turned out well. But at first we suffered! We had to stay seven days in Mexico City between the two appointments. The money that you [Cristina] gave me for the trip wasn't enough, but Kinal helped me by giving me food and a room so that I could stay in the hotel with the other women from the organization. While we waited, the women went to a meeting. It was lucky for us because it was the time of year when Kinal has meetings. Although I wasn't a representative, I had to try to listen to what they said in order to pass the time.

That's how it went. It was difficult. I thought, "The workers in the embassy don't have any respect for us Mexicans. They are inside Mexico, my country! They should respect us. It's very unjust that the people of Mexico don't receive respect within their own country from foreigners. The embassy should have a worker who speaks Spanish, who is kind to the Mexican people." The man who rejected us was old, and he seemed angry. He didn't respect me. He treated me like I was an animal.

12 NOVEMBER 2002

The millions of little dots below begin to take the shape of shops and houses in a big city as our plane makes its descent into Juárez. I expect Antonia to brace herself for the landing, but she takes it in stride. I am especially concerned because while on the flight we got onto the topic of 9/11 and the plane that the passengers brought down so that it wouldn't crash into the White House. Antonia had a lot of questions about the tragedy, and I felt obliged to answer her questions to the best of my ability without scaring her.

Antonia's first visit was filled with many joyful moments. One of the happiest for me was going around Hobby Lobby looking at all the Christmas tree decorations. Antonia seemed overwhelmed by the quantity of colors and glittery things, but delighted by the festive feeling. The anthropologist in me felt obligated to explain to her the consumer-driven nature of Christmas in the United States, but mostly we just feasted our eyes and examined how ornaments were put together. We left the store with a new idea for an ornament that the weavers in her community could make to sell.

Antonia met with many groups of people, but one gathering was especially memorable. Don Pepion, director of American Indian programs at New Mexico State University and a member of the Blackfoot tribe, arranged for Antonia to meet with a diverse group of American Indian students. At the gathering students asked Antonia about her life and shared with her their struggles as native people in the United States. After everyone told Antonia what tribe they were from, she described a bit about life in her community and then asked the students for questions. One student asked Antonia if her people have drinking problems. Her reply led to a lengthy discussion about problems with alcohol in native communities in both the United States and Mexico.

Eventually the conversation turned to respect. One of the students tried to convey to Antonia the challenge American Indian students face in showing each other proper respect. "We struggle to create a respectful environment for native people here at the university. Look at where we are meeting tonight, in a classroom. We don't have a comfortable place to talk with you, and we don't know what foods we should offer to welcome you. We have punch and cookies, but we don't have other foods for you. We don't even know what foods to offer each other because we come from so many different tribes. We don't know how to show each other proper respect in an environment where showing respect isn't an important part of life."

Antonia nodded as I translated the student's words. I don't remember her exact reply, but I remember that she tried to reassure the students that wanting to show respect for others is important in itself, even if one can't always do it according to tradition.

On her first trip Antonia enjoyed taking photos with her disposable camera and keeping notes in a little notebook that she stored in the folds of her belt. I joked with her about how she had become an anthropologist. She agreed, and added that in my country we had reversed roles. "Here I'm like your little child. You aren't giving me your breast, but you're feeding me."

I like going places, meeting new people, and learning new things. Although I wanted to see other places, I thought that it would never happen. I never thought in my life that I was going to travel by plane, but I've flown now four times. In my community we think that nobody is going to fly in an air-plane. Each time when a plane passes over in the sky, we look up and say in jest, "I'm going to travel in a plane, too. The buzzard is going to come soon for me." Those who dream that they are flying in a plane say that it means that they're going to die soon because the airplane symbolizes death. They say that it's the coffin that carries people to heaven.

When I was growing up, we went to San Cristóbal by foot to buy things and to take toasted tortillas to my brother when he was studying there. About two or three in the morning we began to walk on the trails, and about eight or nine in the morning we arrived. We were *very* tired when we ar-rived. Each store that my parents entered, I would sit outside on the curb waiting for them because my feet hurt. Later the bus came to Chenalhó. But only one bus passed by our house each day, and sometimes it was too full, and I had to wait until the next day.

For many years, from when I was a teenager, I only traveled back and forth to San Cristóbal. The majority of women don't know San Cristóbal. They only know the village of Chenalhó. In their communities they mostly go out to see their *milpas* or go to the market. They don't go to a city or another township very often. But I always went to the city to sell. It was a question of needing to leave my house because I had to work as representa-tive of the cooperative. I always went there to sell weavings, to run errands, no? But I was the only one of the sisters in my family like this. I was the only one who turned out different.

Later, when I knew Carolina, she took me on a trip to Villahermosa, Ta-basco. Little by little, I went farther and farther away. In 1995 my Zapatista support base elected me to go to a consultation in Oaxaca.[2] Seven years later I went to Mexico City to get my visa. That's how I climbed the ladder in a few years. My first step was traveling within my state, the second to another state, the third to the capital of my country, and the fourth to another coun-try. For example, right now I'm very far from my village, no? That's the way I've been learning.

Chapter 10

The International Folk Art Market

I opened my mind a little with the many artists in Santa Fe. I saw that it's very important to share our cultures.

Antonia

JUNE 2005

Antonia's second visit to New Mexico was in 2005 in order to attend the International Folk Art Market in Santa Fe. Las Cruces-Chiapas Connection held numerous fundraisers in the spring of 2005 to raise the money to bring Antonia to represent two weavings cooperatives, Tsobol Antzetik and Mujeres por la Dignidad.

Hoping to make the visa application process less painful this time, I accompanied Antonia to Mexico City, along with her sister-in-law Marta and Marta's daughter. We hiked around the city, visiting the National Palace, the Shrine of the Virgin of Guadalupe, and a market called Tepito where Antonia and Marta bought used clothes to resell. But before that we had to obtain Antonia's visa, which turned out to be not without its stressful moments.

Late on the night of June 13, after we arrived in Mexico City, we realized that we hadn't paid for the visa appointment, and we were really worried, sitting on the bed in the hotel thinking about what was going to happen to us. We talked about lying, but Cristina called Michael, and he said that it wouldn't be a good idea. So at 7 a.m. the next morning we went to the embassy and asked what we could do.

The man at the gate said, "Why didn't you pay? It's necessary to pay beforehand." But all was not lost, because then he said, "You're not the only ones who forgot to pay. Go to the bank. If you get back here by 10 a.m., you're okay. But after 10, you're out of luck."

So we went to the bank that was close to the embassy. But it wasn't open

(FACING PAGE): Photo courtesy of Michael O'Malley, 2010.

yet, so we drank coffee and ate donuts for a while. When the bank opened, we got into line to pay. At 9:30 we left, and I got into a long line at the embassy with thousands of people.

You [Cristina] were waiting outside the fence. Two or three times I went over to the fence to ask you for help, and I lost my place in the line. When I returned to the line, the person who was in my place didn't want to let me back in. But others felt sorry for me and gave me a place in line with them. If they hadn't given me a place, I would have gone way back. They were very kind.

I was in line about five hours before I got inside the building. At the building entrance they explained to us that we had to fill out some papers, and if we didn't, they would reject us. There was a space that I didn't fill out, but I couldn't go back to ask you, so I asked a person name Alejandra.

When I entered, I wasn't afraid like in 2002. That time it was horrible. I didn't know what was going to happen to me. But in 2005 I knew that if we got rejected, we could pay for another appointment.

I waited my turn. Then when my number came up, it wasn't hard for me to get the visa. The woman who talked to me didn't ask me anything, and she offered me a ten-year visa! She was very kind. She even complimented me on my blouse. "Ah, what a beautiful blouse you're wearing!" she said.

When I was about to leave, she said, "Now you have your visa for ten years."

Then I went out another door to ask for the receipt to pick up my visa. But they told me that it's necessary to pay an additional 85 pesos to pick up the visa! "I don't know what I'm going to pay with because I don't have 85 pesos," I told a woman in line with me.

"Ah, you don't have it," she said.

"I just have 50 or 60 pesos."

The woman gave me 20 or 30 pesos to make up the difference. I felt happy because I finally had all the money I needed. If she hadn't given me the money, I wouldn't have been able to pick up my visa. There were a lot of kind people there inside the embassy.

Then they gave me a receipt to pick up my visa in Tuxtla when it was ready, and I left the embassy like 2:00 or 2:30 in the afternoon.

Now I feel content that I have a ten-year visa. I'm just waiting to see if someone can help me travel again. I think that I'll go, while I'm still alive.

An unexpected aspect of the Folk Art Market was the rich exchange between Antonia and other artists about struggles for social justice. With two wood-carvers from Peru, Antonia learned about the violence and injustices in their country. With Caesar, a Zulu man from South Africa, she heard about apartheid and was shocked to find out that Caesar had been in jail twenty-two times. Caesar left us with the words, "The pen is the way toward peace, not the gun."

The market in Santa Fe opened our eyes to the struggles and hopes of artisans throughout the world. It also brought Antonia and me closer, perhaps because it was the first time that we were alone together in unfamiliar territory. Although several volunteers from the Las Cruces-Chiapas Connection came to help Antonia sell, we arrived first and had to figure out many things together. Sales didn't go as well as we had hoped. We learned that blouses sold best, along with nursing mother dolls, and little drawstring bags embroidered with plants and animals and their names in Spanish and Tzotzil.

On the last day, crossing the parking lot from the Sage Inn to Wild Oats, where we were going to eat, Antonia put her arm around me and laid her head on my shoulder. I wasn't used to physical affection between us, nor did I expect her to say, "I can't ever thank you enough for bringing me here and for being my friend all these years."

When I went to the Santa Fe Market, Cristina and I had to leave at 9 in the morning. It took about five hours to get to Santa Fe. On our way I saw the hills and how everything is desert. I got sad thinking about the people who cross the desert in July without papers. In July there's so much heat! It seems that there's no place for people to rest. How could they bear it? I don't know how their feet can bear it because the earth is pure sand, not like in Chiapas.

Cristina told me that a man passed behind her house in the night. I'm impressed by the people who cross here. I thought that they crossed in other places, but no, they also cross where Cristina lives. So we talked as we drove along about how sad it is that they have to cross the border because there's a lot of poverty in Mexico.

Later, as we were driving, I was looking at everything. In Chiapas everything is green. Here there's just hills and desert. When we got close to Santa Fe, there were a few bigger trees, and the hills looked a little greener, and there were many elegant houses.

We arrived around 2 p.m. in Santa Fe and looked for information about where the market was and where they were going to put us up. Cristina did me the favor of helping me with everything in Santa Fe. If it weren't for her, I wouldn't have been able to be there in Santa Fe. That's why I want to thank her a lot. It's as if she did more than my own mother would do for me. She also helped me by translating because they don't speak Spanish very well there. They mostly speak English.

On Friday we had to leave early in the morning to arrange all our products for the market on Saturday. Friday was a little difficult for me and Cristina. At first I was just looking at how we could accommodate all our things in the little space we had. It was about three meters square. But we made it work out, and it ended up looking pretty when we had all the weavings and everything arranged. Around noon it was all ready.

After that we went to rest in the hotel for a while, and at night we had an invitation to the governor's mansion for dinner. That night we began to get to know each other, all the people participating as artists. I don't know how to describe it. It was amazing. Before that day I thought that there were a lot of traditional clothes in the world, but I didn't know how people around the world looked. That night the artists wore their beautiful traditional clothing. I opened my mind to how people are, how the world is. We were all happy to be knowing each other, and everyone was very friendly.

That night the governor [Bill Richardson] came to talk in front of all the artists, but I couldn't understand what he said. I just watched while he talked. After the talk many artists went up to him to offer him gifts. I didn't have anything to offer. I just asked for a photo with him and his wife. We were there a long time, and then we returned to the hotel to rest.

On Saturday we had to get up about 5 or 5:30 a.m., something like that, in order to be ready to leave on the bus at 6:15 a.m. to arrive with plenty of time at our booth. The market in Santa Fe was very well organized. We felt very good there. Everything was free, the hotel, the bus, the food. There was a lot of food.

In the morning we also had to carry our posters on the bus to show how life is for the weavers in Chiapas. So we had a little work to do when we arrived putting the posters around. Then we waited for the people to arrive.

We began to sell on Saturday at 8 a.m. There were a lot of people coming in to buy that day—12,000! But they didn't buy too many of our products because there were a lot of other things from other countries. There was too much.

The work on Saturday and Sunday was a little tiring because we had to stand around waiting for people. But I left the booth for periods of time to see the dances. I saw that it wasn't that important that I was in the booth all the time since I can't speak English. My helpers helped me a lot, many women, some friends of Cristina's—Melissa, Meghann, Mari, Janet, many women helped me.

It was the same on Sunday. Only we were a little worried because we saw that we weren't going to sell everything that we had brought. But everything came out well. Afterward, in the late afternoon, there was a farewell party. We were all very happy, all the artists together eating a big meal. Those who like to drink drank beer, and there was music and dancing. It was all very good. Well, it was a bit of both sides, happiness at times and sometimes moments of tiredness.

In Santa Fe we had the chance to meet many people, but I couldn't talk with people because many don't speak Spanish. I only talked a lot with people from Peru because they speak Spanish well. For example, Nilda and Lourdes. Lourdes was my first friend, no? She was very friendly. But I couldn't understand her Spanish very well because it's very different from Mexican Spanish. Later we began to talk with two brothers from Peru, Pedro and Javier. Before talking with them, I liked their way of being. They seemed like men from Chenalhó, humble and honest people. I felt as if they were my family. We talked a lot about how life is in Peru in comparison with Chiapas. It seems that in all countries there's injustice and war. Javier told me that many in Peru have been killed, detained, and disappeared. I told them about what happened in Acteal, that many people died there and that they were only praying.

With others on Monday I talked about the violence that has happened in nearly the whole world. Ceasar talked with me about how things have changed in his village in Africa, but only through much effort, with arms, and with letters sent to the government and to other countries. All kinds of political work are necessary. It's important to be well organized. The government in Mexico isn't well prepared to use a variety of political approaches, like what Ceasar and others from South Africa did. The government in Mexico only sends the army and uses economic force. Mandela, the leader in South Africa, seems the same as Marcos. That's why they could win with such a leader. But it was difficult. Ceasar showed us the scar on his head. He was in a demonstration, and in the middle they were attacked. Many people have scars from the aggression.

After this talk we said goodbye to our *compañeros*. We had to separate ourselves by countries. At 8 in the morning we left the hotel and went to a foundation where we collected the check for what we had sold at the market. From there I went walking a bit with Cristina in the plaza. We had a chance to meet a *compañera* called Mary who lives in Santo Domingo Pueblo. We talked with her, or rather Cristina talked with her, because Mary didn't speak Spanish very well. We exchanged products. She makes things of metal and beads, necklaces and earrings, and she said that if I wanted to exchange something with her, we could do it. I took one of her necklaces with a silver cross on it. I liked it a lot. I gave her one of the blouses that I made. We took a photo, and she gave us her address in case we want to communicate later.

Mary used to drink a lot. It's only been two months that she stopped drinking. Her cousin is in jail because she drank a lot. She pushed her husband off a building, and he died. That's why she is in jail, where she is suffering. How sad for her.

I saw in Santa Fe that there are men artisans who also know how to make things well. In my opinion it would be very good if the men in my community would make whatever they want to make. But men don't know how to make things. They only go to work in the fields with their machetes and spades. Although some men are carpenters, they only know how to make tables, chairs and beds.[1]

In Santa Fe I saw that they know how to make many things to recover their cultures. Javier and Pedro told me about their traditions in the past. Their grandfathers and grandmothers knew how to make things, and their fathers and mothers learned from them. And perhaps Javier's and Pedro's children are going to learn, too. Until today they are continuing the traditions.

In my community we could make dolls of men and women and put traditional clothes on them, like Javier did when he made a dancer from Peru. For example, we could make a figure of Sm'etik Suyil.[2] In the past when we went to the lake where Sme'tik Suyil appeared, we carried many gifts to adorn her cross. We dressed her in a blouse, shawl, skirt, and belt, as if Sme'tik Suyil were a woman. When they were done, she looked like a real woman! To dress the cross like a man, they put on his red scarf like men in Chenalhó use, and also a hat with ribbons and the tunic that men wear. That's how they did it in the past. Now we don't put clothes on crosses. It's a traditional thing, an old custom, but we can recover it, and perhaps the wood figures will sell.

It would be good for my sons to make things of wood or clay because I've seen that all kinds of things made of wood, clay, and metal are sold. Sebastian learned to weave. He can make things, copy old things. He's just working in the fields, but now he has a wife and a family. That's why I want him to know how to earn a little money, to be an artist.

But who knows if my sons will want to, because they only seem to want to spend money. Right now that I'm in Santa Fe, they're only thinking of gifts. "Give me something! Give me!" they tell me. Nothing more. They don't want to work. It's difficult for them and for me, too. But I would like my sons to learn to make things, to be artists.

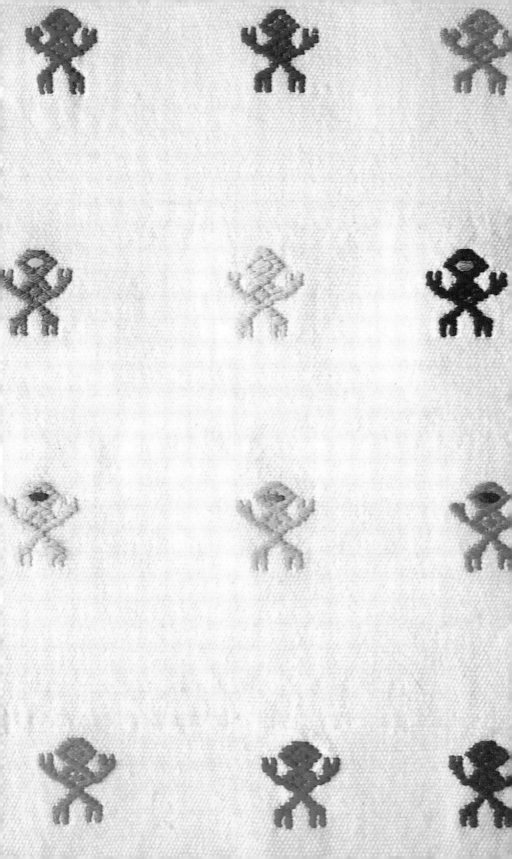

PART III

Gains and Losses,
Lessons Learned

(FACING PAGE): Symbols of a saint on a cloth woven by Antonia in 1988. Collection of Christine Eber. Photo courtesy of Michael O'Malley, 2010.

Chapter 1

Envy

During my initial fieldwork I found that talking about envy and witchcraft with Pedranos was difficult. Most people acknowledged that it was a part of life, but many in the Word of God and Protestant religions seemed to feel ashamed of it, to regard it as a part of their ancestral heritage better forgotten. Nevertheless, envy in Chenalhó seems to be connected to a moral discourse related to promoting egalitarian and cooperative relations, which Pedranos have continued to rework in the context of their changing lives. In the 1980s, when I lived with Antonia, Pedranos valued conformity and viewed unbalanced social and economic relations as precursors of envy that could bring illness and death.

Envy in Tzotzil-Maya communities is connected to an assumption that others' true beliefs and motivations are not easily accessed. This idea stems from a conception of self as composed of extensions, such as the part of one's soul that wanders off in sleep, illness, coitus, and drunkenness. These various aspects of self have qualities and volition that exist apart from the social person whom one sees and interacts with on a daily basis.[1]

I first learned about the power of envy and the volition of self-extensions one evening in 1987 when I overheard Domingo praying in Tzotzil in the sleeping house. Curious, I walked by the half-open door to see him kneeling at the back of the house in front of a row of white candles. Several sweet gum boughs formed a protective wall behind the candles. At Domingo's left, fingers of smoke drifted up to the ceiling from a pottery incense burner. Domingo's humbled body and husky speech spelled urgency and fear. Many nights I had fallen asleep listening to Antonia and Domingo praying, but this prayer was different. On other occasions Antonia and Domingo also prayed rapidly and knelt humbly, but they did not change their tone of voice, nor sing their prayers as Domingo was doing now. The other prayers had passages of Spanish, too. This prayer was all Tzotzil and contained many words I did not know.

I asked Antonia what was going on, why Domingo was praying this way.

(FACING PAGE): Photo by Christine Eber, 2010.

Antonia told me what I feared: that Domingo was asking God and the saints to keep his family safe from the harm that envious neighbors were wishing on them. I knew that neighbors had been talking about my enriching Antonia and Domingo. When I pressed her, Antonia told me some of the rumors that were circulating. In a particularly creative one, Antonia and I were manufacturing money. Although even Antonia was amazed at the ridiculousness of the rumor, after recalling the afternoon a neighbor came to visit, I understood how the rumor might have begun. That afternoon I was writing in my notebook with a technical pen. Antonia, Domingo, and the boys were used to looking at my pen, and all had tried it out at least once. Antonia suspected that the woman, who had probably never seen such a pen and didn't know how money is made, thought it might be an instrument to make money, and so the rumor started. Although we weren't making money, I was paying Antonia for room, board, and for transcribing interviews. I was also buying weavings from her and her fellow co-op members and helping them find markets in the United States. I understood how Antonia's neighbor had only to exercise her imagination a little to conclude that we were making money.[2]

Before the evening that I saw Domingo praying against envy, I had not come face to face with its power in Pedrano social life. Afterward, envy was no longer just an interesting aspect of Pedrano beliefs about illness and social relations, but a commentary on my presence in the community. From then on I was anxious about being a burden to Antonia and increasing the chances of her being a target of envy. When I returned to Chenalhó in 1989 for another four months of research, I stayed with a series of different families instead of with Antonia. But I still spent the night with her family from time to time and have continued to return for yearly visits.

It is common knowledge in Antonia's community that she has two *comadres* from the United States (me and Carol-Jean McGreevy). This fact makes her very different from most people in her community. Over the years Antonia has had many confrontations with envious neighbors because of her relationship with me and other foreigners. Some neighbors who have no way to send their children to school past sixth grade envy Antonia for receiving monetary assistance from her *comadres* for her children's schooling.[3] Once, when she hadn't left the house for a while due to an illness, neighbors with whom she had had problems told another neighbor, who then told Antonia, "Antonia must be on her annual vacation to the US."

Antonia has also confronted envy in the context of the religious and political differences that have proliferated in Chenalhó since the 1980s. Envy was especially worrisome during the time of heightened religious and political conflict in the 1980s and 1990s, when organizations began to expand and contest the status quo. Although all of Antonia's family members support the resistance movement, their different allegiances to the EZLN and Las Abejas have created tensions among them. Antonia has been justifiably concerned that I might inadvertently tell something that she has told me to someone who might use it to hurt her or others in the resistance movement. In the late 1980s, members of the Word of God co-op store held special prayer sessions to counteract envy against the progressive Catholic movement in Chenalhó. Similar prayer sessions to protect against envy are held today in the Zapatista support base in Antonia's community.

Many Pedranos who are not in the resistance movement seem to accept that economic differences are inevitable consequences of "progress" and modernity. Most Pedranos, even in the resistance movement, desire some of the accoutrements of modernity, including the latest electronic equipment. But in the 1980s, if a family could acquire the cash to purchase a TV or tape cassette player, they were careful not to put it on display. Such possessions were covered with a large woven cloth when not in use to avoid drawing attention to the fact that the family had funds to buy something that not everyone could afford.

With increased migration and access to education and various forms of media, social and economic inequality has become a part of the fabric of life in Chenalhó. Today people no longer try to hide their TVs, and now DVD players, although they may adorn them with woven cloths. Two-story houses with trucks parked beside them—an unheard-of display of difference a couple of decades ago—don't raise eyebrows now. In 2010 Antonia acquired a telephone.

Antonia has skillfully used her membership in cooperatives and in the Word of God and Zapatista movements to negotiate a place for herself that accommodates her more independent mind and spirit while protecting herself and her family from the worst effects of envy. Her ability to manage envy through cooperative work seems pivotal to how Antonia has been able to work with me and other outsiders, and also deal with members of her community who are threatened by her activities.[4] Her integration into cooperative work also helps her reconcile her more outgoing personality with traditional conceptions of humility.

The concept of *xmayet* (humility) in Tzotzil-Maya culture is similar to that found in other agrarian cultures distant in time and place. The Sanskrit word for humility is *bhumi* (earth). The Latin root of "humility" is *humus* (soil or ground). From the Latin comes the English human. In Tzotzil-Maya beliefs, walking and working together on the ground of the place to which one belongs is fundamental to one's personal and collective identity. Pedranos come to know and trust each other through being visible on a daily basis walking on footpaths, their feet firmly planted on Earth's face, interacting humbly and respectfully all the while.[5] Walking on unknown paths, in body and mind, has made it difficult for Antonia to assure her *compañeros* of the value of her evolving identity and broadening humanity, as well as her humility.

Antonia's struggle to feel respected both within and outside her society reflects the difficulties that indigenous women of Chiapas face in achieving autonomy and freedom from domination. Even women sometimes undermine the rights of other women, as evidenced by Antonia's attitudes toward her daughters' different desires, and in the way some women distance themselves from Antonia, threatened by her assertive style.

I always remember during the years when you [Cristina] and Carolina came to my house there was a lot of envy in my community. It was very strong. People envied me having foreigners in my house, because before no one had come to our community from other countries.

They used to say, "Ah, a rich woman has come. You're making money from her." The people said many things. In our culture, not just in Chenalhó, but also in other townships, a person who has lots of money causes envy in people. They resent that person, and that brings envy. They say, "Ah, that's great that that person is rich, but I'm not rich."

For example, when I returned to my community from New Mexico in 2006, I asked my sister if she wanted to receive a little salary for being representative of the weaving co-op because we talked about this when I was with you [Cristina]. She answered, "No, because the other women will envy me."

When people here in my community are paid on a regular basis, it's as if they become like the teachers in the school who receive a salary. In the past teachers came from other townships, and most of them were mestizos. Some of them didn't respect the community's rules and behaved badly. Today many teachers are from Chenalhó. They show respect and don't behave like they did in the past. Some participate in the fiestas, like Carnival.

When a woman travels to another town, there's a lot of criticism, lots of ridiculing. That's why women don't want to go. They don't want anyone to make fun of them or envy them. I always bear up under the criticism, the ridicule from my *compañeras*, my relatives, my countrymen and -women. But it hurts me each time someone says something. Since the beginning there has been a lot of ridicule of me. But it has calmed down. They got used to how I am. Domingo had to bear it, too. At times he got angry at the ridicule. But it was my desire, no? I had to leave my community.

Envy comes in chains. One person says something about another, and the person who hears them comes to tell me, "This person was saying something bad about you to another person and I overheard them."

There are some who say, "Ah, that woman, let her fail. It's not good what she does."

Envy can bring much damage. It can cause serious illness and even death. The tradition to prevent envy from entering the body is to pray to God to ask for help. When the late Don Bartolo was alive, he would pray for the cooperative store. Since he was in the Zapatista support base, we asked him to pray for the store. He prayed so that a lot of envy wouldn't come to the store, so that the cooperative members could make progress with the store, and so that the members wouldn't have problems with each other. He prayed a lot for the store when he was alive and was very committed to each prayer. When he died, many problems began in the store. The owner of the land where we built the store began to get angry and to say bad things about us. Later, after Don Bartolo was dead, the landowner became envious of us and threw us off the land. I think that happened because Bartolo was not there, praying against envy. We had to move the store from the land we rented to other land.

Envy is not a good thing to think, to do, to feel. If you feel it, just ask God for help. He's the only one who defends us against envy. That's what Domingo taught me. When I think, "Why that person? Why not me?" Domingo tells me, "Don't think that way. If you continue to think like that, you'll be worse off than you are now."

I don't like to feel envy as it's not right to envy others because God doesn't like us to do this. I believe that each person has different talents. We can't copy another person.

Chapter 2

Suffering

Well, the greatest suffering I have had was because of my husband. The second level of suffering was for my children. I don't think there was any more suffering. Ah, but there is another kind of suffering. It's not my private suffering, but the suffering we share in common because we are indigenous people.

Antonia, June 10, 2006

When I was conducting research in the 1980s, I accompanied Antonia and other Pedrano friends as they crossed geographic and ethnic boundaries. Traveling from their rural communities to the city of San Cristóbal, they entered a cultural world where indigenous people were second-class citizens. I was haunted by stories from anthropologists who had conducted their fieldwork a couple decades before me. They told of mestizos swatting indigenous people off the high sidewalks, if they were bold enough to walk on them. The sidewalks were for mestizos, the streets for dogs and Indians.

Even in the headtown of Chenalhó, where many mestizos were *compadres* and trading partners with Pedranos, they often treated them like children. On many occasions I heard mestizo shopkeepers talk down to respected Pedrano elders, but as an outsider I was uncertain of an appropriate response. Although I became friends with some very kind mestizas, I did not enjoy being in the headtown because I often felt torn between them and my Pedrano friends. Mestizos often questioned me about why I would choose to live in an uncivilized, indigenous community where people eat only corn and beans. They had no idea how much more comfortable I felt in indigenous communities, where I did not have to deal with the crossing of ethnic boundaries that life in the headtown entailed.

Still today indigenous women struggle to negotiate diverse boundaries due to the persistent gender ideology in which it is considered proper for women to stay close to their household compounds. To be safe from suspicion when

(FACING PAGE): Photo courtesy of Michael O'Malley, 2010.

leaving their households, women take a child or another relative with them. Accompanying Antonia on trips to San Cristóbal, I marveled at her courage in dealing with disrespectful bus drivers and shop owners. Once when a bus driver told a crowd of boarding passengers to hurry up and move, Antonia raised her voice enough for him to hear her and said, "We're not like cattle, like animals that you can push around."

Despite experiencing what academics refer to as the "triple oppression" of racism, classism, and sexism, Antonia does not see the suffering that she experiences as a woman in her society as an important cog in a machine of oppression. She focuses instead on the oppression she shares with her husband and other kin as a result of being poor and indigenous. She is skeptical of embracing the individual rights focus of Western feminism for fear it will undermine the larger liberation project of the resistance movement. Although Antonia holds individual men responsible for oppressive actions against herself and other women, she focuses more blame on the government than on her kinsmen for women not receiving equal rights and proper respect.

Many mestizas and indigenous women in Chiapas, especially younger ones, are searching for ways to achieve their own liberation as women within the larger struggle. Many of these young women see their mothers as having known nothing but suffering. They would not understand how Antonia could support arranged marriages and not do everything within her power to keep her daughters in school. The clash in perceptions is, in part, generational, but also regional. In the lowland areas of Chiapas where the Zapatista movement took shape, communities are composed of migrants from diverse ethnic groups, many of whom have lost all connections to their communities of origin in the highlands.[1]

Calixta Guiteras-Holmes (1961: 63–64) writes that in the mid-twentieth century, before the economic crises of the 1970s and '80s, Pedranos did not consider poverty a permanent condition. Like wealth, poverty could come and go. The measure of high economic position in Chenalhó during this time was having one's health and a large family. People power, not goods, was the foundation of well-being. This understanding of poverty frames it as a part of the human condition that can be dealt with through traditional practices such as hard work, prayer, and sometimes witchcraft, if one is resentful. This conception contrasts sharply with the historical, political, and economic perspectives that Antonia and her *compañeros* are developing through participation in the Word of God and the Zapatista movement. More and more they see poverty as linked to social injustice and economic inequality, not as a normal, albeit temporary, condition.

The suffering that Antonia often talks about as part of the "holy struggle" seems to be suffering with the purpose of bringing an end to poverty and racism and other forms of oppression. From this perspective, one who suffers does not seek pity, only fellow strugglers to accompany them on their journey.[2]

They say that in the past in Chenalhó there was a lot of racism. Mestizos treated indigenous people as if they were children. My father explained to me that the mestizos deceived them and hit them. If we wanted to sell something, the mestizos didn't pay us what we asked. They paid what they wanted to pay.

In my time there was also racism with the bus drivers. They didn't respect their passengers. They treated us like cattle. But today I don't see as much racism. Although there are some racist mestizos, not so many as before. Now we are more like equals.

People learn about racism when they go out into the cities. When people only stay in their houses, they don't learn about it. Like in my village, many women don't know about racism. But I learned how it is because I left my community and traveled to San Cristóbal, Tuxtla, Mexico City, and the US. When I went to the embassy in Mexico City to get my visa, I learned a lot about racism there. When I passed through Mexico City on my way to the US, I saw how people treat us. They could see that I didn't know the city, and because I'm indigenous and poor, they thought that I'm not worth anything except to take advantage of. During all of that time I learned about racism. But many people from my country, they don't know about it. They don't understand because they just stay in their houses.

The Mexican government exploits indigenous people in a lot of different ways. For example, in my community we don't pay for electricity because we say it isn't fair that Chiapas is a major source of electricity for the nation, but many poor people in the state don't have it. The president was even thinking about selling our electricity to another country. That's why the people of Chiapas are angry, because it's our resource.

The president of Mexico [Ernesto Zedillo] doesn't think about how to help the poor people. He just thinks about controlling them. He uses taxes to send soldiers to Chiapas. Chenalhó was full of soldiers for a long time. The government spent a lot of money putting soldiers and arms here. The government also receives money from the US for airplanes and guns.

The government doesn't give a good price for products to the producers, and the money that it receives for the public good, I think that officials put it in their pocket. Also, the government is taking land from poor people to construct highways and other things without the people's approval. The majority of people where I live don't have enough land to plant their *milpa*.

Although it's not good to sell our land, people do it because they have to. Maybe they lack corn or other food or have a grave illness. I know a family from my community that had land in the past, but the husband got sick and sold their land. They even sold their house. Afterward, when they didn't have anything, they moved to San Cristóbal to live. Right now I don't know how they are, if they are still renting or have their own house.

It happened with us, too, when Domingo got sick. We already owed a lot of money, and we had to borrow money to pay for the doctor visits and medicine. After that we couldn't find another way to pay back the debt except to sell a little piece of our land. My children regretted that we sold the land. "You shouldn't have sold it. We have to have land, too," they said. I didn't like it that the children were feeling this way. They need their inheritance. Also, Domingo regretted selling the land when he was sick. "Ah, if I hadn't been sick we wouldn't have had to sell the land," he said. A few months ago with some weaving and coffee money, I bought another piece of land to replace the land we sold.

In my village we are very connected to the land. Those who know how to pray on the land to ask for food say that Mother Earth gives us her breast. When one sells part of the land, it's as if we sell part of our mother.

You [Cristina] aren't tied to a particular land. Although you own your own home, it isn't inheritance from your grandfather, because you bought it. Our land is going to be my children's inheritance, and my children are going to give it to their children. That's how it happens when one has a fixed place on the land, a certain place where we are. It helps us work together because we're always living in the same place. It's not the same as you who move from place to place.

Domingo didn't plant a lot this year. Now he can't work in the fields much because he works a lot in the autonomous township government. He can't hire helpers because we don't have the money to pay them. We always have to buy beans and corn because the harvest doesn't give us much corn. I rarely make *chenkulvaj* because we don't have beans. Everyone here—my relatives and neighbors—they all buy corn. But the price is always going up. Now 16 kilos costs 65 pesos. If the family is big, it's necessary to buy a lot of corn. For example, we are sometimes five or six people and we buy 32 kilos each week.

Many families don't have enough corn to make tortillas, and they have to grind a banana root or *sbuk*, a round and thick root. We search for it in the Earth and pull it out. Then we peel it and grind the pieces. It doesn't look like corn dough and has a different flavor, but you can eat it. What I like to eat a lot is banana root. It has a little flavor. Also, flower of the *milpa*, we eat that, too. It has flavor, but I don't like it very much. When I was about twelve or thirteen years old, I had to eat it because there wasn't any corn. Also, you couldn't buy corn at that time. The little that we had in the house, we made a few tortillas and *matz* with it. My mother counted out three tortillas per person and a little ball of *pozol* because it's not fair if one person eats more and another less. She thought it was better to make the portions equal.

Today I follow my mother's example with the things that I don't have a lot of, for example, pineapple, oranges, and apples that I buy in the market. I divide these into equal parts. If I just leave them out someplace, one person could finish the whole thing! At times I put my part aside, and when I see that the children want more, I divide up my portion. With the other foods that I have a lot of, like *chayotes* [a type of squash], I just leave them in a basket or a bucket, and my family takes what they want to eat.

JUNE 10, 2006, TULAROSA, NEW MEXICO

We meet Heather at a Buddhist center in Tularosa, a village in the mountains near Las Cruces. The folks at the center are kindly letting us stay here to work on the book, and our friend Jean has organized a weaving sale at a local gallery. Jean left a big bowl of fruit on the counter to welcome us.

I don't know how long I've been thinking this. I see a lot of fruit here in the houses in New Mexico. In Cristina's house, there's always apples, bananas, and I don't know what other fruit. She tells me, "Eat some, take some." But I don't feel like eating them because I'm full. I don't crave fruit because nearly all day I'm full.

Then I think about my life back home. "It's because we don't have enough food, that's why I crave fruit. If I were with my children eating a lot, like I am here, my children wouldn't crave fruits and other foods," I said to myself.

Then I began to think that we are almost like dogs, because my dogs eat whatever there is, whether it's good or bad. Like I told Cristina, although the beans are sour, we eat them. Why? Because we don't have enough food. My children are always craving things. I know that they're hungry all the time. It's not fair, but we can't do anything about it.

When I explained to my children that I didn't feel like eating all the fruit that was in front of us in Santa Fe, they said, "You should have brought it to us, Mami! You should have brought us all the food!"

"How am I going to carry it?" I told them. "How am I going to carry it with all my other things? All the fruit will spoil," I told them. "Besides, they won't let it cross the border."

They can feel how life is here, how it is when a person is full, how they don't crave anything. I've eaten a lot of meals with you [Cristina], and I don't crave anything. Although I see food, I don't want it.

Each day that I am here, my children don't have enough food. It's not fair that I'm eating so much and my children go hungry. If I were in my home with fruit, it would rapidly disappear. That's a big difference between life here and in my village.

As she finished speaking, Antonia lowered her head and wept.

Forgive me for crying for my children. But I'm not crying only for my children, I'm crying for everyone. It's a very sad life in my village, all over Mexico. Many people can't bear the poverty. That's why they cross the border to find a more dignified life.

Chapter Three

A Difficult Trip

It seems that I don't want to come back here again.

Antonia

Antonia's words break my concentration as I tally earnings from the weavings we've sold over the past two weeks. She's leaning toward me, a wry smile on her lips as her eyes widen and then narrow. Although she laughs a little as she speaks, we both know that she means what she says. She is rarely this honest with me. Although it hurts, I need to hear how she feels. I have been worried about her since she got off the plane. I would never have asked her to come to New Mexico had I known that she was still recovering from a serious illness, that Paulina had just gotten married, and that two of her nephews had died when their new bicycle went off the road and struck a tree. They didn't know how to make it stop.

"I'm really sorry, Antonia. If I had known all the things that happened to you before your trip, I would have told you to stay home. I know that you only made a little money this visit. And you had a terrible experience in Mexico City on your way here. But soon you'll be home."

Because she was sick before coming to visit me, Antonia couldn't weave and therefore had nothing to sell. While in New Mexico she embroidered some pieces that she sold, but she would go home with very little money. Antonia also didn't receive an honorarium for her visit because she didn't give a public talk. During the first two visits she received an honorarium for presentations she made throughout New Mexico and west Texas. In 2002 Antonia was loathe to accept the money and wept as my friend Lisa and I explained to her how "time is money" in the United States, and that she had given generously of her time and therefore deserved to be compensated. Antonia feared that God would feel that she was not a good person for accepting money for "just talking to people." After Antonia returned to Chiapas in 2006, I put together an honorarium from donations and sent it to her.

In retrospect, it was clear that I should have gone to Chiapas instead of asking Antonia to come to New Mexico. By Antonia coming to New Mexico, we could make progress on the book and sell weavings for her compañeras in Tsobol Antzetik. It seemed like a good plan, but it turned out to be at Antonia's expense.

Antonia returned to Chenalhó on July 12. It was 106 degrees that day along the US/Mexico border. After we said goodbye at the Juárez airport, I felt deep regret about putting her through the trip. I kept remembering her falling asleep on rides from place to place, and becoming quiet in the middle of a conversation. She had coped the best she could, and when she was safely home, we were both relieved.

For cultural and personal reasons, I didn't ask Antonia directly why the trip was so difficult for her. But in different ways throughout her stay she gave me clues. The trip in 2006 was Antonia's third to New Mexico. Although Antonia says that the economic inequalities between life in the United States and in her community are not difficult for her to accept, with each visit she has deepened her awareness of the inequality between us, and I think that the injustice of this weighed heavily on her during the third visit. Antonia glimpsed the economic differences during her first visit in 2002, but the warm welcome, gifts, and new adventures seemed to leave her with mostly positive feelings. On each of her visits she met with Mexican women who had migrated from Mexico to the United States. Those visits were laced with the joy of meeting fellow Mexicans trying to make new lives, and the sorrow of hearing the stories of the racism and poverty they faced. Little by little the contradictions in the United States and the disparity between the material realities of life in the United States and Mexico sank in, and she felt some righteous anger about this. That, too, could have influenced Antonia to say that she didn't want to come back.

Earlier during her visit we had talked about the inequality between us.

The inequality between us isn't a problem, although as you say, you have a lot, you are earning well, and I don't have much. But what can we do about it? You're earning here, you have a job here. I don't earn anything because I don't have a job. That's the life of Chiapanecos, no? I see that it takes a lot of work to sell our weavings, to arrange everything, and to find donations for our projects. You have all sold a lot of weavings for us, and it's a big help. That's why I'm not angry about the inequality between us. Since we're friends, it's great help what you all are doing here.

It's complicated for both Antonia and me that I have much more access to

(FACING PAGE): Photo by Christine Eber, 2002.

money and other resources than she does. Because I am her son's godmother, we have a culturally acceptable framework to help explain Mike's and my gifts to her family, such as the money for Alberto's education. In both indigenous and non-indigenous communities, godparents are a source of economic and moral support throughout a child's life. As Antonia's *compañera* in the struggle for social justice, albeit at a distance, I am a conduit for bringing the political and material realities of the groups that she is a part of to the attention of the organizations that I belong to. Over the years I have brought my family, friends, colleagues, students, and members of Las Cruces-Chiapas Connection to meet with Antonia and members of her co-ops so that they can see that I am only one small link in a large network of people who care about what they stand for and want to assist them in advancing their goals.

If asked whether she would ever return to New Mexico, Antonia probably would have said, "Only God knows." However, in September 2008 she traveled again to the United States with Carol-Jean McGreevy-Morales, who had been in Chiapas for Mariano's college graduation. Antonia spent a week in Pittsburgh and then traveled back to Chiapas with Carol-Jean's husband, Jorge. Her trip to Pittsburgh was just the right length, in the cool fall air, and she didn't travel alone.

TRIP TO NEW MEXICO, 2006

My bus from Chiapas arrived in Mexico City in the morning, and when I got off the bus to catch a taxi to the airport, a man came immediately and asked me, "Where are you traveling?" I didn't know who the man was. I thought that he was a man who helps people who don't know how to travel very well, who guides them to the waiting area. "Come," he said.

In the waiting room he went to one side, and I went to the opposite side to get my backpack. He saw that I had my backpack and came to help me carry it. I told him, "I'm not going yet. I'm going to sit down." I had decided to go to the airport later. "No, come," he said. I thought that he wouldn't let me sit down there in the waiting area. "I'm going to rest someplace. I don't know."

He took my backpack, and I followed behind him until I saw that we were coming out to the taxi stand. When I got there, he threw my backpack inside the taxi. Then I realized that he was a taxi driver. After he put my backpack inside, I told him, "I'm not going to go. I don't want to get in the car." But he said to me, "Get in."

"I'm not going to go yet," I told him. With a lot of effort I took my backpack out, and I didn't get in the car.

I decided to return to the waiting area to spend a few hours because it was still morning. It was still early. I walked about ten or fifteen meters on my return, and another taxi driver came! He said to me, "Let's go. Where are you going? I'll take you there."

"No, I'm not going to go yet. I'm going to wait. Someone is waiting for me," I told him. It was a lie, because no one was waiting to pick me up. I just lied so that I could save myself from the taxi driver. But he said, "Let's go." When we were walking back, he kept trying to convince me to go in his taxi.

Later another man came and asked me, "Where are you going?"

"Well, later I'm going to the airport," I told him.

"Ah, no, come now," he said.

"Leave me alone," I told the taxi driver.

He brought me to a booth. "Come here," he said.

"Okay," I said, as I was afraid of what he was going to say. I didn't know who this person was. I had to listen to him.

"Where are you going?" he asked.

"I'm going to the airport."

"Did you bring your papers?"

"Yes, I have all my papers." I had my passport, my visa, and my identification card in my hand.

"Show them to me," he said.

I didn't know what to do, and I began to show him my passport and some papers.

"You're missing the seal." Something like that, he told me. I didn't hear him well. Then I said, "What seal? I have all my papers."

"No, you're missing some. You have to pay a fine."

"How much?"

"Two thousand pesos."

"But I don't have it. I only brought 200 pesos for my food," I told him.

"No, you have to pay. If you don't pay, I'll have to take you to the office."

"Truthfully, I don't have it. What am I going to pay with? I don't have it."

"Yes, you have to pay. If you don't, I'll have to call the office." He began to call on his cell phone. I don't know how many minutes he talked. He was saying, "I'm checking a woman who didn't bring her papers, her seals. I don't know what name is on the papers." Then, while he was talking, I told him, "I'm going to call, too." And I began to look for phone numbers, and while I was looking, he was calling. I don't know, but I think it was a lie what he was saying. When I was looking for the number, he returned my passport to me. And that was that.

After this man left, another taxi driver came and said to me, "Let's go. I'm going to take you where you want to go."

"I'm going to the airport," I told him.

"Let's go then. You can trust me."

I didn't want to go.

"Trust me. I'm going to leave you where you want to go."

"You mean it?" I said.

"Yes, I'm going to drop you off there."

"Well, how much does it cost then?"

"Whatever the meter says."

I decided to go because I was afraid to return to the waiting area because I wasn't sure which direction it was. There are several areas where you can wait. That's why I was afraid I would go in the wrong direction. I thought, "Well, it's better to go. We'll see what happens, if it comes out good or bad. "Well, what can I do? I'm going."

I decided to go with the driver. I thought that he was a good man, because he was a little older. So I decided to go. I went. But he didn't tell me how much it would cost. Then when I was near the airport, he said, "Pay your fare."

"How much is it?" I asked.

"Pay me 900 pesos."

"Nine hundred pesos?! That's why I asked you, 'How much are you going to charge?' And you didn't want to tell me. I didn't want to go with you, and you just forced me to come in your taxi. I'm not going to pay this amount. I don't have it. I only have 200 pesos," I told him.

"No, pay me. If you don't want to pay, I'm going to take you back, and you're going to pay double."

"I don't have it. I only have 200 pesos," I told him. We went back and forth like that. We were still a bit far from the airport when he began to ask me for the money. When we were near the airport, he said, "Okay, although it's only a little, pay me 450 pesos, that's half."

"But I don't have it." I only gave him 200. "I don't have more."

"Do you want to pay or not?" He was nearly yelling at me.

Since I had 470 pesos I decided to pay him 400. "I will give you 400 pesos, and that leaves 70 for my food." I gave him the 400 and with that I got out. But he didn't leave me very close to the airport, at the entrance to the airport. He left me at a distance of about 40 meters, I think.

When I got out, I met two men. "Why are you getting out here?" they asked me.

"Because the taxi driver didn't want to leave me at the airport. I wanted to go to the airport but I got out here because he wanted me to pay him 900 pesos for the ride," I told them.

"You shouldn't have paid that," one man who spoke very well told me.

He was very kind. "You should have asked for help. You should have made a sign with your hand, and I could have come to help you."

"I don't know how to do that," I said.

"You should have taken his registration number," the man said.

But in that moment I didn't know what to do. I was afraid. So I went by foot to look for the airport, and soon I could tell that it was an airport. The men showed me how to get there.

When I arrived in the airport, it was easy for me. Although I waited all day in the airport, I was safe. If it wasn't for the taxi drivers, well, it would have come out fine. By asking questions, I could have done it alone. I have seen how when you arrive in the waiting area at the bus station, you go to buy the authorized taxi ticket. I've seen how to do that. But the taxi driver came to try to persuade me to go with him. That's when it started to go bad.

I arrived about 9 in the morning in the airport. I was there many hours alone, waiting, and bored from waiting many hours. But I wasn't afraid anymore. Later, around 2 or 3 in the afternoon, a very friendly woman sat near me, and we began to talk. After we talked over a half hour and I told her everything that had happened to me, she said, "Do you want to eat something? Let's see if there's something to eat." But I had already bought my taco with my 70 pesos. The woman invited me to eat a sandwich, too, and I went with her. She was very friendly.

"You might want to carry the sandwich on the plane because sometimes they don't serve food," she told me. I didn't want to be ungrateful for the sandwich, so I said, "Yes." Then she bought me the sandwich. I don't know how much she spent on me.

Then she left, and I remained. Later another woman came. She recognized my blouse. "And where are you from?" she asked me.

"I'm from Chiapas."

"I'm from Chiapas, too, from Tapachula!" she said. We began to talk about everything, and she also invited me to eat a sandwich that she had brought with her. After all my troubles, I didn't go hungry.

Chapter 4

Faith and Love

I am a Catholic and a Zapatista, no? But I will always be Catholic because God is the rock.

Antonia, June 28, 1998

Antonia didn't have a cargo dream calling her to work in the Word of God, as her husband did. When Domingo was still single, he would often get drunk and end up in jail for fighting. One day not long after leaving jail, he met a catechist who invited him to enter the church to hear the Word of God. Although Domingo didn't take him up on his offer, about a month later he had a dream that he considers his calling to become a lay preacher.

In Domingo's dream, Saint Peter found him in the town square and brought him before an assembly of elders and asked their permission to give him the *cargo* of making balls of incense. The elders agreed, and Domingo set to work making incense balls and lighting them so that their smoke rose to heaven as an offering to the saints. Soon after this dream, Domingo had another one in which the elders told him that he was going to enter church to hear the Word of God. Three or four weeks later he did just that. Domingo continued going to church, and little by little he gave up drinking completely.[1]

Despite not having a cargo dream, Antonia never turned away from her commitment to Word of God Catholicism after she attended her first service at age seventeen, nor has she abandoned the many traditional beliefs and practices aimed at maintaining peace with her fellow humans. Antonia's beliefs about God, community, and justice became part of her being long before the Zapatistas arrived in her community. They were important preparation for her more overt political activity in "the holy struggle."

Today Antonia's faith is based on a skillful balancing of parallel and often contradictory worldviews that create a framework of beliefs and practices in which spiritual and practical matters, and Mayan and Catholic worldviews co-

(FACING PAGE): Candles and incense lit for a service in a community chapel. Photo courtesy of Bill Jungels, 2009.

exist but do not merge. Like many women in the Word of God and Zapatista movements in Chiapas, Antonia has found a way to be Catholic and Tzotzil-Maya on her own terms, appropriating elements of both worldviews that are relevant to her life and that benefit her, while leaving other elements behind.

Pox is an element of traditional ritual that Antonia and other believers in the Word of God maintain should be left behind. They argue that *pox* is easily abused and drains family resources. Also, the material outlay for prayers and saints' feasts can drain collective resources. Word of God Catholics still participate in saints' feasts and do not consider the expenses exorbitant, but they maintain that *pox* offered in feasts and the *pox*, chickens, and other accoutrements of prayer are unnecessary. Candles and incense are all that God needs, they say. Sodas will do instead of rum.[2]

Another less apparent drawback of the traditional idea about reciprocating with deities is fear about offending them by neglecting to respect them properly through prayers and offerings. This fear also extends to social relationships, which must constantly be kept in balance through reciprocal giving. Antonia gains some relief from anxiety in the Word of God, which places the focus on working together in community with the understanding that the Christian God will provide for all his children. Nevertheless, she continues to reciprocate in a variety of social contexts, such as in *joyol*, the traditional bride petition.

Antonia grounds her faith in prayer and fasting. She divides prayers into two kinds—*k'opetik* (*rezos*, traditional prayers) and *oraciones* (Word of God prayers). The distinction she makes between these prayers reflects a key tension in her life between traditional Mayan beliefs and practices and those of the Word of God.

There are different kinds of prayers. Prayers that preachers in the Word of God pray are called *oraciones*. Believers in the Word of God are in favor of these kinds of prayers. In these prayers we don't use *pox*, just candles. We Catholics don't like *pox*. Not only the Catholics, also the other religious ones, like the Presbyterians and the Pentecostals, they don't like it either.

There are other kinds of prayers that the believers don't like—for example, if a person is sick and he wants a *j'ilol* to pray for him, and the *j'ilol* asks for a chicken and *pox*. *J'iloletik* usually ask for *pox* when they're going to pray for another person. We call these prayers *rezos*, or traditional prayers.

A *rezo* is very difficult to do because it requires witnesses—four people, two on each side of the *j'ilol*. The witnesses cleanse the sick person with the chicken. Domingo doesn't like it when a chicken is used in prayers either. He says, "It's better to have an *oración*, because it comes out the same. Both the *j'ilol* and we talk to God. That's what matters."

Also, some *j'iloletik* become like a witch. They can do things in many ways, from good to bad. If the *j'ilol* uses prayer for good, well, that's fine. We just don't agree with the *pox* and using prayer to hurt people.

In an *oración* no one gives food to those who come to pray for a little while and then return to their homes. We don't make meals for them. When Domingo was sick in 2002, many people, both Catholics and Protestants, came to pray, and they stayed all day and night. That's why we had to feed them. But most of the time when a person is very sick, people only come for a little while and then go home. They don't ask for food or anything.

We have a tradition in my township that we always fast. Fasting for me is when I eat once a day at six or seven at night. For some people it is when they give up eating but still drink water or soft drinks. For others fasting is when they don't take anything until the middle of the day for three days. On the third day they begin to eat again. We make promises and put out candles and incense and pray.

They say that it's best to fast three times a year, at the beginning of the year in January, again in June, and then at the end of the year in December. At the beginning of the year we ask for a blessing, for good things all year, and to continue living until the end of the year. Later, in the middle of June, we give thanks that everything has been fine for the past six months, that we haven't been sick a lot, and that no one in the family has died. We also ask God that no sickness will come, because *vo'olaltik* [the rainy season] is the time when many people have diarrhea. Then at the end of the year, we give thanks for everything that the Earth has given us to eat all year long, and we ask forgiveness for any mistakes we have made because we know that we are only human beings. It's necessary to ask forgiveness for everything bad that we have done.

According to the ancestors, couples must agree on whether to fast or not, but I think differently. At times I want to fast alone from my own thoughts and ideas. I want to ask for something about my own life, and I have the right to do that. For the past three years I fasted by myself each December. I asked the Mother Virgin of Guadalupe for her blessing because December is when her feast day falls. We respect the images of the Virgin of Guadalupe, the Apostle Saint Peter, and all the saints. We pray for what we need and they help us. The Virgin of Guadalupe helps women especially. She is very strong. We women respect her a lot.

At times we also fast in the Zapatista support base to ask for justice. We make an agreement that on such and such a day we will all fast together. Sometimes we get together in the church. We put some money together to buy candles, or we buy our own candle to carry to church. Together we pray to God that another war doesn't begin, that another massacre doesn't come to pass.

Before coming to live with Antonia, I didn't have a strong sense of my own spiritual path, except for a belief in the power of love. But when I was in Chenalhó, I didn't always recognize love, perhaps due to the lack of the physical expressions of it that I was accustomed to, such as hugging and kissing, or saying "I love you." From my understanding, I saw love in the affection lavished on babies, in the casual physical intimacy between people, and in children and parents looking after one another on a daily basis. I also saw love in the willingness to listen for hours to fellow villagers discuss a problem, and in the passion for working in collectives despite differences and tensions.

Love undoubtedly holds different meanings for Antonia and other Tzotzil-Mayas than it does for me. Antonia's and my ideas of love seem to be most alike in the ways we experience close interdependence between people and in how we understand the message of love in the life of Jesus Christ.

Through reading the Bible, Antonia has learned about Christian love, *kanum bail*. Antonia seems to see this form of love as an extension of feelings of close interdependence with kin. During one of our last talks for this book, Antonia clarified her understanding of love by distinguishing between the romantic love that her children are influenced by and the love that she has known that grows over time from living in daily contact with kin. For Antonia, the latter kind of love entails feeling another's pain. "K'ux ta yo'onton smalal" (She loves her husband) means literally "her heart hurts for her husband."[3] Antonia added that this way of saying that one loves another means that one also esteems or respects the other person. She maintains that romantic love lacks esteem, respect, and empathy. Often romantic love entails no more than wanting another person, as in "skanoj smalal" (she wants her husband), which is how her children described their feelings for their prospective spouses. In Antonia's petition on behalf of Sebastian for his future wife, two lines show her effort to reconcile the two contrasting conceptions of love as desire, empathy, and esteem: "It's that my son here, he fell in love with your daughter. That's why we want to appreciate your daughter" (see Part 2, Chapter 4, page 95).

In Word of God Catholicism, Antonia has also learned about forgiveness. She has found in it forgiveness for her own transgressions and the importance of pardoning others for theirs. In Chenalhó it is difficult to live up to high standards of comportment in family, community, and spiritual arenas. Antonia empathizes with those who stop going to church or meetings in the resistance movement because she, too, has stopped going for periods of time and has struggled to show love to people and feel united with them. The Catholic teachings about social justice have helped Antonia see that above all one must love others and struggle together for a better life through creating social and economic relationships in which no one is oppressed or excluded.

While Antonia hopes that the lessons of the Zapatista movement will be-

come a part of the nation's conscience and constitution, she sees the movement as dependent on people who, unlike God, have feet of clay and do not
endure. Antonia's motivation and strength to participate in the holy struggle
seem to come primarily from believing in a God of the people who wants his
children to love one another and work together for peace with justice, irre-
spective of political movements.

Christ came to free the suffering people and to reveal injustices. It says in
the Word of God that only here on Earth can we act the way Christ says we
should. For example, I'm here in the desert, and you give me a glass of water
so I won't die of thirst. In the end Christ will say to you, "Thank you for giving me water when I was thirsty, for giving me food when I was hungry, for
giving me shelter when I had no place to stay." He says this even though you
did these things to me, not to God.[4]

The Bible says something about God being with the poor, right? He says,
"When two or three persons come together, I am in the middle."[5] God is
with his children. He doesn't want any of us to be exploited or to be treated
unjustly. When at times we have sadness and pain, God helps us overcome
this by giving us strength to do good things. God gives us everything that we
need. If God were talking to us, I think he would say, "I am with you. I'm not
going to abandon you if someone comes to threaten you. I'm accompanying
you."

That's why we continue to try to act like Christ. Although some people
say we aren't acting according to the Word of God, we think that we are acting as God would want us to. Of course, at times we fall into temptation because we're just people. But we know that there is only one God who makes
everything.

I think that Domingo is with God. If God were to talk to Domingo, I think
that he would say, "You are my chosen child." Look how Domingo is suffering. He's sacrificing his time and money to go to different communities. He
has to borrow transportation money in order to do his work. But we say that
his *cargo* isn't an ordinary one. It's a sacred *cargo*. The holy struggle we call it,
because in this struggle we bear it all, whether it's good or bad. At times people criticize and make fun of Domingo, but he keeps on going. Sometimes I
get discouraged and tell him, "It would be better if you stayed home because
you're just spending money." But he never gets discouraged. He never gives
up. He has a great deal of spirit to do his work, and he is totally committed.
I believe that Domingo will never leave the holy struggle until he dies. I have
to stay in the struggle with him, too. I have to back him up.

In the Word of God it says that a person standing on a living rock won't
fall. Even if wind comes, it won't carry her away. But a person standing on

sand, when the wind comes, it will quickly carry her away. When one is well prepared for problems, when something comes on top of a person, they won't feel anything. The problem can't make them fall. But if one isn't well prepared, if they are only standing on sand, they will easily fall. They'll go with the wind. They die. Those who aren't with us anymore in the holy struggle, it's as if they have died.[6]

For a while I didn't go to church or to meetings of the support base because I felt discouraged and that I was wasting my time. I had lost my faith and inspiration, and I felt that it was better to stay at home and make a little money.

But it seems that God makes it come out the same whether we stay at home or go to the meetings. Even if I stay home and work, I don't make more money than if I went to church and to the meetings. Besides, if I had gone to the meetings, I would have felt more like working at home. When one has faith or is inspired, it's easier to work and time doesn't matter. Domingo and I have been thinking for a while that even if we don't make much money, God will repay us in the end. Sometimes one receives more than one gives.

I want to go back again to the meetings to share my faith and love with others. Although in my heart I still have faith, I don't share it if I don't go to meetings. When we go to meetings, we show our faith, friendship, love, and thoughts. We have to love one another. We take each others' hands to keep going.

It's been two or three months since my *compañeros* elected me to be a preacher. But I have learned about myself that it's easy to talk. What's hard is to act according to the Word of God. I want to uphold the truth, but at times what I do isn't good. I fall into temptation, as it says in the Lord's Prayer. Although I hear what God says, it's not enough to just listen. We have to analyze what's happening and act. I find that very hard. That's why I didn't accept becoming a preacher. But I'm not sure if it was good for me to decline the *cargo*. Maybe I did it because I didn't want to answer God's calling.

Although I'm not a preacher like Domingo or Guadalupe, I need to share God's words with my *compañeros*. Those who hear my voice might act on what I say. That's all the more good. Later they'll advise me if I don't act the way I talk.

There's a new liberation today. I understand the holy struggle, not like those brothers and sisters who don't. They don't think about why Jesus came to Earth, to liberate his children. It's sad for us that they don't realize that they suffer, too, that they are also exploited. For example, in the time of Jehovah, Moses came to the Earth to free his Israeli brothers and sisters because they were being manipulated by the bad government. Today some people don't see that the same thing is happening to them. The government is trying to divide people by offering handouts. Those who leave the resistance movement receive help from the government. But one can't get rich from government handouts. Although a family receives them, they seem to live more or less the same as us. Even though we don't take government handouts, we're not dying of hunger. Whether one takes the government handouts or not, it balances out. No one is very rich or very poor in our community.

Those who give up the struggle don't feel love anymore for their brothers and sisters. They don't want to help others, to struggle with others. Misunderstandings happened in the time of Israel, too. When Moses came to liberate the Israelites, some became angry and scolded Moses because they were suffering, hungry, and thirsty. All that they suffered in the past, we are suffering now.[7]

Chapter Five

Exodus

And I will bring them out from the peoples,
and gather them from the countries,
and will bring them into their own land,
and feed them on the mountains of Israel
by the watercourses, and in all the inhabited
parts of the land.

I will seek that which was lost,
and I will bring back the strayed,
and I will bind up the injured,
and I will strengthen the weak.
But the fat and the strong I will destroy.
I will feed them with justice.

Ezekiel 34:13 and 16

APRIL 2009

The phone rings. It's Alberto, Antonia's son and my godson. I haven't heard from him in a while. He's in North Carolina now, in Cherokee country. Each time he moves to a new place, I wish I could help him get to know the people, especially now, when he's around other Native Americans. But he tells me that he stays pretty much inside his apartment and the restaurant where he works. He always seems to meet one or two locals, young men with motorcycles, who give him rides to the store or the emergency room.

Last time he called, he wanted to know what kind of supplement he could take to make his muscles big. He told me that he wants to buy a car and build a house like other men who return from El Norte.

I want other things for him, including that he be cared for by people who

(FACING PAGE): Shawl left behind in the desert near Sasabe, a border community in Pima County, Arizona. Photo courtesy of Molly Molloy, 2005.

respect him, but these seem out of his reach. Why can't I accept that he is carving out his own life in the United States in his own way, even if he is transient, on the margins, and focused on material things? How can I expect him, without English and knowledge of my culture, to somehow see the emptiness of our consumer culture and join some local social justice group?

"Madrina, it's me, Alberto."

"Ah, Alberto, I've been thinking of you. How are you?"

"Well, more or less okay. But I'm thinking of leaving North Carolina. My boss doesn't pay me very well. I'm going to Atlanta. I've heard that I can find a better job there."

"Don't you want to stay where you are since you haven't been there very long? Perhaps your boss will give you a raise in time."

"Yes, but even then I won't make as much as the last restaurant I worked at. I'm sure I can make more money in another Chinese restaurant somewhere else."

Following Alberto's migrations around the United States has deepened my sense of how divided my country is—between rich and poor, and between people with skin the color of the Earth and cream-colored skin like mine. It has also made Chenalhó more like another home, and my own country more like a foreign place. Each time Alberto moves to a new place, I get on the Internet and find out about the town so when he calls I'll know about resources to help him. I've become quite knowledgeable about some little towns in several southeastern states. I even tried once to visit him. I had my ticket and a rental car reservation, but he left that town just before I was scheduled to arrive.

Over the years I have watched Alberto cross the ethnic and geographical boundaries of highland Chiapas and now the US/Mexico border. His view of the world began to expand when he attended middle school and high school in the town center of Chenalhó. Gradually he became estranged from his own culture and the movement for social justice that his parents had brought him up in. Alberto craved the things of the mestizo world to which he had not had access in his home when he was younger, such things as sodas, chips, and name-brand sneakers. Antonia regretfully told me that he spent the money that Mike and I sent him for his midday meal at school on coca-cola.

Once or twice when his older brothers were working in Mexico City, Alberto took a bus to visit them—his first experience outside of the state of Chiapas. The Cristóbal Colón bus line carries thousands of indigenous people back and forth from rural areas to the nation's capital and other cities and farms where they work for periods of time. Before Mexico's debt crisis in the 1980s, indigenous families in Chiapas were also on the move, but usually by foot or in the back of trucks. They had to travel to work for periods of time on distant sugar plantations, cattle ranches, or public works projects to augment semi-subsistence farming. These jobs were demeaning and necessitated being away from their families for months at a time, but they kept hunger at bay (Rus 1995; Rus and Collier 2003).

The exodus from Chiapas to the United States snuck up on me and Antonia. Starting in the 1990s, Antonia began to hear about men in her community who had left for the United States. When I moved to New Mexico to teach in 1995, I used *Shadowed Lives*, Leo Chavez's book on migrants in southern California. As border enforcement became stiffer in California, migrants found more remote routes to cross into the United States, many through the Arizona and New Mexico desert, closer to my home. Reports of deaths became more common in local newspapers, and groups began to form to confront the humanitarian crisis.

My awakening to the crisis came in 2007 when I went with Sally Meisenhelder, a friend who had been volunteering with "No More Deaths" in Tucson, to the port of entry in Nogales, Sonora, to provide assistance to returned migrants. I was shocked by what I saw and heard. Together we listened to stories of traumatic experiences crossing the desert and being detained and removed. We eventually wrote an essay that was translated into Spanish. I distributed it to all my friends in Chiapas in the hope that the migrants' sad stories would influence them not to leave Mexico.

Then the day came in February 2008 when I got an e-mail from Mariano telling me what I had been fearing for a long time:

hello cristina
how have you been? I hope in good health. This is the message from my mother:

Hello *comadre*. How are you? How is Michael? And all of my friends there. I send a warm greeting for them. . . .

In truth, I feel sorry to have to write to you now. I am a little sad, because what I have to tell you is something sad. I feel very bad having to tell you this. But I believe it is necessary.

My son Alberto did not want to study anymore. He left school. We pleaded with him so much, his father and I, but we could not convince him. He just doesn't want to stay in school.

But the worst is, he decided to go to the United States. He left last Wednesday and today, Sunday, they were going to begin walking.

The truth is that we never wanted this, but he decided to do it this way.

We are so very worried that something will happen to him or that he will not be able to cross, or that he will not be able to bear the walk through the desert.

You see, he called us Friday, he was still in Sonora and today they were going to start walking and it would be four or five nights they would walk and we are so very worried. . . .

The only thing we want now is that he is able to pass and we pray so much for him. Perhaps he wants a better future but we know that it is not necessary for him to go that far to make life better, but this is what he wanted.

I am so sorry for all the work that you did to help him get the scholarship. I know that he just did not know how to make the most of it and in truth, I want to apologize to you for my son and for myself because I could not convince him not to go.

As soon as he calls us again, we will let you know. There is so much more to say, but for now I will say goodbye.

Your *comadre*, Antonia

P.S. This is my mother's message explaining to you my little brother's situation. Disgracefully, he left school and decided to go to the United States as a wetback.

I read and reread the message from Antonia, feeling panic at not knowing where in Sonora Alberto had called from and where he was headed to in the United States. I struggled to reconcile how he was coming into my country for the first time with how I always imagined he would come, with papers and with my assistance.

Mariano's description of his brother as a *mojado* (wetback) saddened me, but I understood his perspective. He has staked his future on education and can't let other options tempt him.

Antonia's words reminded me of the great loss most parents in Chenalhó feel when their children leave them and their communities. Those in the resistance movement badly need their young people's spirits and energies to keep the movement strong.[1] All parents depend on their older children's assistance with housework and fieldwork. Reading Antonia's letter, I also remembered the night of Alberto's sixth grade graduation, when Domingo wept upon hearing his son's decision to go on to middle school. He felt despondent about losing Alberto's help in the fields and in cutting firewood. But then as now, Domingo and Antonia feel Alberto's absence because they love him and fear for him. They will not be at peace until he returns. Although cash is a critical need, for mothers like Antonia it doesn't compensate for the loss of a son.

After the news from Antonia sank in, I called Sally, who was in Nogales, and asked her to be on the lookout for Alberto. She spoke with all the migrants from Chiapas. Unfortunately, they were from different townships and did not know Alberto.

After ten days we still had no word of Alberto. We suspected that he was headed to a community of Chiapanecos or perhaps had already arrived. Over the past few decades many Chiapanecan communities have formed throughout the United States (Gómez López et al. 1995).

On March 2, 2008, I received an e-mail from Mariano that the man who had helped Alberto cross the border came to see his parents to tell them that he had made it across safely and was working to pay off the debt he incurred to cross ($2,500). About a week later Alberto called his parents and told them that he was okay and had a job picking fruit in an orchard in Florida. A month or so later I learned that Alberto had called to say that he was now working with his uncle and cousin, who had been in the United States awhile. They found each other among people from Chenalhó working in the same area, as they had not crossed together.

Ironically, although Alberto's uncle managed to find his nephew in a foreign country, I was unsuccessful in my attempts to locate Alberto until he finally called me on June 2, 2008. He was no longer working in Florida but living in Springfield, Massachusetts, waiting for work to begin on a tobacco farm. He was sharing a small room with his uncle and cousin and five other men. Food was running out. Could I send $100 to tide them over until they received their first paycheck?

In July 2006, two years before Alberto left Chiapas, Antonia shared her thoughts on immigration.

My children aren't going to live in other countries as you do. Even if they go to work in Cancún or Mexico City, they're only going to other states, not other countries. They always return. Mariano isn't going to live here in Chenalhó if he continues his studies, but the rest are going to stay here.

Look how they are enforcing the border right now. They aren't letting people cross the border. And so people are going to be afraid, and not many are going to cross. They're giving up the idea, they're staying, I believe.

For me the border enforcement is a good thing because I don't want my children to cross that way, without papers, because they could die. I've seen how it is there. I don't want my children crossing without papers. I'm afraid for them.

But many are still leaving. I think they just don't want to suffer as we're suffering. They don't want to wear just any shoes. Now they want to wear shoes that cost a lot and expensive clothes. Now they want to have cars, a two-story house—they want to have everything. That's why many are leaving for the other side. Meanwhile the family that stays suffers a lot. And those who go, they suffer crossing the border. And when they are over there, they suffer, too.

That's why the young people need money. But us, we're fine with simple things. We can survive with that.

Alberto has been thinking about going. He was going to go together with his cousin, but I didn't help him get the money for his travel. If I had helped him with his passage, he wouldn't be here any longer.

Maybe he'll go. One of them, of the four boys, maybe they'll leave. They're thinking about it.

There are *polleros* [human traffickers] in Chamula. Many from my community have already crossed with them. I don't know exactly if the people who left are in Florida or in other places. I don't know. Because one of my nephews tried to go to Michigan. That's why I don't know if everyone is in Florida or in other cities.

Those who owe money, well, I say that it's worth going because if they stay in their houses, how are they going to pay off their debt? I don't know how. But those who don't have debts, it's not necessary to leave. They're just going to suffer. That's why, as I've told Alberto many times, "It's fine just being here. Although we don't have enough money, we're happy."

"No, but I want to have a car, I want to have a good house. While I'm still young, I can do it. Later, I can't do it," he says. "Besides, I'm not going to find work after I complete my studies. Perhaps it's better that I just go work now."

Since I didn't let him leave, he's making the effort to study. But I don't know if he's going to continue or give up his studies.

"After a while they aren't going to let people cross," he says. "It's better that I go right now, not wait," he says.

"I don't want you to suffer because I know with my own eyes how it is over there. It's very hot and you're going to suffer," I told him.

"Well, why don't you give me some money?" That's all he answered.

"The way I grew up no one gave me money, but I'm alive right now," I said. "I grew up with suffering, too, but right now I'm alive, and if there's only tortilla that's enough," I told him. "Work here in the fields. There's a little land for you."

"Many here have a car, and I'm not going to have one," he said. "It's my dream to have a car."

"Well, sure, cars look pretty, but if we don't have one, it's okay."

"I'll see, while I'm still young," he said.

It seems that Alberto doesn't want to suffer. He says that he suffers from everything, that he doesn't have money, that he doesn't have clothes, and I don't know whatever else he needs. We can't give him money because we don't have money ourselves.

The children want to change their lives. They don't want to live like we have lived. They don't want to eat the way we eat, the way we nourish ourselves.

MARCH 2009

For a year I was able to convince Alberto not to go. I kept telling him, "You can't make it across. It's very sad and difficult. You might die of thirst, hunger, or heat. They might return you or beat you. Your feet will be blistered from walking in the desert. You're going to suffer."

But I was only able to convince him to stay for one year. The following year, in 2008, he started to talk with those who know how to transport people, the *polleros*. They were saying that a person can make a lot of money up there, that there's a lot of work, and I don't know what else the *polleros* say to find a lot of people to take across.

In February 2008 Alberto started to talk about going. He didn't want to tell us about it much before this. He only began to talk about it four or five days before he left. First he only told me, "I'm going to the United States. Help me find the money."

"Why do you want to leave? Don't you see that there are no other sons left in the house to help your father?" I told him.

"Yes, but I want to earn some money."

He didn't want to tell his father because he knew that his father wouldn't let him go.

When the man who was going to take him came to the house, Alberto told me, "The man who's going to help me is here, and he wants the money for my ticket. I'm going to go."

"As you wish. How much do you need?" I said.

"A thousand dollars."

And so I gave him the money that I had put away, and the rest I began to borrow. He had already thought out what he was going to do. He had planned it out. There was nothing else I could do.

Then two or three days before he left, he told his father, "I'm going to go to the United States."

His father couldn't say much because Alberto was on the point of leaving.

"Well, if that's what you've decided, then what can I do, because you don't want to be like me. Although I'm poor, I'm living with my poverty," Domingo said.

"No, look, there's nothing else that I can do here to earn money, and you always suffer a lot. I don't have money for my clothes, and we owe a lot. While I'm still young, I have to go to find my work," he said.

At that point Domingo couldn't say much.

"That's fine if you want to go, but you're going to leave me alone," Domingo said, and he began to cry. He was sad because Alberto is his last son who can help him in his work.

What I cried about is that he left school. I didn't want him to give up his studies.

"It seems that I'm not getting anywhere with my studies. I'm going," he said.

On Tuesday I began to prepare his things. I washed all the clothes that he had. On Wednesday in the morning I began to make his toasted tortillas. I wrapped his tortillas in a bag, and we made them in pieces so he could carry a large quantity. I also gave him medicine for a cold, alcohol to clean wounds, and a needle in case he got a splinter. The *pollero* told him that he needed those things. And with that he said goodbye. February 14th he left.

After two or three days he arrived in Altar, Sonora. He called us, "I'm here in Sonora now. Tonight we're going to set off."

"Good. We've been worrying about you. When are you going to call us again?"

"Not until I'm in the United States."

"Okay."

After that we were waiting for the call. No calls for fifteen or twenty days. No calls. We were worried. "What happened to him? Is he alive or dead? Are they walking or resting? Where are they? How are they?"

But there was no call. No communication.

Then after I think it was twenty days, he called, and the owner of the telephone near our house came to let me know.

"Are you going to answer your son's call?"

I went running. Which son could it be? Because I didn't know who it was. Could it be Alberto? It was Alberto.

"Mamá, I'm here now in the United States. I made it," he said.

"And how are you?"

"Really tired. I got here really tired, and I hurt my hand," he said. "I think that I hurt my hand because you were really sad for me."[2]

"Ah, but we aren't that sad," I told him. "I'm not crying," I told him. "Is your wound serious?" I asked him.

"Yes, it's big. I don't know when I hurt myself because I didn't feel anything because I was so afraid," he said.

"How did it happen? How did it go for you?"

"Well, it's really dangerous. But, yes, I was able to cross. I made it here," he said.

"Do you have work yet?"

"We still haven't found any yet because we just arrived."

So after that we began to feel happy because he made it alive and he achieved his goal. I was sad when he left, but now, although I miss him, since he's not dead, I think that he'll return. It's not the same as when one dies. Then you're never going to see them again or hear their voice. But since he's just a long ways away and still alive, I'm not very sad. I'm only sad for his illness, because he got sick there. I don't know if they are able to cure him or how he's going to be.

September 10, 2009

Last weekend I flew to the small Alabama town where Alberto is working. After my failed attempt to see him in July, until I saw his face behind the counter in the restaurant, I was afraid he wouldn't be there. But there he was.

I almost didn't recognize him because his face was so light. I was looking for a face the color of milk chocolate, but his was almost as light as those of his Chinese coworkers. I learned that his work schedule doesn't leave much time to be in the sun. He works from 9:30 a.m. to 9:30 p.m. and has one day off. He doesn't go outside from the time he leaves for work in the morning until he returns at night, and he spends most of his day off resting inside his apartment. He prepares food for himself at the restaurant when he is hungry. He shares an apartment with the Chinese workers where he sleeps on a mattress on the living room floor. He rationalizes not having his own room and the grueling work routine because his food and rent are free. He accepts his situation as the price he must pay for a job in the United States. The days go fast, he says.

Each time Alberto receives his pay, he walks across the street to Western Union in Wal-Mart and sends about $100 home to his parents and an additional payment for the car he asked them to buy with money he sends home. He only keeps a little to buy the things he needs.

During my weekend with Alberto we accomplished many things, but we were often blocked by his lack of a photo ID. I never realized how important one is in the United States until we tried to get him a library card, a cell phone, and a return visit to the clinic, where they agreed to see him once without a photo ID but not after that. (A very kind doctor who spoke some Spanish prescribed him some antibiotics to clear up his infection.)

Soon after I arrived, Alberto told me that when he returns to Chiapas, he wants to go back to school to study social work, the career he was pursuing when he dropped out. He asked me to tell his mother when I send the photos of our visit that he really means it when he says he is going back to school.

I am sad to see Alberto have to endure more time in the United States away from family and friends in order to pay off a car and feel that his one trip to El Norte has been worth the sacrifice. But he has gone through a lot to be in my country and seems to feel that when this chapter of his life is over, he will put it all behind him and start life again in Chiapas, with a car and a house. But these won't be something to be proud of, he says. Pride will come with an education and being able to live a dignified life as part of a family and community again.

Chapter 6

Death

Of all the topics in this book, death embodies how alike, yet different, Antonia and I are. One of the greatest differences between us is that death is much more a part of Antonia's life than it is of mine. Antonia never lost a child, which makes her fortunate among women in her community. But since childhood she has spent countless days and nights accompanying sick and dying relatives and neighbors of all ages. In contrast, my life has not involved daily contact with illness and death.

I was visiting Antonia when Domingo was gravely ill in 2002 and witnessed the outpouring of support that the couple received. I joined the dozen or more friends and relatives sleeping on straw mats on the floor in the kitchen house for several nights. One photo that I took during that time symbolizes for me the experience of illness and death in Chenalhó. In the photo, eight-year-old Rosalva stares at a mountain of firewood stacked against the wall of her house. The wood arrived load by load on the backs of male relatives and neighbors who knew that Domingo couldn't provide firewood for his family and visitors while he was sick.

While people experience death personally in whatever culture they live, Antonia's experiences with death are profoundly communal in contrast to mine. Antonia shares with her family and community beliefs and traditions that carry her through the days, months, and years of an illness and after a death. *Cham*, the Tzotzil word for "death," is the root of *chamel*, "illness," conveying the sense that illness begins the process of dying. In traditional beliefs, soul loss is the cause of illness, and the main goal of healing is to bring lost souls back into people's bodies. When a person dies, the part of the soul that most embodies their unique self leaves them for good.

But Tzotzil beliefs also enable people to reunite with the souls of their deceased loved ones each year in November. Sk'in Ch'ulelal, Fiesta of the Souls (called Días de los Muertos [Days of the Dead] in other parts of Mexico), is a family and community celebration between the living and dead held in cemeteries and in homes. On November 2, families set out chairs in front of tables that they have loaded with tamales, beef, peanuts, oranges, bananas, shrimp, soft

drinks, rum, candles, and marigolds. The next day relatives and friends visit each others' homes to partake of the food.[1]

Antonia lost her father in 1991 after he had been living many years in a weakened state from chronic bronchitis. No one is quite sure how old Hilario was when he died because keeping track of age was not a priority for Pedranos until recently. But Antonia had her father in her life a long time.

We felt very sad when my father died. We missed him. Every morning, every day, we were used to seeing him there in the house. Although I lived apart from my father, each time when I came to visit, I would see him there. After he died, well, we missed him. It was sad. I remember when Felipe was growing up, he always respected my father. My father made him toys and everything. My father was very kind when he was sick. When he drank, he wasn't very kind, but when he was sick, he changed a lot.

When my father died, we got together with a lot of people, about one hundred, I think. We mourned for two nights. We prayed and made food. They also selected people who would stay to care for the house after we took my father to the cemetery. Two couples stayed behind. They had the responsibility to sweep and burn chiles to scare the Devil away, so that he would escape from the house. Right after they brought my father out of the house, the couples started to burn the chiles. When the chiles were burning, they quickly began to sweep.

When it was time to bury my father, some men went to open the ground where he would go. And when the ground was ready to put him in, they came back to carry him there. It's necessary to choose an old man to carry the soul of the dead person. He carries a little gourd of water with three leaves of the *snichim anima* [flower of the dead].

When the dead person is brought out of the house, this old man has to walk three times around the house and call the soul to the cemetery. All the while he says the name of the deceased, "La, Hilario. La." [Come, Hilario. Come.] After he has gone three times around the house, they carry the dead person to the cemetery. The old man is the first to go down the path.

After that, all the people went to the cemetery. There they put some little sticks in the coffin for my father to defend himself, to defend his soul. They say that upon arriving at the cemetery, animals come to attack the soul. That's why they put little sticks in for him to defend himself. There they also put his clothes, not all of them, only the new ones, or the ones that he still used. The oldest ones they burned in the cemetery. It's necessary to burn

(FACING PAGE): Celebrating Sk'in Ch'ulelal (Day of the Dead). Photo by Christine Eber, 1987.

all the things that are no longer any use to the dead person so that he leaves with all his things. That's what they say.

Also, when he was inside the Earth, we had to throw handfuls of earth, three handfuls each person. The Earth is our soul's substitute, so that we won't die, too.

When all that was finished, the men put my father in the Earth and made him a little house. In the past they used to make little houses of straw. But now they use tin for the roof because you can't find straw easily. The little house looks like a new house, not very good like a real house, but it's a little house. And there the deceased person remains.

Then every year in the month of November we go to the cemetery to offer candles, flowers, and food to celebrate Sk'in ch'ulelal.

Do you know what I said to my children? I told them that I don't want a coffin when I die. I've noticed that coffins are decorated, and there's a sheet. The coffins are well made. But while I'm alive, I sleep on wood boards with only a blanket. I have lived with suffering. It's not right that my body rots in the ground inside a special thing.

I'd rather be buried on a board. I want them to put four corn candles at my side and flowers on top of the straw mat they wrap me in because flowers bring me happiness when I'm alive and also because I like flowery things— my clothes, my ribbons, my belt. I want to wear the *sat cu'il* [ceremonial blouse] in my tomb. I'm going to make a blouse like that to be buried in.

I've been thinking about this for many years. I've already told my idea to Domingo and my children. They know. "You're crazy," Domingo says. He says this because now it's common to be buried in a coffin. That's why they want to put me in a coffin.

We'll see if they want to follow my wishes. My children say that they will be ashamed if I go to the cemetery on a board. They think that people will say that they don't want to buy me a coffin. My children say they want to give me more respect with a coffin. They don't want to respect me now, but when I'm dead they want to adorn my body! What use is giving me respect when I'm dead?

"If you want to respect me, then respect me now! If you want to give me something, then give it to me right now! After I'm dead, what use is it? A coffin is just going to rot." That's what I said to my children.

Chapter 7

Life So Far

It's not simple to live in the world.

Antonia

A writer from the New Mexico State University Communications Depart-
ment wrote an article about this book when I was finishing the first draft.
Daniella Deluca tried her best to present the complexities of Antonia's life in
her article and was not in charge of what happened to it after it left her desk.
The day it came out in the Las Cruces *Sun-News*, it was also on New Mexico
State University's web page. I decided to check it out online and was shocked
to see the caption under a picture of Antonia and me: "Professor Christine
Eber returns to chronicle the twenty-year friendship, simple life of a Tzotzil-
Maya woman."

Simple life? No! Please don't perpetuate that stereotype! But the idea is all
too familiar to me. Over the years I have read similar statements in students'
papers. These students assume that agrarian people in so-called "developing"
nations live simple lives because they are not technologically sophisticated and
lack extensive formal education. Sadly, these students only see value in the lives
of people in these circumstances in relation to their romantic notion of a time
when life was simpler, purer, and closer to nature.

At the same time, Antonia and her children sometimes idealize our
modern lives and conveniences. Although Antonia is critical of the trappings
of modernity, several of her children crave those things and don't have a critical perspective about them. I know that there is a more balanced place to be
where we can appreciate the strengths and weaknesses of both our ways of
life. But it is difficult to find balance in our grossly unequal world shaped by
global capitalism.

Although I am distressed by my students' ethnocentric ideas, I empathize
with them. When I was living with Antonia in 1987, I held many ethnocentric
notions and was guilty of assuming that by immersing myself in a dramati-

cally different society, I could strip myself of cultural preconceptions and gain a clearer view of myself and others that I couldn't achieve at home. This is, in fact, one of the reasons we do fieldwork. But once anthropologists are involved in the lives of the people we pledge to understand, it soon becomes clear that life is far more complex in all places and times than we can ever completely grasp. So we embrace ambiguity and complexity at home and "in the field" and call that knowledge. And I think it is, because it encourages us to keep talking to one another to get clearer pictures, to explore our biases and be transparent about them, and to resist constructing a précis of other cultures.[1]

About all the stuff of life that we can't completely understand, Antonia would say, "Only God knows." But at the same time that she places the unknown in God's hands, she is engaged in the life-long process of making her soul arrive while keeping her feet firmly planted in the material realities of life. Antonia shares with those who made their souls arrive in earlier times a conviction that the work of living on Earth should not be a lonely task. Reciprocal exchanges have always been fundamental to life in Chenalhó, but in recent decades working collectively has become a popular strategy to confront poverty and injustice. Still, it is often easier to work alone. Many of Antonia's neighbors have left the resistance movement due to the challenge of collective work. Sometimes Antonia tires of working with others, too.

Antonia isn't as consumed by collective work today as she was a decade ago. In recent years her life has been contracting to some extent, although she is still an active member of Tsobol Antzetik and the Zapatista general store co-op. When we were thinking of titles for this book, one of my proposals was, "A Tzotzil-Maya Woman and Her Expanding World." At the time I was thinking of how Antonia's collaborations with people outside her family have helped her expand her understanding of the world and her place in it. I wasn't thinking about how she has contracted at certain times in her life when she is sick, when life's lesions leave her wounded, or when she needs time to reflect.[2]

Antonia's relative withdrawal from community involvement at this time in her life seems to be about healing from illness and disappointments, as well as

(FACING PAGE): I made a cloth with a chicken design because I felt like learning other designs. I copied it from a curtain from Guatemala that my sister-in-law had. The chicken is a new design for us. I made two of these cloths in 2002 to sell on my first trip to the US. I wanted to make something special so that I could earn more money from my weavings. Molly from Las Cruces bought one of the two. She hung it on the wall of her kitchen, and it looked pretty there. I saw it again after three years, and I felt good that she knows how to respect things. I just want to say to all the people who bought my weavings, I am very happy you bought them so that you will have a remembrance of me and won't forget how I'm working. Photo courtesy of Michael O'Malley, 2010.

reflecting on the meaning of her actions so far, as she did while working on this book.

Antonia often uses the expression "one moment happiness, the next sadness" to describe the flux of her life. This image was presaged by a dream she had before she married Domingo in which a light surrounding his hat represented his good qualities, and darkness the problems that he was to bring into her life. To me Antonia's conception of the dialectic between dark and light, happiness and sadness, is like a butterfly that flutters into her life (or emerges from within her) but doesn't stay very long. Just as she recognizes joy, it departs. Then it returns, now in the form of pain. But it, too, leaves quickly, giving way to joy again.

During the latter stages of our work on this book, Antonia felt sad over problems with her adult children and her own and her family members' illnesses. Watching Felipe and Sebastian struggle to bring their souls to themselves as husbands and fathers while working for periods of time in distant cities has brought her many moments of sadness. In 2007 Sebastian and Juana left the house they had built near Antonia to live in Juana's community, and Felipe and Magdalena divorced in 2009. Antonia deeply regrets an argument with Sebastian that led him to leave his home community.

Antonia has a life-long *cargo* as the guardian of her four sons' souls. In contrast to how most parents in US society look forward to their children being independent when they are grown, in Tzotzil-Maya culture parents maintain that children need them throughout their lives. Antonia's guidance is also vital to her daughters, especially at this time when they are learning to be wives, and in Paulina's case, a mother. Antonia hasn't always known how to advocate for her daughters, especially during their middle and high school years. She is ambivalent about the benefits of education for young women in her community past sixth grade, even though this is what she wanted more than anything else in her life. The choices open to her children today are overwhelming to her. In response, I think that she feels that if her daughters follow in her footsteps, they will be safe and loved, while still being free to work with others in their communities to create a better world.

María, Antonia's own mother, hasn't always known how to guide her, but Antonia deeply values her advice and working alongside her in the weaving cooperative. Although Pedranos say that the saddest death is the death of a spouse, Antonia says that she will be saddest when her mother dies.

If a woman has the desire to do something, she can do it. With desire and faith one can do it. Since I was a little girl, I wanted to leave the house and find work as a teacher. I had a lot of desire to do things, to weave, to go places. It was my dream to leave, to know, to enjoy, and it came true. Like now, I'm out of the house. I know a little about different parts of my country.

Also, like my first child, Felipe, since childhood he wanted to be a driver. Each time when he went to San Cristóbal, where there are a lot of cars, he always inspected them. He acted as if he was a mechanic, looking under the car. That's how he was from when he was less than two years old. His dream was to be a driver, and now he is one.

We have talked about how since you [Cristina] were a child, you always wanted to be an anthropologist. And now you are one. I say that when a person plans something since their childhood, when they have a desire to do something, it's going to come true.

In the past Domingo didn't want me to leave the house, but I went out anyway in spite of the fact that he is easy to anger. Domingo has two sides, his faults and strengths. But now he understands that women have to have rights and be equal with men. He understands how to respect women. In the past he was different, but he has changed. As the Zapatistas say, "It's necessary for men and women to have mutual respect." Domingo has learned a lot about this, and that's why he lets me leave the house to go as far as here [the United States].

I've had freedom with my husband. If I didn't have freedom, my husband wouldn't let me go all the places I have gone. Perhaps he would have tied me up in the kitchen! Other husbands don't give their wives freedom, and also some women don't want it. But my husband and I are equal. God chose for me a man who has good sense, who is very kind to me, no? He loves me a lot, and he lets me go places.

For all these reasons, I haven't had the same situation as most women in my community. Also, I want to be different from other women. It seems that I have always been different from other women. I didn't want to stay in the house like my mother, like she was suffering. I saw that it wasn't very good for her.

Your mother could support you because she was a teacher and had learned things. In comparison, my mom didn't attend school. She didn't know anything about schooling. She didn't understand that I wanted to do more things because she hadn't attended school. She thought about defending herself or others, but she didn't know how or she couldn't do it. It's that my mother is very gentle. She has great respect for others. I love my mother a lot because she's a kind woman. But she can't defend either herself or us. In comparison with me, at times I defend myself more than men do! I don't want anyone disrespecting me.

Also, I talk without embarrassment. I'm a very open person. But my little sisters, no. They're embarrassed. They don't want to talk. They show a lot of respect for people. It seems that I don't have much respect for my people. I mean I'm a mixture. I want to respect my people, but I am a mixture with Ladino influence. The Ladinos and mestizos act a certain way, and I act like them and my people.

That's why I'm here, traveling, seeing, knowing how it is in each country, in each state. When the Zapatistas selected me to consult with the people, I learned a little from this, to know how other people are and how they live. Since it was my first trip to another state, I didn't know how to do things, how to say many things. But what I've learned about myself is that I can travel, I can go to other countries. I also learned that in nearly all the states, in the whole country, there's a lot of poverty.

I don't want to be the only one who has this right to be free to leave the house. I want other women, my daughters, my granddaughters, and my great-granddaughters, to have the same freedom that I have to do what they can do.

But the men's hearts aren't there yet. The majority of the men don't want to make their own food or *matz*. They just want to sit around waiting for their food. But it's better for them to learn how to do housework. I hope that men who don't understand women's rights very well can become like my husband. I want to say to them, "Understand this, learn how to care for the house a little."

Truthfully, men and women have the same body. For example, women have two eyes and men have two eyes. Women have a nose and men have a nose. We women have ten fingers and toes, and men have ten fingers and toes. There's hardly any difference between us. That's why it's better to make things equal.

Leaving the house gives me strength. When I stay closed up in the house, I feel as if I'm sick. I feel very old, and I quickly age. That's what's happening right now. Now I don't feel like walking and going places as much. Sure, I still feel like going out for pleasure. But it's changing. I don't have as much energy as in the past. I'm getting old, and I feel weak from my illness. It seems that I don't want to move my body. When I was young, I was quite thin. But right now I'm getting fat like a pig! Also, I don't leave the house much now because I have a lot of my own work with the store. It seems that I don't have time to go to meetings. That's why I can't struggle more with my *compañeros*. I think that's what's happening with me.

I think about a lot of things when I'm at home. One moment I think about my money, my family, my work, and my life. Everything comes into my mind and makes a mixture of things. I don't know why these thoughts come into my mind, but they come. It's not simple to live in the world.

There are times when I feel passionate, and times when I think that things aren't going to change. But things are changing. For example, in the past nobody used plastic sandals. Nobody used a machine-made shawl. Nobody used a sweater. Long ago women didn't wear ribbons in their hair. But now, there are shawls, sweaters, sandals, and many other things.

In the past, women were embarrassed to wear a dress, pants, and all of that. I wore a dress when I was very little, but then I stopped wearing it when I went to school. Who knows if in the future little girls won't give up their dresses. Maybe the young women will lose their embarrassment about wearing new things. Who knows what will happen in the future?

But we will probably not give up our traditional clothes because with this holy struggle we're recovering and strengthening many of our traditions. The elders are getting together to remember all that we have forgotten. They already know a lot about our ancestral traditions. For example, the masses in the sacred hills when prayer leaders ask for food, we can't forget these. And the feast on June 27th for our patron Saint Peter. It's a very important tradition that we can't forget. And the healers, surely we should respect them. Although they don't come to my house since I pray for myself, they're still useful to us. Also, our language, we can't lose it. Our children need to hear it. If my granddaughters didn't speak Tzotzil, I couldn't advise them. I couldn't give them my words, they couldn't learn my wisdom. Although we have to learn Spanish, the children need to study both Spanish and Tzotzil. They need to know how to write Tzotzil, too.

I don't think that we're going to forget all the good traditions. But if it weren't for the holy struggle, we might forget everything about our traditions.

Epilogue

In June 2010 I went to Chenalhó to go over the final draft of Antonia's words with her and catch up on all the changes in her life since my last visit in early 2009. As this book goes to press in 2010, Antonia and her family are continuing their passage over the Earth.

Felipe now lives in a new house he built on the foundation of the house he shared with Magdalena, who received the house boards in the divorce settlement. There he lives with a new woman and their infant. Felipe's six-year-old son lives with Antonia, and his four-year-old daughter lives with Magdalena's parents. Felipe is still drinking.

Sebastian continues to travel for periods of time to find work in other states in Mexico. Recently he began to carve wooden crosses that Juana is dressing in traditional clothes to sell through the weaving co-op. He is trying to stop drinking.

Mariano obtained a job in another state using his degree in computing. He met a woman there, and together they had a son in 2010. Although he lost his job just before his son was born, he found another soon after.

Alberto is still working in the same Chinese restaurant in Alabama but plans to return to Chiapas at the end of 2011. He will return to a cement block house with a cement floor that his parents are building with money he sent home. The used car that his parents bought with Alberto's earnings is a great help to his family, including his brother-in-law Antonio, who uses it as a taxi.

Paulina is dedicated to developing her weaving skills in order to help her family survive. Her husband, Antonio, works whatever job he can find in the area. He is supportive of Paulina and helps take care of their son.

Rosalva dropped out of high school soon after her fifteenth birthday to be with a young man who left his wife and new baby to be with her. Antonia and Domingo were distressed by the situation but allowed Rosalva to go live with the man in his community. When he started to beat her, Rosalva returned to live with her parents.

Domingo has not lost an ounce of his commitment to the Zapatista movement. Antonia says that God keeps him strong to help him keep working hard for the holy struggle. Domingo calls the holy struggle "my glass of water."

Antonia was able to take advantage of money saved from selling coffee to buy a *rotoplas*. It has made collecting water much easier. She still suffers from what appears to be Bell's palsy, but the symptoms have lessened. She remains an active member of the weaving and general store co-ops. Despite recent problems with Rosalva, in June 2010 Antonia's house was a lively place, full of joking and laughter.

Afterword

Human lives—the personal and the self—are the yeast that causes the
bread of ethnography, literature, theory or history to rise.

Martha Ward,
A Sounding of Women, p. xv

Antonia's story is part of the larger story of how Chiapas and Mexico are changing in this era of globalization and, especially, the important roles of women in these changes. Her words speak to the particular ways that women are creating and bearing witness to change, and in the process expanding their worlds beyond anything that their foremothers could have imagined. Few sectors of Mexican society have been more silenced than indigenous women. Most of them live out their lives under the weight of poverty, racism, and patriarchal beliefs and structures. Yet, many, like Antonia, resist this oppression and find moments of joy in the process.

In highland Chiapas the traditional gender ideology restricts women's place to the house and hamlet, and associates women with traditional beliefs and practices.[1] However, since the Word of God and artisan cooperative movements of the 1980s and the Zapatista movement of the 1990s, indigenous women have begun to reconceptualize gendered notions of space and place through contesting their confinement to homes and hamlets.[2] Antonia's life illustrates this dynamic process.

Antonia's story also highlights the role of women as change agents. In indigenous communities of Chiapas, women are active participants in critiquing cultural traditions that serve their interests and those that do not. In the process they contest stereotypical conceptions of women as bulwarks of tradition, and efforts by kin to bind them to traditions that do not respect their human rights in order to bolster claims of ethnic sovereignty (Speed et al. 2006). In the Zapatista support base and the cooperatives that Antonia helped form, women evaluate those traditions and cultural symbols that no longer serve their well-being, such as using alcohol in rituals and not sending girls to school. Nevertheless, Antonia and other women stress the important roles they play in cultural and material survival through passing on valued practices and beliefs to future generations. Antonia has been strengthened by many traditions—such as weaving ancestral designs—and hopes that her daughters and granddaughters will carry these on.

Feminist scholars have coined the term "grassroots feminism" to describe the myriad ways in which women such as Antonia and her *compañeras* respond to male dominance within the contexts of their unique cultures, histories, and social systems (Eber and Kovic 2003: 20). These women's efforts call into question definitions of feminism based on assumptions that women's actions must challenge gender norms in order to be considered political or feminist. Antonia is not aware of these debates or concerned about outsiders' labels for her actions, but her life's work illustrates the value of grassroots feminism. Antonia's efforts and those of other women in her Zapatista support base illustrate a kind of feminism rooted in women's strategic positions on the front lines of providing for their families. Their conception of feminism stresses collective struggle to overcome racism, poverty, and sexism. Within this communal context women work together to understand and speak out against gender inequality to foster greater mutuality between men and women (Stephen 1994).

Antonia did not need the Zapatista movement to open her eyes to male dominance, but discussions about the Revolutionary Women's Law in her local support base gave her a formal context within which to join with women in her own and other communities to confront the negative aspects of traditional gender norms. The Zapatista movement has been unusual in Latin American liberation struggles for its commitment to integrating women's rights into its overall agenda. Nevertheless, women base members still feel pressure to subordinate their rights as women to those of their kinsmen's or to the organization. Zapatista support bases can rarely find enough women to fill leadership positions because of the time-consuming nature of women's household-based work and men's reluctance to take over more of this work. Antonia was elected to serve as one of the women leaders of the support base in her community, but she already had more work than she could handle, and Domingo did not offer to take over more of her work.

The collective efforts of women in highland Chiapas highlight the need for forms of feminism that address the ways in which local and global realities interpenetrate and, in the process, reveal alternative stories of difference, culture, power, and agency (Mohanty 2005). Antonia's story provides insight about collective conceptions of development that link people in chains of social and economic exchange across cultural, class, ethnic, and national borders. Through Antonia's life we learn about the importance of think-

ing and acting in terms of mutuality, co-responsibility, and common interests—anchors of feminist solidarity (Mohanty 2005: 87).

While working on this book with Antonia, Heather Sinclair and I became aware of some emotional aspects of mutuality that scholars have paid
less attention to. During one of our talks soon after the Zapatista uprising,
Antonia asked me the meaning of *mutuo* (mutual). She had heard the word
at a support base meeting in reference to men and women creating gender
equality. In the definition I gave her, I focused on people respecting each
other's needs and striving to work together in reciprocal exchanges. As the
years passed, Antonia and I talked about mutuality in our own relationship
in terms of its materiality, but we did not explore its emotional qualities.
Taking both emotional and material aspects of mutuality seriously seems
fundamental to developing reciprocal and long-term relationships in our
globalized world. But this is a topic for another book.[3]

Migration and Transnational Networks

Neither Antonia nor I anticipated how the forces of capitalism and globalization would transform and merge our lives. The Zapatista uprising in 1994
took Antonia by surprise as much as it did me. An exodus of migrants from
Chiapas in the twenty-first century was unimaginable in the 1980s. Twenty
years ago we could not have envisioned the complex ways in which our fates
and those of the people of our two regions would become intertwined. During her visit to New Mexico in 2005, Antonia's sons asked her to measure
the width of the Rio Grande to see if they could swim across it. These men,
little boys when I first met them, are now fathers. They have scarce means to
support their families without leaving them for months at a time to work in
cities in Mexico or the United States. Antonia's youngest son, Alberto, has
been in the United States nearly three years.

Antonia's words throughout this book reveal challenges that parents in
most rural areas of the world face as they work to support their families on
the land and, in the process, conserve valuable connections to places and
people. Writing about his family's history in the Texas Hill Country, Paul
Syring (2000: 185) speaks of his hope that readers will be inspired by his
stories to live "a meaningful, gathered life in a chaotic time." Much as most
parents in highland Chiapas want their families to stay united and on their
land, it has become increasingly hard to do so amidst the chaos of poverty,
migration, and political factionalism.[4]

Seasonal work on plantations and migration to places as far away as the
United States are a well-established pattern in the highlands (Rus 1995). In

recent years, however, migration has intensified (Rus 2008). Increased migration in search of wage labor has brought indigenous people from different regions into contact with each other. In the process, township-based identities have broadened to include categories of shared ethnicity based on migrants' languages, for example "Tzotziles" and "Tzeltales" (Rus and Collier 2003; Rus and Vigil 2008).

In studies of migration and identity, scholars have rightly critiqued bounded notions of culture that map cultures onto places. But the current scholarly focus on fluidity and mobility runs the risk of neglecting important analyses of people like Antonia with strong connections to places. Antonia's life story illustrates the tension between attachments to places and valued cultural traditions and the need to travel far from home to find cash to survive. In addition to her husband and sons having to migrate to find work, Antonia has had to reach foreign markets to sell her own and others' weavings for the cooperatives she belongs to. She has also left her community for short periods of time to participate in activities of the transnational civil society movement. Although Pedranos differ in their perspectives—for example, youths show a lessening commitment to semi-subsistence farming, while elders are often concerned about losing connections to the land— their discourses are embedded in a framework of experience that still values land-based identities and the continuity of languages and traditions.

As we finish this book, a rural city is being constructed in Chenalhó. It is one of several in Chiapas already finished or underway in the first phase of Project Mesoamerica, an $8 billion project involving nine countries. The government maintains that by concentrating people into rural cities, it will be able to offer communities much needed services such as schools and health clinics; however, to sell one's land and move to such a city would mean that Pedranos would have to abandon their stewardship of the land and their identities as campesinos.

Living in closely packed houses with no yards or land, Pedranos would no longer be able to raise animals or feed their families from their corn and bean fields, nor from the many other edible plants that grow wild or that they cultivate. They would be forced to work in large agribusinesses or factories. Moving to the rural city will end people's identifications with their local communities and weaken, if not destroy, the social justice organizations that they have created. Not surprisingly, Pedranos in the resistance movement see the rural city as one more particularly menacing government plan to open their lands for resource extraction and development by multinational corporations, and to crush their autonomous initiatives and alternative visions of development.[5]

One of the motivations guiding this book was to increase solidarity between the United States and Mexico. Antonia's story joins with other testimonies from Latin American activists involved in liberation struggles to advance a dialogue of solidarity between people of other nations and these activists and their *compañeros*. This dialogue expanded greatly with the Zapatista uprising, which seemed to reach to the farthest corners of the world. As described in this book, Antonia and I became involved in transnational solidarity networks that over the years have gone through many permutations. For the past eight years we have both been supported in our endeavors by the Las Cruces-Chiapas Connection, a committed volunteer group in Las Cruces, New Mexico, that sells weavings for women's cooperatives and educates consumers about the link between feminism and fair trade, and the negative effects of globalization, for example, the rural cities project. This organization is a part of Sophia's Circle, a nonprofit women's art and cultural organization founded in Las Cruces in 2003. In addition to assisting artisan collectives on the US/Mexico border and in Chiapas to sell their work through fair trade, we also bring members of these groups together in conversations about how to create a stronger solidarity economy and social network among ourselves. This network also draws inspiration from the model in both indigenous and non-indigenous Mexican communities of kin and *compadres* supporting one another throughout the life cycle. When health or other personal emergencies arise among cooperative members here on the border or in Chiapas, our network in Las Cruces mobilizes to find funds to respond to them.[6]

Life Histories, Oral Histories, and Testimonial Literature

Antonia's life story adds to a growing movement of collaborative writing across class and ethnic borders in the interests of decolonization. Within this body of literature, her story illustrates some common themes in women's oral histories and testimonial literature, as well as ways of talking about her life that are unique to her culture and personality.

Like many women who have committed their stories to oral and written records, Antonia tends to focus on who she has done things with, rather than on *what* she has done and *when* (Armitage 1983). Early on I learned that the significance of Antonia's life lies in her commitment to life as a process of working with others, not in any particular act at a specific time or place.

Antonia's story also shows strength and affirmation despite suffering and victimization, a quality evident in many women's oral histories (Armitage 1983). Antonia refers often to suffering and struggle, but she does not frame herself or her *compañeros* as victims. She speaks about "our mind, our struggle, our imagination" (Part 2, Chapter 1), evoking the determined and creative actions that her community has taken to solve economic and political problems without recourse to competition or dependence. Where she speaks about working in collectives, Antonia shows how she is in a conversation with her *compañeros* about a new way to belong to the world that is not dictated by want, suffering, or victimization. For as long as Pedranos can remember, they have been in subordinate positions. They have had to act small for fear of offending those in power. In their contemporary autonomous communities and collective conceptions of development, Pedranos are acquiring the capacity to act in a larger way in the hopes of transforming social, economic, and political relations with one another and with their state and nation. But all the while, they seek to remain in humble and respectful relation to one another lest they fan the flames of envy. A very difficult balancing act.

Antonia's story also shares with women's testimonies from Latin America a concern for integrating personal and political dimensions of life, as well as private and public spheres of action. Reflecting on the life of Salvadoran activist María Teresa Tula, Lynn Stephen (1994) discusses how the personal tragedy that Tula experienced when her husband was detained and then assassinated was the catalyst for her political involvement.

In contrast, Antonia's introduction to political activism evolved more slowly, emerging over more than two decades, beginning with her awareness of the need to create weaving cooperatives to avoid being exploited, and then her awakening to social and economic injustices as a progressive Catholic, and culminating in her radicalization as a member of a Zapatista support base. Over the years her identities of mother, weaver, Catholic, and cooperative organizer have commingled in Antonia's growing awareness of the right of all people to be free from manipulation and domination. In the late 1980s and early 1990s, when coffee didn't seem as viable an option for earning cash, she turned to her weaving and invested more energy in organizing women into cooperatives and attending meetings of the Word of God. In the early 1990s she seemed more worried and discouraged than she had in previous years. The Zapatista uprising in 1994 gave Antonia a tremendous boost, and by connecting to it, she regained her spirit to struggle for social justice. As government repression increased in the wake of the Zapatista uprising in 1994, she refocused her energies away from the cooperative that she had formed with her mother and sisters, composed of both Zapatistas and the Bees, toward projects within the Zapatista movement, including organizing displaced women into weaving cooperatives. All the while, her identity as a Catholic remained central to her sense of self and her place in the world. "God is the rock," Antonia maintains.

Antonia's story reflects an additional blending of identities, or merging of commonly opposed spheres of life, that of producer/consumer with spiritually attuned being, coached since birth in the proper ways to ensure balance in human affairs. Since childhood, Antonia has had an entrepreneurial bent that as an adult she has put to the service of organizing cooperatives. In cooperatives and meetings of the Zapatista base, Antonia and her *compañeros* integrate prayer, fasting, and fellowship into their work. Antonia refers to this work as "the holy struggle." Conceptualizing community organizing as sacred may come as a surprise to outsiders who are sympathetic with the Zapatistas but have not spent time in their communities and do not understand how members of Zapatista support bases imbue their struggle for autonomy and justice with spiritual significance. The image of Zapatistas praying before meetings and reading the Bible together challenges popular assumptions that religion is an antirevolutionary force (Eber and Kovic 2003: 111). For Antonia, participating in a local Catholic group was an important step on her path to more overt political activity in a Zapatista support base.[7]

Antonia's story also shares in common with other testimonies a focus on telling aspects of a group's story. But in contrast to women such as Rigoberta Menchú, the Guatemalan Mayan Nobel Peace Laureate, Antonia intends her story to be foremost about her life, not about her community's history. When Rigoberta told her life story to Elisabeth Burgos-Debray in 1982, she made it clear that she was telling her people's story. In contrast, Antonia took pains to help me understand that she does not speak for others, nor tell a group story. Over the years I have often heard her say, "Remember, that's just how I see it. Others may have different ideas, may tell it differently."

Despite not intending to tell a larger story, Antonia teaches us a great deal about her people's recent history and culture, and what it means to resist oppression as a group. Her story renews appreciation for indigenous people's subjectivity in the context of widespread repression, and encourages us to rethink ethnocentric conceptions of resistance that portray indigenous people as only reacting, not acting (Rus 2002: 1025). Her descriptions of daily life reveal how resistance builds in moments rarely noted by historians, moments of sharing unique discourses and ways of being and knowing. Jan Rus reframes resistance in highland Chiapas as "a long-term strategic commitment" to defend all that the ancestors have handed down since the beginning of time, including land, language, beliefs, and knowledge (Rus 2002: 1026; see also Kovic 2005: 179–191).

One of Antonia's strengths is that she questions what she hears. Through sustained critical reflection she arrives at her own opinions, even if she can't always act on them. For example, when the Zapatista rhetoric is out of sync with the realities of women's lives in her community, she does not defend it, but negotiates a compromise that respects both the spirit of the movement and women's needs and desires. She once compared herself with her husband, who "believes everything he hears." Although she attributes this tendency in Domingo to his lack of schooling, I believe the difference between Antonia and Domingo lies more in Antonia's commitment to developing her critical thinking capacities over years of comparing herself with others and being attentive to how abuses of power shape people's lives—from her father's abuse of her mother, to the mestizo domination of indigenous people and the abuses of the global economy.

The Conversation Continues

This book ends in the middle of a conversation. I am reassured by knowing that my conversation with Antonia will continue, and that by means of this book readers will be able to enter our conversation-in-progress.

This book has also given me an opportunity to honor Antonia, a friend who has encouraged and inspired me along my path as a human being and a feminist anthropologist. It has also enabled me to explore conflicts, complexities, contradictions, and changes in both Antonia's life and my own, and in the lives of others with whom we are engaged in social justice work in Mexico and the United States. I hope that our stories will show readers how we all live in the face of individual and structural tensions, whatever our location in a given social structure, and that an important part of the human experience is negotiating these tensions.

I have struggled most while writing this book with how to explore the power differences between me and Antonia that stem from my privilege as a middle-class white woman living in the United States and Antonia's life as an indigenous woman with scarce economic resources living in a nation shaped by extreme poverty and human rights abuses. In the context of the inequalities that inform our relationship, I have learned to accept that part of the human condition is that we all use one another for our own as well as larger purposes. Facing how both Antonia and I have used each other, as well as many others, has been a humbling experience. But it has helped me realize that despite personal and structural constraints, people can work together toward a more just world if we do so with respect, love, and close attention to what inspires the other. What matters is how we use each other, how we pass over the Earth. Antonia taught me this, even if we both fail at times to act as we wish we could.

I also hope that this book will show readers how academic work can be more inclusive, attentive, and powerful by being merged with social justice work. Although I have been involved in this work most of my adult life, I entered it more deeply and broadly through knowing Antonia. More than anyone, she helped me develop a feminist praxis that unites my scholarship, teaching, and activism. I hope that Antonia's life story and pieces of the story of our friendship will embolden readers to make their own connections across even the most troubling differences to work for social justice, or if they have already made such connections, to deepen their reflection on these. The risks of being disappointed, and disappointing and burdening others, are implicit in this work. The acts of reflection and action take courage. But in the process of embracing these challenges, we are blessed with unexpected gifts of spirit and insight, and the opportunity to work together toward a world where everyone has the right to find their authentic place, and freedom to express their passion.

Antonia's Words to Alberto

A message in Tzotzil that Antonia sent by cassette tape to her son working in Alabama, recorded March 3, 2009. Translated from Tzotzil to Spanish by Antonia, and from Spanish to English by Christine Eber.

K'ox ta jk'opanot.
Hijo menor, te quiero platicar.
Youngest son, I want to talk to you.
Tax kalb'ot ti junuk avo'onton xa amtej ti bu oyote avo'onton.
Te voy a decir que quiero que estes contento de trabajar donde encuentres.
I'm going to say to you that I want you to be happy in your work, where you
are working.
K'uxetuk avo'onton ta abamtel.
Animo en tu trabajo.
May you have good spirit in your work.
Tsob'o ataquin yu'un jun no'ox velta la jelo ti ta namal balamile.
Junta tu dinero porque solo una vez cruzaste la tierra lejos.
Save your money because you only crossed over to the faraway land one
time.
Junuk no'ox velta ti laj kat ko'onton avu'une.
Solo una vez puse triste de ti.
I only became sad about you once.
**Jech ti vo'ote junuk nox velta la vich avokol ta xanubal ta vinal ta taki on-
tonal,**
Tu, también, solamente una vez que sufriste de caminar, de hambre, de sed,
You, too, only one time suffered from walking, from hunger, from thirst,
ta xi'el ta skotol ti k'usitik avokol, la jelo-e,
de miedo y todo del sufrimiento como cruzaste.
from fear and all the suffering as you crossed.
Koliyal jtotik ti la jelo laj xk'uxbinot.
Gracias a Dios que pudiste.
Thanks to God that you could do it.

Yu'un laj yil avokol ti abul abae,

Te consuelo porque estabas sufriendo,

I console you because you were suffering,

ti muyuk jtak'intik, muyuk ak'u avex.

que no tenías dinero, no tenías ropa.

because you didn't have money, you didn't have clothes.

Ep abul aba yu'un mu xu' ku'un skotol tax kakbot.

Sufriste mucho porque no pude ayudarte de todo.

You suffered a lot because I couldn't help you with everything.

Ja yo te abil avokol.

Así sufriste.

That's how you suffered.

Pero ta horae kuxetuk avo'onton.

Pero ahora que seas contento.

But now be content.

Ti cha pas xa kanal jutuke.

Estás ganando un poco.

You're earning a little.

Ja no'ox, jech tax kalbot, junuk avo'onton.

Solamente, así te digo, que seas contento.

That's only why I tell you to be content.

Jech vu'un ek jun ko'onton.

Yo también estoy contenta.

I'm also content.

Ja' jechun k'ucha'alo no'ox.

Así estoy como siempre.

That's how I always am.

Jtotik ak'o chi'inot ta aba'mte,

Dios te acompaña en tu trabajo,

May God accompany you in your work,

ta be' ta bu'uk no'ox oyot.

en el camino donde quieres que te encuentres.

on the road wherever you wish to find yourself.

Chi'uk ak'o xa kol ta sventa achamel.

Y también que Dios te salva por tu enfermedad.

And also may God heal your sickness.

Ja no'ox jech yepal la jchi'inota ta lo'il.

Eso es toda mi plática.

That's all my talk.

Ta yan to velta te oyan.

Hasta luego. Allí te quedas.

We'll see each other later. You stay there.

Life Histories from Chiapas and Other Places

The most notable life histories of indigenous people in Chiapas were written in the 1950s: the life story of Juan Pérez Jolote by Ricardo Pozas Arciniega (1962) and the life history of Manuel Arias recorded in *Perils of the Soul: The Worldview of a Tzotzil Indian* by Calixta Guiteras-Holmes (1961). Several decades later, Diane Rus published a book about thirteen Coletas, women descended from the Spaniards who founded the highland city of San Cristóbal de las Casas, *Mujeres de tierra fría: Conversaciones con las coletas* (1997). The next year *Rosa Caralampia: Historia de una mujer tojolabal* (The Story of a Tojolabal Woman) by Delfina Aguilar Gómez was published. Segments of life stories focused on childbirth, religious change, and community organizing are also found in several chapters of *Women of Chiapas: Making History in Times of Struggle and Hope* (Eber and Kovic 2003), including the chapters by Diana Damian, Graciela Freyermuth Enciso, Christine Eber, and Pilar Gil.

Three books that focus on women of Chiapas were published in 2008. K'inal Antzetik, a women's non-governmental organization in San Cristóbal de las Casas, published *Voces que tejen y bordan historias: Testimonio de las mujeres de Jolom Mayaetik* (Voices that Weave and Brocade Histories: Testimonies of Women of Jolom Mayaetik), life stories of women weavers in the cooperative Jolom Mayaetik; Gayle Walker and Kiki Suarez published *Every Woman Is a World: Interviews with Women of Chiapas*, containing the stories in their own words of twenty-eight women from different socioeconomic, ethnic, and cultural backgrounds who have lived in Chiapas for the past 60 to 108 years; and Melel Xojobal, an organization dedicated to social services for indigenous children and teenagers of San Cristóbal de las Casas, published a bilingual book, *"So that you know": Aspirations and Stories by Women of Chiapas*, a compilation of stories created by women for their children.

Antonia's life story also adds to a growing movement of collaborative writing across class and ethnic borders in the interests of decolonization.

In Chiapas, scholars have been collaborating with community members in various publications. *San Miguel Chiptik: Testimonios de una comunidad tojolabal* (1998) resulted from a collaboration among Tojolabales and researchers Carlos Lenkersdorf and Gemma Van der Haar. In 2001 the diary of Sak K'inal Tajaltik (Javier Morales Aguilar), *El diario de un tojolabal* (Diary of a Tojolabal), was translated by Carlos Lenkersdorf. María Komes Péres, a Chamula woman, collaborated with Diane Rus and Xalik Guzmán to write a booklet, *Bordando milpas* (1990), about her work and life as a weaver. Jan and Diane Rus have been involved in a sustained collaboration with Chamula men and women writing about social change through their perspectives (Peres Tzu 2000, 2003). In 1995 Jan Rus and Salvador Guzmán López assisted Santos Gómez López, Mariano Gómez López, and Juan Gómez López in compiling and translating their stories of going to California to find work in *Jchi'iltak ta Slumal Kalifornia* (Chamulas in California). Most recently, the Ruses have been working with indigenous young people living in squatter settlements surrounding San Cristóbal to record elders telling their stories of migration from rural communities to the city.

Several indigenous women have recorded and published their own stories and plays, a reversal of "outsiders" (mestizo or foreign anthropologists) writing about indigenous people's lives. Women playwrights include Ruperta Bautista Vázquez and Petrona de la Cruz Cruz and Isabel Juárez Ch'ix of La Fomma, a women's theater collective. Ambar Past edited a collection of indigenous women's prayers, songs, and stories, *Incantations by Mayan Women.*

A work of autobiography in its own category is *Las andanzas de Miguel: La autobiografía del Padre expulsado de Chenalhó* (1999), by Padre Miguel Chanteau, the Catholic priest in Chenalhó for thirty-three years before he was expelled in 1998 for his alleged political activism.

I have also been influenced by many life histories of indigenous and non-indigenous women of the Americas and other continents. Some particularly inspiring books are: *Mabel McKay: Weaving the Dream*, by Greg Sarris; *Nisa: The Life and Words of a !Kung Woman*, by Marjorie Shostak; *Stolen Life: The Journey of a Cree Woman*, by Rudy Weibe and Yvonne Johnson; *I, Rigoberta Menchú, the Story of a Guatemalan Woman*, edited by Elisabeth Burgos-Debray; *Forged Under the Sun/Forjado bajo del sol: The Life of María Elena Lucas*, edited by Fran Leeper Buss; and *Translated Woman: Crossing the Border with Esperanza's Story*, by Ruth Behar. I am delighted that Antonia's story now can be read and compared with these and other women's life stories.

Notes

Prologue

1. The terms *madrina* (godmother) and *padrino* (godfather) are given to friends and relatives who serve as sponsors for various rites of passage such as school graduation and marriage. Extending the concept of godparent beyond baptism provides much-needed emotional and financial support for important life transitions.

2. *Kox* is the Tzotzil kin term for youngest son or daughter, and also the word for the smallest tortilla in a batch. Most Tzotzil speakers in Chenalhó do not use Christian names when speaking to members of their families and communities.

Background Notes

1. The Zapatista Revolutionary Women's Law was originally published in the official organ of the Ejército Zapatista de Liberación Nacional (EZLN) (the Zapatista Army of National Liberation), *El Despertador Mexicano*, no. 1 (December 1993). For background on how indigenous women participated in creating the law, see Hernández Castillo 1994 and Rovira 1997. For background on how women are interpreting and using the women's law and other aspects of the Zapatista agenda for women's rights, see Eber and Kovic 2003; Olivera 2005; Ortiz 2001; Rovira 1997; and Speed et al. 2006.

2. For more information about the movement in Mexico that has joined under the slogan "Electricity is the People's!" see SIPAZ report, vol. XIV, no. 3 (November 2009), www.sipaz. org/informes/vol14no3e.htm#ENFOQUE.

3. To provide some compensation to Antonia for not using her real name, I will pass on to her all revenue derived from this book. I will also self-publish a separate book for Antonia to distribute to her family that will bear her real name and photos of her and her family. Giving her descendants a record of her life was one of Antonia's motivations for embarking on this project.

4. In addition to Tzotzil, several other Mayan languages are spoken in Chiapas: Tzeltal, Chol, Lacandon, Kanjobal, Tojolabal, Chuj, and Jakaltek.

5. Like myself, Antonia does not always use correct Spanish tenses and other forms of grammar. For this book, I made corrections in grammar so as to convey clearly what Antonia was saying. Most transcriptions and translations of Antonia's words from Tzotzil to Spanish are hers, while most translations of her words from Spanish to English are mine. Heather Sinclair, Rosaceli Ortega, and Mayra Valtiérrez assisted in some transcription and translation from Spanish to English for this English edition.

6. Other sources for this book include my fieldwork journals from the 1980s to the present, and cassette recordings in Spanish and Tzotzil that I made with Antonia in the 1980s and 1990s.

7. Antonia's language lesson about "life" is taken from Eber [1995] 2000: 61.

Part I. Becoming a *Batz'i Antz* (True Woman)

Chapter 1. A Childhood Memory

1. Chamula is the closest township to San Cristóbal de las Casas, and if any indigenous group symbolizes being indigenous to non-indigenous people, Chamulas do. They have often been the brunt of racial slurs, even by their indigenous neighbors.

2. *Ocote* is pitch pine; *tsots te'* is *liguidambarstyraciflua L.*; *lotsob chix* is *uña de gato* or *la vergonsoza* (*Mimosa albida H. & B*). *Valak xik* is a plant with delicate peach-shaped leaves on vinelike branches. It grows to about 2 meters high. During healing ceremonies *j'iloletik* stand branches of *valak xik* in the ground beside rows of candles. They also administer teas made from the crushed leaves steeped in hot water, and make baths with a combination of leaves from *valak xik* and other plants. For background on traditional healing in Chenalhó in the mid-twentieth century, see Guiteras-Holmes 1961: 133–130; and Arias 1973: 45–54.

3. Pedranos consider the number 3 to be *yox* (good luck) (Guiteras-Holmes 1961: 305). The number 3 comes up in many daily and ritual practices, some of which Antonia mentions in this book in relation to her own and others' actions. For additional beliefs and practices surrounding the number 3 in Chenalhó and its association with women and femaleness, see Guiteras-Holmes 1961 and Eber [1995] 2000.

Chapter 2. Parents

1. A story from the neighboring township of Chamula admonishes humans who waste corn, a gift from Father Sun (Gossen 2002: 77–79).

Chapter 3. Learning to Work

1. Antonia's mother recalls that she also used *polots* (*amolillo* [*Agave schottii*]) to make soap.

2. The process Antonia describes involves forming a round disc of corn dough in the air with both hands rather than patting out the dough on a surface.

3. *Batz'i luch* (the true design) is a weaving design that women of Chenalhó claim as their own, but it appears on weavings in several highland Chiapas townships. It is a rendering of a design reminiscent of those on garments of ancient Mayan women depicting a quartered universe moving through time, uniting Earth and Sky. See Morris 1987 for more about the meaning of weaving symbols.

4. Brocading, also called double-weft weaving, is a complex process in which weavers insert colored threads into the weft to make designs, rather than embroidering designs on a completed cloth. For women's recollections about learning to brocade in Chenalhó and Chamula in the early to mid-1900s, see Komes Péres 1990 and Modiano 1973: 67–69. For a long-range study of girls learning to weave in Zinacantán from 1969 to 2003, see Greenfield 2004.

Chapter 4. School

1. For background on the acculturation of indigenous teachers to the mestizo worldview, see Arias 1973. For an ethnography of schooling in highland Chiapas in the 1960s, when Antonia entered primary school, see Modiano 1973.

2. When Antonia was in primary school, it was common for children to graduate sixth grade at the age of fourteen or fifteen. Antonia was fifteen when she graduated. Poor teaching and missing classes because her mother needed her to work alongside her in others' fields were the main reasons she was held back.

Chapter 5. Making One's Soul Arrive

1. I am grateful to Isabel Zambrano for her analysis of *nael* in "Ethnoepistemologies at Home and at School."

2. *Cargos* in highland Chiapas are unpaid positions of leadership or service to one's com-

munity. In Chenalhó they are divided into *abtel patan* (*cargos* in township governance) and *abtel nichimal* (literally "flowery work," service performed as healers, midwives, and in service to saints during fiestas). Members of cooperatives, religious groups, and social justice organizations such as Zapatista support bases and community groups of the Sociedad Civil las Abejas (the Bees) have extended the concept of *cargo* to the voluntary service they perform in their groups. For a discussion of traditional *cargos* in Chenalhó, see Arias 1985 and Guiteras-Holmes 1961. See Rosenbaum 1993: 152–178 for a discussion of women's *cargos* in Chamula.

3. In Chenalhó, mole sauce is identified with mestizo culture. Serving it at graduation meals seems to be a way for Pedrano parents to show respect to mestizo teachers and acknowledge the beneficial aspects of their culture that they have introduced to their children. Often parents decline to eat the mole, preferring to have their chicken in broth with vegetables, but the mothers prepare ample quantities of both.

Chapter 6. Listening to the Word of God

1. For more about the reforms in the Catholic Church in Chiapas see Early 2012; Kovic 2005; McEoin 1995; and Chojnacki 2010.

2. Padre Miguel Chanteau, a French priest who lived in Chenalhó for thirty-three years, until he was expelled in 1998, was an exception in this and many other ways. When Vicente Fox was elected president in 2000, he rescinded deportation orders for foreigners, and Padre Miguel was able to return to highland Chiapas. For Padre Miguel's life story see *Las andanzas de Miguel: La autobiografía del Padre expulsado de Chenalhó* (1999). The current priest in Chenalhó, Padre Marcelo Pérez Pérez, is an indigenous man from San Andrés Larrainzar. Having grown up under the same conditions as those of most of his parishioners, Padre Marcelo understands their suffering and stands beside them in their struggle for social justice.

3. The following sources explore how indigenous people of highland Chiapas have been taking Catholicism into their lives in ways that empower them: Chojnacki 2010; Eber [1995] 2000, 2003a, 2003b; Early 2012; Gil 2003; Kovic 2003, 2005; and Moksnes 2005, forthcoming.

4. La Colonia Nueva Primavera, on the outskirts of San Cristóbal de las Casas, hosts the convent of the nuns of Hermanas del Divino Pastor. It is often used as a retreat center for Catholics from indigenous communities.

Chapter 7. Courtship and Marriage

1. Twenty was considered the proper age for marriage for both men and women in Chenalhó around the time that Antonia married, although it was common for girls and boys to marry earlier (Guiteras-Holmes 1961: 124). Ethnographic background on the bride petition and bride-service in highland Chiapas communities can be found in Collier 1968; Eber [1995] 2000; Flood 1994; Guiteras-Holmes 1961: 124–130; Laughlin 1963; Nash 1973; Rosenbaum 1993: 95–108; and Siverts 1993.

Chapter 8. Learning to Be a Wife

1. Guiteras-Holmes (1961: 130–131) and Rosenbaum (1993: 108–110) discuss separation among couples in Chenalhó and Chamula, respectively. Freyermuth Enciso (2003a) explores the importance of close and caring kin for married women's health and well-being.

Chapter 9. Learning to Be a Mother

1. Many women in Chenalhó do not go to government clinics because they fear being sterilized without their consent. Recent government programs claim to have improved infant and maternal health, and to have reduced the birth rate in Chiapas without coercion. However, Oportunidades (Opportunities), the government's main antipoverty program, requires women to "submit their fertility to official control" (Olivera 2005: 613). Women who register with the program obtain a monthly cash stipend for each child in school in return for their compli-

ance with mandatory health checkups. Women in the resistance movement do not participate in such programs, maintaining that they violate their rights. Antonia and others in the resistance movement go to Zapatista clinics or to Marie Stopes, a private clinic in San Cristóbal, for their reproductive health care. In autonomous Zapatista communities, midwives and female *promotores* (advocates) encourage women to make their own decisions about pregnancy, a right included in the Zapatista Revolutionary Women's Law (Olivera 2005: 614; see also Forbis 2006). For background on pregnancy, childbirth, and care of infants in Chenalhó in the mid-twentieth century, see Guiteras-Holmes 1961: 102–111. For factors contributing to high rates of maternal mortality in Chenalhó and other indigenous townships, see Graciela Freyermuth Enciso 2001 and 2003.

Chapter 10. Learning to Manage a Household

1. Jacinto Arias grew up in Chenalhó and has written extensively about the history and culture of the township. His master's thesis, "The 'Numinous' World of the Maya: Contemporary Structure and Change" (1973), gives abundant evidence of the significance of corn to Pedranos.

2. *Sak mes* is *Lavatera acerifolia malvaceas*. Its common name is *malva de risco*.

3. Research indicates that replacing dirt floors with inexpensive cement floors in low-income urban areas improves the health and cognitive development of young children mainly by reducing the incidence of intestinal parasites that are not treatable by common deworming medicines (Cattaneo et al. 2009). Cattaneo et al. also report that adults living in houses with cement floors are happier and experience lower rates of depression and stress. They note that cement floors may be less effective in rural areas where there are no safe water sources and children are undernourished. Given the realities of life in rural communities of Chenalhó, cement floors have considerable drawbacks and health risks. Where water is scarce, such as in Antonia's home, there is no way to clean a cement floor well. In contrast, women usually keep dirt floors well swept and sprinkled with a little water to keep the dust down. When infants urinate on a dirt floor, as most do not have diapers, mothers simply dig up the soiled area and throw it outside. On a cement floor a soiled area may stay there for quite some time until water can be obtained. Also, children who fall onto concrete floors are not cushioned in the same way that they are when falling on dirt. And there are considerable health risks to walking on cement floors, including foot discomfort, lower leg pain, hip degeneration, lower back pain, and skin rashes on the soles of feet.

Part II. Contesting the Status Quo, Creating a Different World

Chapter 1. The Time of Fire

1. For background on the economic and political changes leading up to signing of NAFTA and the Zapatista uprising, see Harvey 1998; Higgins 2004; Rus and Collier 2003; and Womack 1999. For background on NAFTA and its effects on corn production, see de Ita 2008.

2. Background on the formation of Las Abejas and the relationship between this group and Zapatista support bases within the context of the paramilitarization and militarization of Chenalhó in the mid to late 1990s is covered in Arriaga Alarcón et al. 1998; Eber 2003a; and Moksnes 2005 and Moksnes forthcoming.

3. In the context of a stalemate between the government and the EZLN over the government's failure to implement the Law on Indigenous Rights and Culture agreed upon during the peace talks, Zapatistas have focused on creating autonomous townships in five regions of Chiapas. These townships, such as San Pedro Polhó, provide health care, assistance with dispute settlement, and alternative schools that base their curricula on valuing native worldviews.

4. In June 2010, while reviewing this manuscript for publication, I asked Antonia to clarify when she began to refer to her work on behalf of social justice as the *santa lucha* (holy strug-

gle). Antonia explained that before she was involved in the Zapatista movement, no one in her community used the Spanish word *lucha* (struggle) or another comparable word in Tzotzil to describe their work for social justice. After joining the Zapatista support base in 1994, she and others came to call their movement for justice a *santa lucha*. Looking back on her involvement in the Word of God in the 1980s and early '90s, Antonia says that this work, too, was a *santa lucha*, but at the time she didn't have the words to call it that.

5. Marcos, a subcommander of the EZLN, is a non-indigenous man from central Mexico who went to Chiapas in 1983 to join a handful of mestizo and indigenous people to form the Zapatista Army of National Liberation. Marcos was transformed by the experience of living among indigenous people and learning their conceptions of history and humanity, especially those of the wise elder Don Antonio (see Marcos 1999). Within this context of intercultural dialogue, the Zapatista movement began to build. For a discussion of Marcos's role in the Zapatista movement, see Higgins 2004: 156–169.

Chapter 2. 1997

1. For a historical perspective on beliefs about animal soul companions, see Gossen 1994.

2. Pedranos also participated in lynchings and were suspected of being head-cutters prior to the Zapatista uprising. I thank Heidi Moksnes for bringing this fact to my attention.

3. For discussions of this incident, see Gorza 2002 and Freyermuth Enciso 2002.

4. E-mail sent on December 23, 1997, by the National Commission for Democracy in Mexico (moonlight@igc.apc.org) to chiapas-l@profmexis.sar.net. For background on the massacre, see Arriaga Alarcón 1998; Hernández Castillo 2001; and Moksnes 2004.

Chapter 3. International Encounters

1. Aguascalientes, now known as Caracoles (literally "snail shells"), are five regional political centers of the Zapatista movement in the state of Chiapas. These centers are the seat of the Juntas de Buen Gobierno (Councils of Good Government), alternative governing bodies replacing the traditional township governing structure. "Center of the Zapatista Heart Before the World," located in the community of Oventik, is the name of the *caracol* located in the autonomous township of San Andrés Sakamch'en de los Pobres, about an hour and a half drive from where Antonia lives. The autonomous township of San Pedro Polhó pertains to this *caracol*. For background on the formation of Caracoles and the Juntas de Buen Gobierno, see Ross 2006.

2. *The Struggles for Women's Rights in Chiapas: A Directory of Social Organizations Supporting Women in Chiapas* (2009), a publication of Lilla: International Women's Network, provides a list of the various organizations in Chiapas that have formed to address women's concerns and issues. The resource also offers information about contacting these organizations.

Chapter 4. Sons

1. Money was not included among the gifts given in *joyol* during the mid-twentieth century. Domingo did not give money to Antonia's parents when he petitioned to marry her. Only foodstuffs were given to the bride's parents as a symbol of their daughter's value to them. Often parents returned the food so as not to appear too eager to marry off their daughter, and to make it clear that if the marriage did not go well, the girl would be welcome to return to her parents (Guiteras-Holmes 1961: 124–128).

2. *Bik'it snuk*, or *jich'il*, is a falsetto tone of voice that people use when requesting something, such as in *joyol*, and when speaking with their seniors, especially respected elders. Spoken well, the words have a songlike quality.

3. Alberto, Antonia's youngest son, is the focus of Chapter 5 in Part 3.

Chapter 5. Daughters

1. Three Crosses is not the real name of the young man's community.

2. Antonia says there is a trend among contemporary young men to try to control their wives, perhaps in response to young women's growing assertiveness and independence. Fortunately, Antonio has not attempted to control Paulina, as Antonia feared. The couple are creating a fairly egalitarian marriage.

3. Until 2009, when it ended its scholarship program, Las Cruces-Chiapas Connection provided approximately $45 per month for children in middle school, about three-quarters of the actual costs. In 2010 the Maya Educational Foundation inaugurated a scholarship program in Chenalhó that funds part of the schooling expenses for four young people in Chenalhó to attend middle school and high school. MEF scholarships amount to about $45 per month to support a student in middle school, $85 a month in high school, and $180 a month in university. For information about this program and other programs of the Maya Educational Foundation, see www.mayaedufound.org.

4. This discussion with Antonia about Rosalva took place in June 2006.

Chapter 6. Daughters-in-Law and Grandchildren

1. Antonia prepared a tea of *valak xik* leaves for Juana to drink after she gave birth in order to help the placenta come out. She simply crushed the leaves and put them in boiling water to steep.

Chapter 7. Cargos

1. Eventually Zapatista base members in Antonia's community decided that only single women should serve leadership roles because it is too difficult for married women to fulfill their responsibilities to both their households and the base.

2. While I use the word "stress" to describe how Antonia experienced the many demands on her, it has no equivalent in Tzotzil. In a conversation with Paulina and Antonia about the concept, the closest words they came up with were *jvokolil* (suffering) and *soket sjol*, a state in which one's mind and heart are a mixture of sadness and anger. I now think that I should have physicalized my explanation more when trying to explain stress, as it seems likely that Pedranas like Antonia who juggle many roles experience stress by falling ill. In fact, Antonia told me that she thinks perhaps the numbness she now has in her face may have resulted from crying so much about the problems she experienced with her sons in 2008. Robert Dentan explores links between stress, illness, and social inequality in *Overwhelming Terror: Love, Fear, Peace, and Violence Among Semai of Malaysia* (2008).

3. It is customary in Chenalhó to present sodas or *pox* when asking for something. This gift is called *vokaroil*.

Chapter 8. Cooperatives

1. For more information about cooperative economic ventures in indigenous communities, see Castro 2003; Earle and Simonelli 2005; Eber and Rosenbaum 1993; Eber and Tanski 2002; Forbis 2003; Vargas 1999; and O'Donnell 2010.

Chapter 9. Traveling

1. For the history of the relationship between Kinal Antzetik and Jolom Mayaetik, see Castro 2003 and O'Donnell 2010.

2. In 1999 five thousand civilian Zapatistas traveled throughout Mexico to consult with fellow Mexicans on the San Andrés Peace Accords.

Chapter 10. The International Folk Art Market

1. Men in Chenalhó also make the *nuti*, a macramé shoulder bag made of cotton thread or maguey fiber with a leather strap, carried by men, women, and children.

2. Stories throughout highland Chiapas tell of a girl, Suyil, who fell into a lake and returned as the Virgin Mary, Sme'tik Suyil. After a big storm in Takia k'um, Chenalhó, a large lake formed, after which Pedrano elders announced Suyil's return. Soon an elder had a series of dreams in which Suyil came to him as the Virgin Mary, Sme'tik Suyil, demanding that a fiesta without alcohol be held in her honor (Eber [1995] 2000: 209–212). Antonia attended the fiesta with her parents. Respected Pedrano elder Manuel Arias tells his version of the story in Guiteras-Holmes 1961: 203.

Part III. Gains and Losses, Lessons Learned

Chapter 1. Envy

1. Tzotzil-Mayas maintain that *chu'lel*, one's essential soul, can leave the body during sleep in search of adventures. In dreams the soul sees what is not visible to the physical self when awake—for example, one's own and others' motivations and intentions. In dreams the *chu'lel* can bring harm both intentionally and unintentionally to itself or others (Pitarch 2010).

Envious people can also bring illness or death by going to a cave with candles and rum to ask the Earth Lord to make the person they envy fall sick, or die, or fail in whatever venture they are involved in. In the process, one aspect of the envious person's soul is believed to turn itself into a *nagual*, the animal soul companion of a witch—usually a four-footed domestic animal—which symbolically devours the envied person's soul (Laughlin 1988: 7).

For a discussion of envy and personhood, see Groark 2008. Groark explores conceptions of social knowing and selves in Tzotzil-Maya communities that relate to the challenges facing Antonia, who holds both traditional Tzotzil-Maya conceptions of soul and personhood, as well as a more Westernized Christian conception.

For information on envy and social relations in the mid-1900s in a Tzeltal township, see Nash 1985.

2. This story is recounted in Eber [1995] 2000: 151–153.

3. Carol-Jean McGreevy and her students at Shady Side Academy in Pittsburgh, along with Kathy Scigliano at Fox Chapel High School, also in Pittsburgh, raised funds for Mariano's education from middle school through college. My husband and I paid for most of Alberto's schooling until he dropped out of high school in 2008, and the Las Cruces-Chiapas Connection provided Paulina's and Rosalva's scholarships to attend middle school and high school. In 2010 I worked with the Maya Educational Foundation to set up a scholarship program in Chenalhó to reach out to more children whose parents cannot afford to send them to school. MEF scholarships do not cover all of the expenses of education, requiring students and parents to provide additional funds. MEF's philosophy is to provide a large number of children partial support for their education rather than supporting a few children fully. This philosophy helps minimize envy and encourages parents to become involved in their children's education.

4. Like earlier cooperatives in townships such as Amatenango del Valle, contemporary cooperatives in Chenalhó socialize gains, counteracting the forces of envy by making it difficult for a witch to pray against all the members, as envy usually targets individuals (Nash 1985: 86).

5. Writing about Tzotzil-Maya Catholics in the Word of God, Christine Kovic (2005) describes how these men and women speak of walking together on footpaths to symbolize their experience of working together with one heart for social justice.

Chapter 2. Suffering

1. For a historical perspective on changes in gender identity since the Zapatista uprising, see Olivera 2005. For perspectives of Zapatista women on the suffering of their mothers and grandmothers, see the video *We are Equal! Zapatista Women Speak* (Chiapas Media Project, 2003).

2. See Moksnes 2005 and forthcoming for in-depth discussions of both traditional Pedrano conceptions of suffering and those influenced by more politicized analyses of suffering as the result of poverty caused by unjust government policies. Moksnes (2005: 588–589) summarizes how Pedranos have talked to her about suffering over the past two decades:

> It [poverty] constitutes an intrinsic part of Pedrano identity, and villagers commonly describe themselves as a "suffering people." The suffering, I was informed, is caused by the hard work, the meagre food, the bad housing, the mud during the rains, and the lack of infrastructure. Suffering is associated with disease and the death of infants, children and adults. In short, their suffering is seen as a consequence of poverty. The term commonly used in Tzotzil to describe this suffering is *vocol* or *jvocolil*, which literally means "difficulty," "hardship," or "anguish," but is usually translated as "sufrimiento" when villagers speak Spanish.

For additional insights on the concept of suffering in Chenalhó and in other highland Chiapas communities, see Chojnacki 2010; Eroza Solano n.d.; and Kovic 2003. Of special interest is Kovic's discussion of workshops on human rights in indigenous communities. Like Antonia, participants in these workshops distinguish suffering on different levels—the family, community, and township (Kovic 2003: 109–110).

Chapter 4. Faith and Love

1. The full story of Domingo's *cargo* dream is in Eber *Women and Alcohol in a Highland Maya Town: Water of Hope, Water of Sorrow* ([1995] 2000), pp. 52–56. See Chojnacki 2010 for an analysis of how catechists in Santa María Magdalena, an *agencia* or political sub-unit of Chenalhó, have used participation in the Word of God as a substitute for *cargo* service and the drinking that accompanies it.

2. Candles symbolize life, and candle smoke carries people's petitions to God. Sodas have become an accepted substitute for *pox* in rituals in highland Chiapas townships. Padre Marcelo Pérez Pérez, the priest in Chenalhó since 2002, is a Tzotzil man who witnessed alcohol abuse firsthand. Padre Marcelo empathizes with women's concerns about problem drinking. He goes so far as to refuse the sacraments to people who are known to drink excessively after leaving church.

3. Many statements of emotion in Tzotzil can only be expressed by referring to one's heart as the seat of emotion— for example, "My heart is sad, happy, angry, etc." For a beautiful book in words and woodcuts of twenty expressions that begin with "My heart . . ." see *Mayan Hearts* (2003) by Robert Laughlin et al.

4. Antonia refers here to Matthew 25:35–40:

> For I was hungry and you gave me food, I was thirsty and you gave me something to drink, I was a stranger and you welcomed me. I was naked and you gave me clothing, I was sick and you took care of me, I was in prison and you visited me. Then the righteous will answer him, "Lord, when was it that we saw you hungry and gave you food? Or thirsty and gave you something to drink? And when was it that we saw you a stranger and welcomed you in, or naked and gave you clothing? Or when was it that we saw you sick or in prison and visited you?" And the King will answer, "Truly, I tell you,

just as you did it to one of the least of these who are members of my family, you did it to me."

5. Antonia refers here to Matthew 18:20: "For where two or three are gathered together in my name, there am I in the midst of them."

6. Antonia refers here to Matthew 7:24–27:

Everyone then who hears these words of mine and acts on them will be like a wise man who built his house on rock. The rain fell, the floods came, and the winds blew and beat on that house, but it did not fall, because it had been founded on rock. And everyone who hears these words of mine and does not act on them will be like a foolish man who built his house on sand. The rain fell and the floods came, and the wind blew and beat against the house, and it fell—and great was the fall!

7. Antonia's comparisons between Zapatistas organizing for a better life and biblical figures in the Old and New Testaments bear a close resemblance to how María Elena Lucas describes her view of farmworker organizing in the United States in *Forged Under the Sun / Forjada bajo del sol: The Life Story of María Elena Lucas* (1993).

For a comparison between Antonia's faith and that of a non-indigenous Catholic woman of San Cristóbal, see Eber 2003b.

Chapter 5. Exodus

1. Zapatista supporters are not supposed to leave their communities to find work because their absence weakens the base of support. If a Zapatista base member has no choice but to migrate, they must find someone in their community to assume their work for the Zapatista movement while they are gone.

2. Antonia says that it is common wisdom in her community that if someone worries about another person, it can put that person in harm's way. This belief is embedded in an overall awareness that most things are outside of one's control, except one's own behavior, hence it does no good to worry about others or try to control their thoughts or actions.

Chapter 6. Death

1. For an ethnographic account of traditions surrounding death and remembering the dead in Chenalhó, see Guiteras-Holmes 1961: 33–34, 139–147.

Chapter 7. Life So Far

1. In reference to presenting others' cultural realities, Robert Dentan (2008: 234) states: "We should produce biased accounts that state our biases as honestly as we can because that's the best we can do. Perfection is beyond us. We're not going to get to 'final accounts' but we'll get better as long as we keep talking with each other."

2. I thank Pete Benson for encouraging me to consider cycles of expansion and contraction in Antonia's life.

Afterword

1. For studies of women and gender in indigenous communities before the Zapatista uprising, see Devereaux 1987; Eber [1995] 2000; Garza Caligaris 1999; Nash 1973; O'Brian 1994; Rosenbaum 1993; and Rus 1990. See also Alaka Wali's 1974 honors thesis, which explores male dominance in Zinacantán through the life stories of four women.

2. For more background on recent reconceptualizations of gender and women in Tzotzil-Maya communities, see Eber 1999; Eber and Kovic 2003; Garza Caligaris 1999; Hernández

Castillo 2001; Olivera 2005; Ortiz 2001; Rovira 1997; Speed et. al 2006. For a comparison of indigenous women in Chiapas with women throughout Mesoamerica, see Rosenbaum and Eber 2007.

3. See Mills 1998 for a discussion of the complexities of creating postcolonial feminist theory and practice, and Lugones and Spelman 1983 for an account of the role that friendship can play in this process.

4. For additional background on parents' and young people's perspectives on immigration to the United States, see the documentary film made by Bill Jungels in Chenalhó, *Broken Branches, Fallen Fruit: Immigration in the Family* (2009).

5. For background on Project Mesoamerica, see Centro de Investigaciones Económicas y Políticas de Acción Comunitaria, A.C. (CIEPAC), *Chiapas al Día*, no. 585 (June 21, 2010) (ciepac@laneta.apc.org) and "Housing and the Mesoamerica Project" by Jamie Way, *Global Justice Monitor*, May/June 2010, pp. 5–7. For background on the rural city proposed for Chenalhó and letters from the Parish of Chenalhó, see www.lascwny.org/rural-cities.html. Tom Hayden (2003) provides a concise overview of the new globalism in Chiapas beginning with Plan Puebla Panama. For insight on the lack of fit between conceptions of fragmentation, mobility, and deterritorialization, and the discourses and historical consciousness of place-based peoples, see Nash 2001.

6. See O'Donnell 2010 for a book-length discussion of transnational solidarity connections with weaving cooperatives and other women's organizations in highland Chiapas.

7. Antonia's experience of faith shows that it inspires her to work with others to create inter-community and intra-community networks, and in the process facilitates her own and others' political mobilization. Her experience resembles closely those of members of a Catholic Maya community displaced from their lands, who collaborated with Christine Kovic in her research on human rights in highland Chiapas (Kovic 2005, esp. pp. 150–154).

Glossary

Acteal—a community in the north of the township of Chenalhó where forty-five people died in a massacre on December 22, 1997.

Autonomous township—a township created by Zapatista supporters in order to establish local control of juridical and administrative affairs.

Batz'i antz—true woman.

Batz'i vinik—true man.

Cabecera—the administrative center of a township; literally, "headtown."

Campesino—a peasant farmer.

Cargo—work (usually without a cash reward) on behalf of one's community; literally a "burden" or "weight."

Catechist—a lay leader in the Catholic Word of God movement.

Chiapanecos—people from Chiapas.

Comadre—the godmother of one's child.

Comal—the clay griddle women use to make tortillas (*semet* in Tzotzil).

Compadre—the godfather of one's child.

Compadres—plural form for *comadre* and *compadre*.

Compañero—a friend or companion.

EZLN—Ejército Zapatista de Liberación Nacional (Zapatista Army of National Liberation).

J'iloletik—native healers who use herbs and prayer to heal.

Ladino—a non-indigenous person of Spanish descent.

Madrina—term of reference for one's godmother.

Marcos—non-indigenous subcommander of the Zapatista army.

Matz—a staple drink made of ground corn.

Maya—a cultural group with its roots in the ancient Mesoamerican civilization that existed in the contemporary nations of Belize, El Salvador, Guatemala, Honduras, and Mexico.

Me'—female linguistic marker; also means "mother" and "wife."

Mestizo—a person of mixed Spanish and indigenous blood. Indigenous people of Chiapas use this term interchangeably with "Ladino" to refer to a non-indigenous Mexican.

Milpa—a plot of land planted with corn and beans, and sometimes squash and chile.

Paramilitaries—armed groups of civilians.

Pedrana—an indigenous woman from San Pedro Chenalhó.

Pedrano—an indigenous man from San Pedro Chenalhó.

Peso—the Mexican currency.

Pox—alcohol made from sugarcane.

PRI—the Institutional Revolutionary Party, the political party that held power in Mexico throughout most of the twentieth century.

Rotoplas—a large polyethylene tank placed on the roof or beside the house to collect water.

San Cristóbal de las Casas—a city in highland Chiapas.

San Pedro Chenalhó—an indigenous township in highland Chiapas.

San Pedro Polhó—the headquarters of the autonomous Zapatista township within the territory of San Pedro Chenalhó. Formed in 1995.

Sk'in Ch'ulelal—Day of the Dead; literally "Feast of the Souls."

Sociedad Civil Las Abejas (Civil Society [of] the Bees)—a Catholic social justice organization that formed in Chenalhó in 1992.

Tuxtla Gutiérrez—the capital city of Chiapas.

Tzotzil—a Mayan language spoken in Chenalhó and other highland Maya townships.

Word of God—the progressive branch of the Catholic Church in Chiapas with its roots in the liberation theology movement of the 1960s.

Zapatista—a civilian supporter of the EZLN, the Zapatista Army of National Liberation.

Zapatista support base—a civilian group that supports the EZLN.

References

Note: Bible translations are from the New Revised Standard Version published in 2007 by HarperCollins.

Aguilar Gómez, Delfina. 1998. *Rosa Caralampia: Historia de una mujer tojolabal.* Mexico City: CIESAS-DEMAC-IVEC-IOC.

Arias, Jacinto. 1973. *The "Numinous" World of the Maya: Contemporary Structure and Change.* Master's thesis, Catholic University, Washington, D.C.

———. 1985. *San Pedro Chenalhó: Algo de su historia, cuentos y costumbres.* Tuxtla Gutiérrez, Chiapas, Mex.: Publicación Bilingüe de la Dirección de Fortalecimiento y Fomento a las Culturas de la Subsecretaría de Asuntos Indígenas.

Armitage, Susan. 1983. The Next Step. *Frontiers*, vol. VII, no. 1: 3–8.

Arriaga Alarcón, Pedro, Rodrigo González Torres, and Carlos Morfin Otero, editors. 1998. *Acteal: Una herida abierta* [Acteal: An open wound]. Tlaquepaque, Jalisco, Mex.: Instituto Tecnológico y de Estudios Superiores de Occidente (ITESCO).

Aubry, Andrés, and Angélica Inda. 1998. Acteal antes del 22 de diciembre. In *Acteal: Una herida abierta* [Acteal: An open wound], edited by Pedro Arriaga Alarcón, Rodrigo Gonzalez Torres, and Carlos Morfin Otero, 71–83. Tlaquepaque, Jalisco, Mexico: ITESCO.

Behar, Ruth. 1993. *Translated Woman: Crossing the Border with Esperanza's Story.* Boston: Beacon Press.

Castro, Yolanda. 2003. J'pas joloviletik-Jolom Mayaetik-K'inal Antzetik: An Organizational Experience of Indigenous and Mestiza Women. In *Women of Chiapas: Making History in Times of Struggle and Hope*, edited by Christine Eber and Christine Kovic, 231–252. New York: Routledge.

Cattaneo, Matias, Sebastian Galiani, Paul Gertler, Sebastian Martinez, and Rocio Titiunik. 2009. Housing, Health and Happiness. *American Economic Journal: Economic Policy* (American Economic Association), vol. 1, no. 1 (February): 75–105.

Chanteau, Miguel. 1999. *Las andanzas de Miguel: La autobiografía del Padre expulsado de Chenalhó.* San Cristóbal de las Casas, Chiapas, Mex.: Editorial Fray Bartolomé de las Casas, A.C.

Chávez, Leo. [1992] 1998. *Shadowed Lives: Undocumented Workers in U.S. Society.* Fort Worth, TX: Harcourt Brace College Publishers.

Chiapas Media Project. 2003. *We Are Equal! Zapatista Women Speak*. Video. Chicago: Chiapas Media Project.

Chojnacki, Ruth. 2010. *Indigenous Apostles: Maya Catholic Catechists Working the Word in Highland Chiapas*. Amsterdam and New York: Rodopi.

CIEPAC. 2005. In the Crossfire: Mesoamerican Migrants Journey North. *Chiapas Today*, bulletin no. 454 (February 23). Chiapas, Mex.: CIEPAC.

Collier, George, with Elizabeth Lowery Quaratiello. [1994] 1999. *Basta! Land and the Zapatista Rebellion in Chiapas*. Oakland, CA: Food First Books.

Collier, Jane. 1968. Courtship and Marriage in Zinacantán, Chiapas, Mexico. *Middle American Research Institute Publication* (Tulane University, New Orleans) 25: 149–201.

Damian, Diana. 2003. Learning Everything I Can About Freedom: Testimony of a Social Worker and Popular Educator. In *Women of Chiapas: Making History in Times of Struggle and Hope*, edited by Christine Eber and Christine Kovic, 221–228. New York: Routledge.

Dentan, Robert Knox. 2008. *Overwhelming Terror: Love, Fear, Peace, and Violence Among Semai of Malaysia*. Lanham, MD: Rowman and Littlefield.

Devereaux, Leslie. 1987. Gender Difference and Relations of Inequality in Zinacantán. In *Dealing with Inequality: Analysing Gender Relations in Melanesia and Beyond*, edited by Marilyn Strathern, 89–111. Cambridge: Cambridge University Press.

Earle, Duncan, and Jeanne Simonelli. 2005. *Uprising of Hope: Sharing the Zapatista Journey of Alternative Development*. Walnut Creek, CA: Alta Mira Press.

Early, John D. 2012. *Maya and Catholic Cultures in Crisis*. Gainesville: University Press of Florida.

Eber, Christine. [1995] 2000. *Women and Alcohol in a Highland Maya Town: Water of Hope, Water of Sorrow*. Updated and revised edition with epilogue. Austin: University of Texas Press.

———. 1999. Seeking Our Own Food: Indigenous Women's Power and Autonomy in San Pedro Chenalhó, Chiapas, 1980–1998. *Latin American Perspectives*, issue no. 106, vol. 26, no. 3: 6–36.

———. 2000. "That they be in the middle, Lord": Women, Weaving, and Cultural Survival in San Pedro Chenalhó. In *Artisans and Cooperatives: Developing Alternative Trade for the Global Economy*, edited by Kimberly F. Grimes and B. Lynne Milgram, pp. 45–64. Tucson: University of Arizona Press.

———. 2003a. Buscando una nueva vida (Searching for a new life): Liberation Through Autonomy in San Pedro Chenalhó, 1970–1998. In *Mayan Lives, Mayan Utopias: The Indigenous People of Chiapas and the Zapatista Movement*, edited by Shannon Mattiace, Rosalva Aída Hernández Castillo, and Jan Rus, 135–159. Lanham, MD: Rowman and Littlefield.

———. 2003b. Living Their Faith in Troubled Times: Two Catholic Women. In *Women of Chiapas: Making History in Times of Struggle and Hope*, edited by Christine Eber and Christine Kovic, 113–129. New York: Routledge.

Eber, Christine, and Christine Kovic, editors. 2003. *Women of Chiapas: Making History in Times of Struggle and Hope*. New York: Routledge.

Eber, Christine, and Sally Meisenhelder. 2008. Border Crossings, From Theory to Practice: Looking for Floriberto. *Practicing Anthropology*, vol. 31 (1): 25–29.

Eber, Christine, and Brenda Rosenbaum. 1993. "That we may serve beneath your hands and feet": Women Weavers in Highland Chiapas. In *Crafts in the World Market: The Impact of Global Exchange on Middle American Artisans*, edited by June Nash, 154–180. Albany: State University of New York Press.

Eber, Christine, and Janet Tanski. 2002. Women's Cooperatives in Chiapas: Strategies of Survival and Empowerment. *Journal of Social Development Issues*, vol. 24, no. 3: 33–40.

Eroza Solano, Enrique. n.d. Las visiones contestatarias de la vida social: Las narrativas del padecimiento entre los chamulas. Manuscript in possession of author.

EZLN (Ejército Zapatista de Liberación Nacional). 1993. *El Despertador Mexicano*, no. 1 (December).

Flood, Marielle. 1994. Changing Patterns of Interdependence: The Effects of an Increasing Monetization on Gender Relations in Zinacantán, Mexico. *Research in Economic Anthropology* 15: 145–173.

Freyermuth Enciso, Graciela. 2001. The Background to Acteal: Maternal Mortality and Birth Control, Silent Genocide? In *The Other Word: Women and Violence in Chiapas Before and After Acteal*, edited by Aída Hernández Castillo, 57–73. Copenhagen: International Work Group on Indigenous Affairs.

———. 2002. Violencia y etnia en Chenalhó: Formas comunitarias de resolución de conflictos. In *Estudios sobre la violencia: Teoría y práctica*, coordinated by Witold Jacorzynski, 183–204. Mexico City: CIESAS.

———. 2003a. Juana's Story. In *Women of Chiapas: Making History in Times of Struggle and Hope*, edited by Christine Eber and Christine Kovic, 37–46. New York: Routledge.

———. 2003b. *Las mujeres de humo: Morir en Chenalhó: Género, etnia generación, factores constitutivos del riesgo durante la maternidad*. Mexico City: CIESAS and INM.

Forbis, Melissa. 2003. Hacia la autonomía: Zapatista Women Developing a New World. In *Women of Chiapas: Making History in Times of Struggle and Hope*, edited by Christine Eber and Christine Kovic, 231–252. New York: Routledge.

———. 2006. Autonomy and a Handful of Herbs: Contesting Gender and Ethnic Identities Through Healing. In *Dissident Women: Gender and Cultural Politics in Chiapas*, edited by Shannon Speed, Rosalva Aída Hernández Castillo, and Lynn M. Stephen, 176–202. Austin: University of Texas Press.

Garza Caligaris, Anna María. 1999. *Pluralidad legal y género en la vida cotidiana de San Pedro Chenalhó*. Master's thesis, Instituto de Estudios Indígena, UNACH, Chiapas, Mex.

Garza Caligaris, Anna María, et al. 1993. *Sk'op Antzetik: Una historia de mujeres en la selva de Chiapas*. San Cristóbal de las Casas, Chiapas, Mex.: Centro de Estudios Indígenas.

Gil, Pilar. 2003. Irene: A Catholic Woman in Oxchuc. In *Women of Chiapas: Making History in Times of Struggle and Hope*, edited by Christine Eber and Christine Kovic, 149–154. New York: Routledge.

Gómez López, Santos, Mariano Gómez López, and Juan Gómez López. 1995. *Jchi'iltak ta Slumal Kalifornia* [Chamulas in California]. Compiled and translated by Jan Rus and Salvador Guzmán López. San Cristóbal de las Casas, Chiapas, Mex.: INAREMAC.

Gorza, Piero. 2002. El anhelo de conservar y la necesidad de perderse: "Cortacabezas" en San Pedro Chenalhó, Chiapas, México, 1996. In *Estudios sobre la violencia: Teoría y práctica*, coordinated by Witold Jacorzynski, 169–182. Mexico City: CIESAS.

Gossen, Gary. 1994. From Olmecs to Zapatistas: A Once and Future History of Souls. *American Anthropologist* 96 (3): 553–570.

———, editor and translator. 2002. *Four Creations: An Epic Story of the Chiapas Mayas.* Norman: University of Oklahoma Press.

Greenfield, Patricia. 2004. *Weaving Generations Together: Evolving Creativity in the Maya of Chiapas.* Santa Fe: School of American Research.

Groark, Kevin. 2008. Social Opacity and the Dynamics of Empathic In-Sight among the Tzotzil Maya of Chiapas, Mexico. *Journal of the Society of Psychological Anthropology*, vol. 36, no. 4: 427–448.

Guiteras-Holmes, Calixta. 1961. *Perils of the Soul: The World View of a Tzotzil Indian.* Chicago: University of Chicago Press.

Harvey, Neil. 1998. *The Chiapas Rebellion: The Struggle for Land and Democracy.* Durham, NC: Duke University Press.

Hayden, Tom. 2003. Seeking a New Globalism in Chiapas. *The Nation*, April 7.

Hernández Castillo, Rosalva Aída. 1994. Reinventing Tradition: The Women's Law. *Akwe:kon Journal* 18 (1): 67–70.

———, editor. 2001. *The Other Word: Women and Violence in Chiapas Before and After Acteal.* Copenhagen, Denmark: International Work Group for Indigenous Affairs.

Higgins, Nicholas. 2004. *Understanding the Chiapas Rebellion: Modernist Visions and the Invisible Indian.* Austin: University of Texas Press.

Ita, Ana de. 2008. Fourteen years of NAFTA and the Tortilla Crisis. *Americas Program, Hungry for Justice: How the World Food System Fails the Poor* (#5), http://americas.irc-online.org/am/4879.

Jolom Mayaetik. 2007. *Voces que tejen y bordan historias: Testimonio de las mujeres de Jolom Mayaetik.* San Cristóbal de las Casas, Chiapas, Mex.: K'inal Antzetik.

Jungels, William. 2009. *Broken Branches, Fallen Fruit: Immigration in the Family.* Documentary film. http://brokenbranchesdoc.com/prem.html.

Komes Péres, María, with Diana Rus and Xalik Guzmán. 1990. *Bordando milpas.* In Tzotzil and Spanish. San Cristóbal de las Casas, Mexico: Instituto de Asesoría Antropológica para la Región Maya.

Kovic, Christine. 2003. Demanding Their Dignity as Daughters of God: Catholic Women and Human Rights. In *Women of Chiapas: Making History in Times of Struggle and Hope*, edited by Christine Eber and Christine Kovic, 131–146. New York: Routledge.

———. 2005. *Mayan Voices for Human Rights: Displaced Catholics in Highland Chiapas.* Austin: University of Texas Press.

Laughlin, Robert. 1963. Through the Looking Glass: Reflections on Zinacantán Courtship and Marriage. Ph.D. dissertation, Harvard University, Cambridge, MA.

————, compiler and translator. 1988. *The People of the Bat: Mayan Tales and Dreams from Zinacantán*. Washington, D.C.: Smithsonian Institution Press.

Laughlin, Robert, Naúl Ojeda, Ambar Past, and Taller Leñateros. 2003. *Mayan Hearts*. San Cristóbal de las Casas, Chiapas, Mex.: Taller Leñateros.

Lenkersdorf, Carlos, and Gemma Van der Haar. 1998. *San Miguel Chiptik: Testimonios de una comunidad tojolabal*. Mexico City: Siglo Ventiuno Editores.

Lewis, C. S. 1961. *A Grief Observed*. New York: Bantam Books.

Lilla: International Women's Network. 2009. *The Struggles for Women's Rights in Chiapas: A Directory of Social Organizations Supporting Women in Chiapas*. Sydney, Australia: Lilla and the Edmund Rice Centre for Justice and Community Education.

Lucas, María Elena. 1993. *Forged Under the Sun / Forjada bajo del sol: The Life of María Elena Lucas*. Edited and introduced by Fran Leeper Buss. Ann Arbor: University of Michigan Press.

Lugones, Maria, and Elisabeth Spelman. 1983. "Have we got a theory for you!" Feminist Theory, Cultural Imperialism and the Demand for "The Woman's Voice." *Women's Studies International Forum* 6 (6): 573–581.

MacEoin, Gary. 1995. *The People's Church: Bishop Samuel Ruíz of Mexico and Why He Matters*. New York: Crossroads.

Marcos. 1999. *The Story of Colors*. El Paso, TX: Cinco Puntos Press.

Melel Xojobal. 2008. *"So that you know": Aspirations and Stories by Women of Chiapas*. San Cristóbal de las Casas, Chiapas, Mex.: Melel Xojóbal.

Menchú, Rigoberta. 1984. *I, Rigoberta Menchú, An Indian Woman in Guatemala*. Edited and introduced by Elisabeth Burgos-Debray. Translated by Ann Wright. New York: Verso.

Mills, Sara. 1998. Post-Colonial Feminist Theory. In *Contemporary Feminist Theories*, edited by Stevi Jackson and Jackie Jones, 98–112. New York: New York University Press.

Modiano, Nancy. 1973. *Indian Education in the Chiapas Highlands*. New York: Holt, Rinehart, and Winston.

Mohanty, Chandra. 2005. "Under Western Eyes" Revisited: Feminist Solidarity Through Anticapitalist Struggles. In *Women's Studies for the Future: Foundations, Interrogations, Politics*, edited by Elizabeth Lapovsky Kennedy and Agatha Beins, 72–96. New Brunswick, NJ: Rutgers University Press.

Moksnes, Heidi. 2004. Factionalism and Counterinsurgency in Chiapas: Contextualizing the Acteal Massacre. *Revista Europea de Estudios Latinoaméricanos y del Caribe / European Review of Latin American and Caribbean Studies*, no. 75 (April): 109–117.

————. 2005. Suffering for Justice in Chiapas: Religion and the Globalization of Ethnic Identity. *Journal of Peasant Studies*, vol. 32, nos. 3 and 4 (July and October): 587–607.

———. Forthcoming. *Trapped? Rights-Claiming Mayas and the Scope of Citizenship.* Norman: University of Oklahoma Press.

Morris, Walter F., Jr. 1987. *Living Maya.* New York: Harry N. Abrams, Inc.

Nash, June. 1973. The Betrothal: A Study of Ideology and Behavior in a Maya Indian Community. In *Drinking Patterns in Highland Chiapas*, edited by Henning Siverts, 89–120. Bergen: Universitetsforlaget.

———. 1985. *In the Eyes of the Ancestors: Belief and Behavior in a Maya Community.* Prospect Heights, IL: Waveland Press.

———. 2001. Globalization and the Cultivation of Peripheral Vision. *Anthropology Today*, vol. 17, no. 14: 15–22.

O'Brian, Robin. 1994. The Peso and the Loom: The Political Economy of Maya Women's Work in Highland Chiapas. Ph.D. dissertation, University of California at Los Angeles.

O'Donnell, Katherine. 2010. *Weaving Transnational Solidarity: From the Catskills to Chiapas and Beyond.* Boston: Brill.

Olivera, Mercedes. 2005. Subordination and Rebellion: Indigenous Peasant Women in Chiapas Ten Years After the Zapatista Uprising. *Journal of Peasant Studies*, vol. 32, nos. 3 and 4 (July and October): 608–628.

Ortiz, Teresa. 2001. *Never Again A World Without Us: Voices of Mayan Women in Chiapas, Mexico.* Boston: Epica.

Past, Ambar. 2005. *Incantations by Mayan Women.* San Cristóbal de las Casas, Chiapas, Mex.: Taller Leñateros.

Peres Tsu, Mariano. 2000. Conversaciones interrumpidas: Las voces indígenas del mercado de San Cristóbal. Introduced and translated by Jan Rus. In *Democracia en tierras indígenas: Las elecciones 1991–1998 en Los Altos de Chiapas*, edited by Juan Pedro Viqueria and Willibald Sonnleitner, 259–268. Mexico City: El Colegio de México, CIESAS, and Instituto Federal Electoral.

———. 2003. A Tzotzil Chronicle of the Zapatista Uprising. Translated by Jan Rus. In *The Mexico Reader*, edited by Gilbert Joseph and Timothy Henderson. Durham, NC: Duke University Press.

Pitarch, Pedro. 2010. *The Jaguar and the Priest: An Ethnography of Tzeltal Souls.* Austin: University of Texas Press.

Pozas Arciniega, Ricardo. 1962. *Juan, the Chamula: An Ethnological Recreation of the Life of a Mexican Indian.* Berkeley: University of California Press.

Rojas, Rosa. 1996. *Chiapas? Y las mujeres, qué?* Mexico City: Ediciones la Correa Feminista.

Rosenbaum, Brenda. 1993. *With Our Heads Bowed: The Dynamics of Gender in a Maya Community.* Albany: Institute for Mesoamerican Studies, State University of New York at Albany.

Rosenbaum, Brenda, and Christine Eber. 2007. Women and Gender in Mesoamerica. In *The Legacy of Mesoamerica: History and Culture of a Native American Civilization.* Revised and updated edition. Edited by Robert Carmack, Janine Gasco, and Gary Gossen, 810–875. Upper Saddle River, NJ: Prentice Hall.

Ross, John. 2006. *¡Zapatistas! Making Another World Possible: Chronicles of Resistance 2000–2006.* New York: Nation Books.

Rovira, Giomar. 1997. *Mujeres de maíz.* Mexico City: Ediciones Era.

Rus, Diane. 1990. *La crisis económica y la mujer indígena: El caso de Chamula, Chiapas.* San Cristóbal de las Casas, Chiapas, Mex.: INAREMAC, A.C.

————. 1997. *Mujeres de tierra fría: Conversaciones con las coletas.* Tuxtla Gutiérrez, Mex.: Universidad de Ciencias y Artes de Chiapas.

Rus, Diane, and Jan Rus. 2008. La migración de trabajadores indígenas de Los Altos de Chiapas a Estados Unidos, 2001–2005: El caso de San Juan Chamula [Migration of indigenous workers from highland Chiapas to the United States, 2001–2005: The case of San Juan Chamula]. In *Migraciones en el sur de México y Centroamérica,* coordinated by Daniel Villafuerte Solís and María del Carmen García Aguilar, 343–382. Mexico City: UNICACH and Miguel Ángel Porrúa.

Rus, Jan. 1995. Local Adaptation to Global Change: The Reordering of Native Society in Highland Chiapas, 1974–1994. *European Review of Latin American and Caribbean Studies* 58 (June): 71–90.

————. 2002. Afterword. *Four Creations: An Epic Story of the Chiapas Maya,* edited and translated by Gary Gossen, 1019–1026. Norman: University of Oklahoma Press.

————. 2004. Rereading Tzotzil: Recent Scholarship from Chiapas, Mexico. In *Pluralizing Ethnography: Comparison and Representation in Maya Cultures, Histories, and Identities,* edited by John W. Watanabe and Edward F. Fischer, 199–230. Santa Fe: School of American Research.

Rus, Jan, and George Collier. 2003. A Generation of Crisis in the Central Highlands of Chiapas: The Cases of Chamula and Zinacantán, 1974–2000. In *Mayan Lives, Mayan Utopias: The Indigenous People of Chiapas and the Zapatista Movement,* edited by Jan Rus, R. Aída Hernández Castillo, and Shannan Mattiace, 33–61. Blue Ridge Summit, PA: Rowman and Littlefield.

Rus, Jan, and Diego Vigil. 2008. Rapid Urbanization and Migrant Indigenous Youth in San Cristóbal de las Casas, Chiapas, Mexico. In *Gangs in the Global City,* edited by John Hagadorn, 152–183. Urbana: University of Illinois Press.

Sak K'inal Tajaltik (Javier Morales Aguilar) and Carlos Lenkersdorf. 2001. *El diario de un tojolabal.* Mexico City: Plaza y Valdés.

Sarris, Greg. 1994. *Mabel McKay: Weaving the Dream.* Berkeley: University of California Press.

Shostak, Marjorie. 1981. *Nisa: The Life and Words of a !Kung Woman.* Cambridge: Harvard University Press.

Siverts, Kari. 1993. "I did not marry properly": The Meaning of Marriage Payments in Southern Mexico. In *Carved Flesh / Cast Selves: Gendered Symbols and Social Practices,* edited by Vigdis Broch-Due, Ingrid Rudie, and Tone Bleie, 225–236. Providence: Berg.

Speed, Shannan, R. Aída Hernández Castillo, and Lynn M. Stephen. 2006. *Dissident Women: Gender and Cultural Politics in Chiapas.* Austin: University of Texas Press.

Stephen, Lynn, editor and translator. 1994. *Hear My Testimony: Maria Teresa Tula, Human Rights Activist of El Salvador.* Boston: South End Press.

Syring, Paul. 2000. *Places in the World a Person Can Walk.* Austin: University of Texas Press.

Vargas Cetina, Gabriela, 1999. Flexible Looms. Weavers' Organizations in Chiapas, Mexico. *Urban Anthropology*, vol, 28, nos. 3 and 4, 299–325.

Wali, Alaka. 1974. Dependence and Dominance: The Status of Women in Zinacantán. A.B. honors thesis, Radcliffe College, Cambridge, MA.

Walker, Gayle, and Kiki Suarez. 2008. *Every Woman Is a World: Interviews with Women of Chiapas*. Austin: University of Texas Press.

Ward, Martha. 1998. *A Sounding of Women: Autobiographies from Unexpected Places*. Boston: Allyn and Bacon.

Weibe, Rudy, and Yvonne Johnson. 1998. *Stolen Life: The Journey of a Cree Woman*. Toronto: Knopf.

Womack, John. 1999. *Rebellion in Chiapas: An Historical Reader*. New York: The New Press.

Zambrano, Elizabeth, and Patricia Greenfield. 1999. Ethnoepistemologies at Home and at School. In *Culture and Competence*, edited by Robert J. Sternbergh and Elena Grigorenko, 251–272. Washington, D.C.: American Psychological Association.

Index

Page numbers in italics refer to photos.